Pray for Lucy

CARMELITE MONASTERY

W9-AFL-486

Christmas 1957

From Fashions to the Fathers

From Fashions to the Fathers

THE STORY OF MY LIFE

by Hilda C. Graef

THE NEWMAN PRESS
WESTMINSTER IN MARYLAND • 1957

Copyright © 1957 by The Newman Press
Library of Congress Catalog Card Number: 57-10749
Printed in the United States of America

Foreword

ONE evening, as my mother and I were exchanging reminiscences, she said to me: Why don't you write your autobiography? The idea had never occurred to me, and I refused to consider it. But somehow it entered what I ought probably to call my subconscious, and there it took root and grew until, one day, it crossed the threshold that divides the mysterious underworld of our psychology from the clear daylight of our conscious mind and appeared as the resolve to present my personal life to the public.

I feel I ought to apologize for such an impertinence, for I am neither a famous person whose name appears on the newsreel and in the headlines, nor has my life been distinguished by spectacular adventures. It is true, I have had in the course of years to change both my nationality and my religion; yet this is not a conversion story in the usual sense, since many other events are recorded in these pages beside those leading directly to my becoming a Catholic. Unlike many conversion stories, too, this one does not end in a convent. In fact I tried—but far from finding inside the walls the peace and fulfilment that is the happy ending of so many religious autobiographies, I have to confess that they gave me an unbearable feeling of claustrophobia.

If despite these drawbacks I have tried to write this book as frankly as I could and without, I hope, undue self-dramatization, I have done so because I thought it might be of interest to record how a naturally religious Protestant child lost her belief so utterly as to be a scoffing agnostic for twenty years, and by which stages she came to find the fullness of the Christian faith in the Catholic Church. In the course of my life within the Church I have sometimes been involved in controversy, notably in the disputed case of the Bavarian stigmatic Therese Neumann. Here I have set down how my book on her came to be written. Work on this and on a Lexicon of the Greek Fathers (the latter occupied me for the first fourteen years of my life as a Catholic) led me to an ever deeper appreciation of the relations between reason and faith. This was another motive for writing the present book: to make my own however humble contribution to the large body of evidence that the Church does not fetter the minds of her children but rather stimulates their critical faculties and encourages independent research, though this may not always be appreciated by her rank and file.

Yet this book is in no way a kind of "apologia." For the first thirty-three years of my life I have very nearly lived without any religion, and naturally these had to come into this book as well. They were spent for the greater part in Berlin, between the "Kaiser" and the "Fuehrer," and are a veritable hotchpotch of literary studies, political interests, love affairs and journalistic efforts. As I was writing about these, my reminiscences seemed to belong to a different life, almost to a different person. It seemed incredible that I should have been the small girl delightedly mingling with the revolutionary Berlin mob of 1918, the teenager queuing up for hours to get a cheap seat in the theatre and making sentimental poems, or the young woman dancing through the night and flirting with her fellow students. The twofold separation, first from my native country and even from my native language

—for German has by now become quite foreign to me—then from my deep-rooted skepticism and agnosticism has brought about a change that makes my former self almost unrecognizable to me.

Yet, as I went on writing this book, I began to see the pattern in the various strands that make up the web, the rebuilding of an interior life that had once been shattered by a rude shock which it was then still too young to sustain. In the strange welter of revolution, inflation, Third Reich, emigration and the rest, something was at work rebuilding what had been all but destroyed. I have not in this book dotted the i's and crossed the t's—I think the reader can do that much better than I. But I hope this narrative will make it sufficiently clear that the power at work was nothing in my own natural self. Christianity has a name for it: it is grace.

HILDA GRAEF

Oxford, Feast of St. Peter's Chair in Rome

Contents

From Fashions to the Fathers

1. *Secure Childhood*

IT IS doubtful whether I should have chosen Berlin for my native city, had I been asked my opinion on the matter. Berlin, this citadel of Prussian militarism and upstart among the European capitals, with its straight, uninspiring streets lined with grey blocks of flats and Wilhelminian monuments, could never compare with the charm of Paris or Vienna, the glory of Rome, or with London's unique blend of ancient tradition and modern efficiency. Yet it had its points: attractive surroundings of forests interspersed with lakes, spotless cleanliness, and inhabitants who, almost alone among their rather heavy-going countrymen, were endowed with a keen sense of cockney humor. Whether I liked it or not, into this city I was born to the accompaniment of marching music played by a military band under the windows of the maternity home just at the crucial moment, so my mother later informed me, punctually at eight o'clock in the morning. She had taken it into her head to call me Hiltgunde, a name fitting a fair-tressed Valkyrie, and which she staunchly refused ever to abbreviate. But are Valkyries born on St. Valentine's Day?

It is fashionable nowadays to describe one's childhood in terms that give delight to psychoanalysts: distant fathers and uncomprehending mothers, domestic scenes and precocious awareness of sex, cruel teachers and an all-pervading sense of frustration—the setting of the scene for future neuroses. However conscientiously I may search the first years of my life for any such indications, I fail to find them—but then I have never been psychoanalyzed. My own retrospect impression of peace and happiness is, however, corroborated by a complaint our maid once made to my mother: "I have never been in such a boring household—Herr and Frau Doktor never quarrel."

The only dramatic elements were provided by my three aunts, sisters of my mother, who were all very excitable in different ways. One of them fortunately lived in Vienna, and hence appeared only rarely; another had been forbidden by my father to enter our house, though mother sometimes took me to her flat. She had been very beautiful as a girl and finally married a man who was something of a gambler. She was highly temperamental and was always borrowing money from somebody. The third, very intelligent but given to frequent tantrums, had inspired my father to write a poem beginning: "Please, remain cross with me a little longer; you cannot know how blissful is this peace!" It appeared in one of the Berlin weeklies, but she never guessed that she herself had inspired it. She had the most charming and devoted husband, a very clever doctor, as calm and peaceful as she was emotional. When I lay in bed, feverish with measles or chickenpox, I needed only to hear his voice in the hall to feel I was already beginning to be better. They had an only son, Werner, who was six years older than I and very brilliant. The whole family admired him, as he was invariably head of his class and intellectually very precocious. Naturally I looked up to him and took him for an oracle, though this did not prevent me from being sometimes jealous, because he was always in the foreground whereas I, being 'only a girl,' had to play second fiddle. My mother's mother, the only one of my grandparents I have known, simply doted on him and nourished the frequently expressed desire that we should marry each other later. In fact we were often together, and being both only children, grew up rather like brother and sister.

I saw much less of my father's family. His father and mother, both painters, had died long before I was born. His sister, Sabine Lepsius, was a very remarkable woman. She remained rather distant while I was a child, but became a powerful influence when I was a young girl. Though my father had studied literature and history, his inclinations were literary and artistic rather than scholarly. He sang well and wrote plays which remained forever in the drawers of his writing table, except when they went on unsuccessful journeys to publishers. After his marriage, when he was already nearing fifty, he became a teacher at a girls' school at Weissensee, a northern suburb of Berlin.

My mother, too, was a trained teacher, determined to apply to her own child what she had learned from her textbooks. I therefore had the benefit of a very consistent upbringing. There were few things that were definitely forbidden, and it would never have occurred to me to question a parental order. One of the taboos of my childhood was that I was never allowed to sit on a sofa. "Children do not belong on a sofa," my father informed me. The only exception to this strictly enforced rule was a special treat I was given on festive occasions, when I might sit between my parents on the sofa and look at a picture book. Another form of restraint imposed on me was that I was not allowed to make any noise in the afternoons, while my father was first resting and then working; I had simply to occupy myself quietly, unless I went for walks with Mother or with Selma, our maid.

According to the theories of many modern educators these restrictions ought to have produced a whole crop of neuroses, but somehow they failed to do so. I loved my parents dearly, and simply accepted whatever they told me. I do not think I was exceptional. Later in life my experience has always been that children appreciate firmness, if it springs from love.

Nevertheless I was far from being in any way subdued. One night, as I was going to bed and Mother wanted me to go to sleep quickly, she said with a big yawn: "Are you as tired as I am?" "But how can I know how tired *you* are?" came the disconcerting reply from her small daughter. Sometimes bits from my parents' conversations would come out in the most inappropriate way. My father tended to divide mankind into educated and uneducated people; so I once confronted our maid with the question: "Selma, do you have educated parents, too?" Fortunately, Selma did not mind.

My mother's ideas were in many ways in advance of her time. Once she profoundly shocked my father by going to town to do her shopping on a hot summer day in sandals and without stockings. She had to promise him solemnly never to do that again. She also rented a lot, so that I should have as much open air life as was possible for flat dwellers, and she did a good deal of gardening there at a time when such pursuits were still considered unladylike in Germany. There I used to play, dig, weed, and pick fruit, and there I was introduced to the "facts of life" in the most natural way. When I was about four, Mother considered it was time for me to know where I myself had come from. She told me no stories about storks or angels having deposited me in my cradle, but took the opportunity of a neighbor's cat having kittens, to tell me the facts as far as I could grasp them. Since these seemed quite plain and satisfactory to me, I cannot recall ever having been interested in this subject again as a child; whereas, had I been left puzzled, I should certainly have tried to find out about it in other ways.

For, like most children, I was not easily put off by unsatisfactory answers. My father used to talk at table about someone called Hugo. Much intrigued by this subject of conversation, I asked him who this was. "Hugo is a little dog," he replied. For a second I was content with this. But then I reflected that in former conversations Hugo had been reported to have said certain things. Now dogs did not talk—on the other hand, Mother had such a passion for truthfulness that she had not even taught me the word 'lie' and had instructed our maid, too, never to use it, since I did not lie myself and should not know it was possible not to speak the truth. In fact it was at school that I first heard the word and came home asking what it meant. But Daddy had said Hugo was a little dog, and Hugo evidently did talk. He had given the reply, however, in such a tone of finality that I did not dare to refer to the subject again. So the question of the speaking dog Hugo continued to puzzle me for some time, until I at last made up my mind to solve the mystery come what may, and asked Mother about it. She realized that it would only make things worse to withhold the necessary information and told me that my father had only been joking, and that Hugo was the name of his headmaster, but that I was on no account to say anything about it all to other people. I was at last satisfied—but the story of the speaking dog Hugo has remained engraven on my mind, whereas I do not even remember the conversation about babies, of which Mother told me many years later.

About this time, my cousin Werner and I invented a strange game, which we played whenever we were together. We called it "playing Jesus and Mary," but we changed the names, so that the grownups should not know what we were doing. We would make up conversations between them; sometimes God the Father came in also. We played this game especially during the summer holidays, which we often spent together, for as Werner's parents liked to go mountain climbing in the Tyrol, he went with us to the Baltic. We used to sleep in adjoining rooms. When my mother had finally left us, usually after, to my great satisfaction, making Werner get up once more to wash his knees properly, we would creep out of bed, open the door and then go back and indulge in our strange religious dialogues until we both fell asleep.

I sometimes dreamed about God, who played the same games with me as my father. I pictured Him as a kind of transparent balloon; no doubt because I had been told that He was spirit, though I can vouch for it that at this time I had never heard of Origen's theory of spiritual bodies being circular in shape.

On our walks Selma and I often passed a Catholic art shop. Though she firmly impressed it on me that all Catholics were deceitful (I had been introduced to the possibility of telling lies by this time), because they did nasty things and then just went to confession and afterwards did them all over again, I loved to stand before this shop and stare at the pictures and statues, especially of the Sacred Heart. Once when I went with my father and stopped before the window, he informed me that all this was trash; but this did not prevent me from looking at these statues whenever I had a chance. I did not know what this flaming red heart on our Lord's breast signified, but is seemed wonderful to me.

The newly confirmed Protestant young girls were another impressive sight. They would parade up and down the streets in their long black dresses, carrying bouquets of flowers, from which flowed long white veils of tulle or lace. Though they were only fourteen, they looked very grown-up to me and behaved with extraordinary decorum. Even more romantic were the little Catholic First Communicants all in white, with long veils, crowns of flowers on their heads and candles in their hands. I was eagerly looking forward to the day when I, too, should be an interesting figure in black; meanwhile I was ransacking mother's sewing basket for pieces of lace to produce at least a veil for my otherwise neglected dolls.

My early religious interests, however, were not encouraged at home. Once, as my father was sitting with folded hands at the table, waiting for dinner, I asked him: "Daddy, are you praying?" He answered almost fiercely: "Certainly not." I was wondering why this question should have upset him so much. Though I had been baptized a Protestant when I was four months old, not in church, though, but at home, I was never taken to church or to Sunday school; but Mother taught me some prayers and Father gave me Scripture lessons. I loved the Bible stories he told me, which I would later read myself in a children's New Testament, though I did not relish having to learn by heart not only the Ten Commandments themselves, but also the long-winded explanations from Luther's Catechism. For, after a brief spell at school, during which I had successively picked up chicken pox, conjunctivitis and diphtheria, my parents had decided to educate me at home for the time being. I learned reading and writing very rapidly, and was soon always to be seen with some book, generally fairy stories by Grimm or Hauff or from the *Thousand and One Nights*, which I loved. I had a beautiful doll's house and a large number of pretty dolls; but I was not very interested in them, and I intensely disliked having other little girls in my nursery, who would play with the doll's house all the afternoon and prevent me from reading.

For I was athirst for higher knowledge. My father had amused himself with teaching me the Greek alphabet. This greatly intrigued me, and then and there I made up my mind to learn Greek.

"Daddy, please can I learn Greek?"

"Yes, my doll (his favorite term of endearment), when you are a little older."

"Daddy, is this a promise that I can learn Greek?"

"Yes, I promise. When you are the right age, you shall go to a school where you learn Greek."

I was satisfied and kept his promise firmly fixed in my mind.

My parents were leading a very quiet life, without much entertaining. One party stands out in my memory, because it involved my first ride in a motor car. It was a luncheon party given by Professor Georg Simmel, the philosopher, who was a school friend of my father's known to me as "Uncle Georg," and particularly dear to me because he used to send me enchanting presents for Christmas and my birthday: wonderful teddy bears, which I vastly preferred to dolls, rocking chairs and the like. I still see myself sitting at the long dining table, the only child among a crowd of grownups, carefully keeping my elbows pressed to my sides, as I had been taught to do, while trying to handle my knife and fork without mishap. It was a great relief when the meal was over and I was sent at last into another room where a collection of toys were waiting for me.

In July 1914 we went once more to the Baltic. Though these holiday expeditions involved only four or five hours train journey, they were nevertheless important enterprises, prepared many weeks ahead. For like many other German families in those days, we took our maid with us and set up a real menage, kitchen and all, in some farmer's house. We travelled with our belongings stowed away in enormous travelling baskets, well secured with iron rods and padlocks. A coachman by name of Boche was hired for the great day to convey us to the Stettiner Bahnhof in his horse-drawn cab, and there was an air of excitement and joyous expectancy when we had eventually found our seats, and the train began to move out of the mass of tall grey blocks of flats into the wooded surroundings of the capital.

This holiday, which began as all others had so far done, was to end very differently. Father was reading his paper with greater attention than he used to; and in his conversations with Mother, the words "Serajevo," "ultimatum," "Erzherzog Ferdinand" and others I had never heard before became more and more frequent. Then yet another word was added to my vocabulary: "Mobilmachung"—mobilization. At this stage my father became very agitated; he would walk to the station at least twice a day, often taking me with him, and always returning rather dejected. Apparently there were no trains running direct to Berlin any more. At last, one morning at the end of July, I remember sitting in a horse-drawn cart that was rattling along through thick forests. I was shivering in the cold morning air; for it was only about three o'clock and still quite dark. We were on our way to a larger station, from which there were still some trains running to Berlin. "There is going to be a war."

My first memory of the first World War is the front page of a newspaper called *Berliner Lokal-Anzeiger,* covered with heavy black print, which my mother handed to me. The page was headed "Aufruf an mein Volk"—it was the Kaiser's proclamation calling his people to arms. Mother told me to learn it by heart. Normally my father did not interfere with her educational measures, but this outburst of patriotic fervor was too much even for his otherwise unimpeachable loyalty. For once he flatly contradicted Mother in front of me: "She need not learn it by heart." And I was saved from encumbering my memory with one of the less inspiring pieces of imperial prose.

At first, war seemed to be a gay affair. It was "frisch-froehlicher Krieg," every man in fieldgrey a hero; the soldiers were marching accompanied by their bands, singing: "Adieu, Louise, wipe your face, not every ball is a hit." Many of them had bunches of flowers sticking out of the barrels of their guns; they were all singing lustily, and Selma and I used to stand staring at them with admiration. "See you again at Christmas," they would call out, for nobody expected the war to go on longer than that. Though my father made a serious face when the *Lokal-Anzeiger* informed him that England had declared war on us, he comforted himself with the idea "England won't do much." Once our gallant troops had reached Paris, which would not take them very long, the war would be over.

At first it certainly looked to us as if this were going to happen. I vividly remember all the names of Belgian fortresses and cities that were besieged and quickly fell, news vendors calling out their special editions: "Maubeuge, Maubeuge fallen—Namur—Liège—Louvain, Louvain taken. . . ." It was wonderful. Our grey boys were carrying everything before them. And at every single victory the flags would come out. Even the trams carried tiny ones. The schools had a holiday. Berlin gave itself up to rejoicing. Once the Kaiser drove in an open car through the main street of Weissensee; we children were lining the road. I had been given a black-white-and-red flag which I waved at him shouting "Hurrah" for all I was worth, and getting a gracious handwave in return. Mother had bought a book of patriotic songs with a glaring black-white-and-red cover. She would often sit at the piano singing with me "Deutschland über alles," "Heil Dir im Siegerkranz"—which was then the national anthem, sung to the same tune as "God save the King"—of course, "Die Wacht am Rhein" and a rather sentimental song which I liked particularly, of a soldier on guard at midnight, wondering whether his sweetheart was still faithful.

It was an intoxicating time, these first months of the first World War. But it did not last long, and we were soon to be given some sobering medicine. Christmas came and went, and there was no sign that the war was going to end. Instead yet another word was added to my vocabulary: "Blockade." Its practical results soon made themselves felt; at first, as far as I was concerned, in a rather exciting way. Selma and I were sent on sugar shopping expeditions. Before universal rationing was introduced, the shops limited their sales to half a pound; so Selma would go into a shop first, while I waited outside. Then I would go in and ask rather nervously for half a pound of sugar. It was the first time I was allowed to go into a shop and buy something unattended, and though it was very thrilling, it was also slightly frightening. Soon, however, the authorities announced that there were to be *razzias* by the police, and any sugar or other hoarded foodstuffs would be confiscated. Mother was frightened, and as there was no other fruit available, she turned all her hoarded sugar into lemon juice.

My dolls were now altogether discarded, and I began to play with soldiers like a boy. I had plenty of them, infantry, cavalry, guns; Germans, French and British, and grand battles were being fought on the floor of my nursery.

The flat above us had recently been occupied by a family with a boy, Heinz Kirschner, who was a year older than I. Soon we became great friends and staged battles together. He was rather quiet for a boy and also liked reading. We used to play games like *Halma* and *Checkers*, at which he nearly always won; but I did not resent that as I should have, had I been defeated by a girl. When I was alone I would draw naval battles. My father, who was very good at drawing, had taught me to draw ships, and so I covered sheet upon sheet with steamers surrounded by bright blue waves and red and yellow flames, some of them half submerged and about to sink.

Towards the end of 1915 my parents decided to send me once more to school. After passing an entrance examination I was allowed to leap one year and so became, and remained, the youngest of my class. I thoroughly enjoyed school at this stage, especially German and Scripture, my favorite subjects. By now I had discarded fairy tales and was reading girls' books like Johanna Spyri's *Heidi*, but I preferred adventure stories. Karl Mai remained somehow outside my scope—I have never read a single book of his—but I read and reread *Gulliver's Travels* and Jules Verne, whose poker-faced Englishman Phineas Fogg became one of my heroes. But the books that attracted me most were those in my father's library. Before supper, when he had finished his day's work, I was allowed to come in for a talk. Then I would stand before his book shelves and ply him with questions. I knew all the names of the principal German authors and their chief works—a game called *Dichterquartett* I used to play, which involved the names of writers and their books, had provided my first introduction to literature—and now I would ask over and over again when I should be allowed to read these works.

My father had very definite views on the suitability or otherwise of books for his "doll." Nothing was allowed me yet; but when I was twelve, I might read some of the works of Schiller; Goethe was not to be approached till fourteen, and his main work, *Faust*, I should not understand till I was eighteen. It was most disappointing, for I should have liked to start at least on Schiller right away. But Daddy remained adamant, and so my literary appetite had to be satisfied with the few books allowed me. Among these were stories about the Greek gods, which did not interest me very much. The Germanic mythology, on the other hand, greatly attracted my imagination. Thor and Odin and their various exploits, especially the former's fight with the wicked Loki appealed to me; and I was enchanted by the *Nibelungen* saga.

In the latter part of 1916 my father fell ill. He had been ailing for some time. No doubt the war, too, was preying on his mind. I still hear him say: "The worst that can happen is that the war will end without a decision." But I could tell from his voice that things were going bad for us, and that he took it to heart. An influenza attack which he had suffered some time before had left after-effects; at last he had to take to his bed. Finally a nurse had to be engaged. Mother was frequently in tears. There was very little food, and I was only too glad to escape from the depressing atmosphere at home to the normal life at school.

Fortunately, Frau Kirschner asked Mother to let me spend most of the day with them. So as soon as I had had my mid-day meal, I would go up to their flat, do some of my home-work there, and play with Heinz. Frau Kirschner was a deeply religious woman, but, as often happens in Lutheranism, her Christianity expressed itself in a rather mournful manner. She always spoke as if she were in pain, and though she was kindness itself and would give me of the homemade cakes that German housewives managed to produce, even in those days, from potatoes and saccharine, I was always a little frightened of her, and began to associate religion with melancholy.

Christmas was a sad feast that year; even I realized that there was little hope that I should ever see my father well again. I had never done any more than to say my—very perfunctory—morning and evening prayers, usually while lying in bed. But now I began to pray without anyone having suggested it. I knelt down beside a chair in my nursery—a very unusual thing to do for a Lutheran child, as we never knelt for prayer—and simply implored God not to let my Daddy die. I used to pray like that for quite a long time, in my own words; but when I heard anyone coming toward my room I quickly got up from my knees so that no one should see what I had been doing.

From time to time Mother took me to see my father, who was lying in bed motionless. He hardly spoke, but would just give me a smile. When she took me in on the day before his death, he was unconscious. I gave him a kiss and went out crying. Next morning my mother came in to tell me that my father had died during the night. She broke into tears and sat down on a chair, sobbing inconsolably. Then I said, trying to comfort her: "But, Mummie, don't cry so hard; we shall surely see Daddy again in heaven."

She answered, with a strange smile: "Yes, my child."

At that moment I knew in a flash: "She does not believe it." I cannot say how, whether it was her smile or the tone in which she spoke, but I had the distinct impression that belief in heaven was something only children were taught, but which grownups knew not to be true.

Though religion had not played an important part in my

life during these last years, this realization came as a great shock, especially as I did not know how to console my mother, seeing she evidently did not believe she would ever meet my father again. Religion was indeed puzzling. I supposed Frau Kirschner believed in heaven, but Mother did not —and of course Mother must be right.

In the afternoon, men in black came and carried my father out. I stood in the dining room, through which they had to pass, staring at the stretcher that was covered with a white sheet, and at the silent men. It was the first time I had met death. It was final, irrevocable and infinitely sad, not least because, during these days, my teachers and school friends treated me with a tenderness and respect which were in some way gratifying, but also embarrassing.

On a cold, dull winter day Mother and I went to the cemetery, accompanied by those of our relatives and friends who had been able to come, for many were absent owing to the war. I remember sitting in the bleak graveyard chapel, trying to swallow my tears, while the clergyman spoke a few words. Then we went to the open grave; the coffin was lowered. Somebody offered me cold, damp sand, which I threw down as I had just seen Mother doing. The sand made a slight, muffled sound as it fell on the lid of the coffin; people came and pressed my hand—then it was all over.

The sadness of it all had been too much for me. There had, of course, been no prayers for the dead, no hint that this parting was not final, that he who had been my father did still exist. All I wanted now was to forget this sorrow, to be a child again, after having been treated almost like a grownup, and to run away and play, read, and resume my normal life. There was school, there were my books, there were my daydreams—I would go back to them as quickly as I could.

2. A World in Ruins

AFTER my father's death things were not quite the same as they had been before. When my mother surveyed our finances she found that her widow's pension together with the interest from our small capital, which had become negligible owing to war conditions, did not suffice to keep the two of us. She therefore decided to go back to teaching. But even so, her income was not sufficient to keep the maid, so our dear Selma had to go. Our flat also was too expensive; we therefore moved to a smaller one in West Berlin, where most of our relatives were living. This naturally involved a change of school for me. I had never forgotten my precocious desire to learn Greek, and now told my mother that she should send me to a school where I could learn that. Mother remonstrated. She was of a very practical bent of mind and could see no use in a classical education for a girl. But I was not to be put off, and I had a very strong argument in my favor: "But Daddy promised me I should learn Greek." My mother could not resist this pleading, and so I was sent to the Koenigliche Augustaschule in Schoeneberg, which was considered the better of the only two girl schools in Berlin where both Latin and Greek were taught as the principal subjects.

Though I had used my father's promise so effectively to gain my object with my mother, I set aside his views in another matter; for my desire to read the works of the famous authors in his library was stronger than my filial piety. Almost immediately after his death, therefore, I embarked on a systematic course of reading, taking as my guide the timetable my father had mapped out for me, with that difference that I started now, at the age of ten, on the books he had scheduled for two years later. As I was a quick reader, I covered in a year much more ground than he had allowed in his curriculum. My mother was far too busy with her teaching and housework to supervise my intellectual activities; nevertheless she thought I was neglecting my homework and was cross when she found me lying on the carpet—my favorite posture —engrossed in some book which she was sure was not a schoolbook. I therefore devised the trick, which she discovered only much later, of having two books before me, one a schoolbook which remained open under the book I was actually reading, and which was immediately placed on top of the other when I heard Mother's steps approaching.

The first winter in our new home was grim, indeed. All Berliners sufficiently old to remember it think of it as the *Kohlrueben-winter,* the winter when turnips were practically our only food. We ate them as a vegetable and we ate them in our bread; we ate them as soup and we ate them as jam, we turned them into fritters and we drank them as 'coffee'—whatever we might call it, we inevitably consumed turnips.

From time to time my mother made the long journey to Weissensee, our former home, where she was well-known at a dairy, in order to bring back a bottle of milk and some butter and cheese to supplement our diet of turnips. It was a hazardous undertaking, for if her shopping bag had aroused the suspicions of an ill-disposed policeman, all would have been confiscated, and she would have been fined or even sent to prison. However, we were spared such a disaster, and always had a feast on her return.

As our new home was not too far from my doctor uncle, I saw more of my cousin Werner than before. He had developed into a brilliantly clever boy and liked to impart most of his newly acquired knowledge to me. As the whole family regarded him as a genius, I had come to accept everything he said as the last word of wisdom. It must have been in the late spring of 1918, when I was just eleven, that we had one of these highly intellectual conversations, standing together before a bookshelf in our sitting room. Somehow our talk turned to the subject of religion, and a remark of mine produced his reproach: "Really, Guggi (an abbreviation used by those members of my family who found "Hiltgunde" too much for them), it is time you stopped believing in all these stories about Moses and Jesus and so on. This is something for babies and old women; but they are no more true than Grimm's Fairy Tales."

For a moment I was aghast. Only last Easter I had drawn a picture for my mother, as I had seen it in some book, of Jesus leaving the tomb, by which an angel was sitting, while three women, all with large haloes, were approaching it. On the back I had written a short poem, an acrostic on the word Easter, which I had made myself, saying that Jesus had risen and conquered the darkness.

And now all I had learned from my Biblical story books, all I had so readily believed, was not true? The shock would have affected me even more if I had not been in some way prepared for it by my mother's attitude when I was trying to comfort her after my father's death. Still, God and Jesus had been very real to me—and now there was no one to pray to even. For Werner was so much cleverer than anyone else I knew. I did not dare to doubt anything he said.

It may have been due to this shock, and to the void left in my life when my religious beliefs had been shattered in a moment, that I developed a strange daydream, which I indulged for a considerable time. I invented for myself an elder brother, who was the epitome of all power, virtue and beauty, and whose principal *raison d'être* seemed to be to protect and entertain his small sister, that is myself. He was called Karl, after one of my heroes, Charlemagne, and was tall, fair and clothed in a kind of dark blue silk uniform embroidered with gold, though sometimes he changed into a red and silver one. He had adventures that took him all over the world, and he would come back with presents for me and tell me all that had happened to him.

I never told any one about this creature of my imagination. Looking at it in retrospect it seems to have been an amalgamation of an unconscious longing of the only child for a brother—though this office was really performed quite satisfactorily by Werner—and of the religious instinct that had lost Christ and needed a substitute; for "Karl" had all the attributes of protective power normally associated with a supernatural being.

Not long after this shattering of my religious beliefs I had another shock. One day I saw an official-looking paper lying about on our grand piano. I looked at it more closely: it was Mother's teaching certificate, stating that she was allowed to teach all secondary school subjects except Scripture. I was greatly puzzled by this curious exception, and when she came into the room asked her the reason for it. Then she told me that she was of Jewish descent, having become a Protestant only after her teacher's examination, before she married my father. This announcement took me completely by surprise. Somehow the Jews had always seemed foreign. The Jewish girls in my form were different from the other pupils; they missed school on certain days which we knew were their feasts, they did not attend our Scripture lessons, and they showed great emotion when the word "Jew" was mentioned, however amiably. And now my own mother belonged to this strange people—one of her grandfathers had even been a well-known rabbi! It took me some time to adjust myself to the new situation; but then I reflected that my mother herself had not changed; she was the same as she had been before I knew of her parentage, and anyway, we were all Christians. It never struck me at the time that I, too, belonged, at least partly, to the race of Abraham.

In the late summer that year, just after the holidays, I had an accident. At games a large ball hit me in the stomach; I took no notice of it and carried on. But on my way home from school I began to have "tummy ache." I could just finish my dinner, but then the pains became so severe that I had to tell Mother. I tried to get up from my chair, but realized that I could hardly move. "I can't walk any more," I moaned, "can't you carry me into bed?" Mother was thoroughly alarmed and telephoned my uncle. After he had examined me he made a very serious face. I had twisting of the bowels, a grave matter, especially as I was badly undernourished, and he only hoped it might right itself without an operation which, so I gathered from his conversation with my mother which I overheard, was extremely dangerous.

For three days I had to remain motionless on my back, being allowed no food, only a sip of what we called "tea" now and again. It was the first time I seriously thought of my own death. Strangely enough this idea did not seem at all terrible. Though I no longer believed in heaven, I did not think death a bad alternative to pain, which was severe at times. I had seen my father die; there had been a series of deaths in the family after his, that of his younger brother and of two of my cousins in the war. Death had become almost familiar, there seemed nothing to be afraid of. However, after three days my uncle pronounced me out of danger, and death soon receded completely from my thoughts.

Since the illness had left me very weak, Mother took me to Brunshaupten, on the Baltic, where we stayed with a peasant couple well known to us. As I had been so ill, Mother asked them to let us have a little butter or bacon. These had become almost a legend to me, but we had seen a surprising stock of them in our hosts' larder. Yet old Frau Uplegger replied to my mother's request: "I cannot let you have anything, for everyone is neighbour to himself, especially in wartime." These hard words remained engraven on my memory. They were, indeed, typical of the German peasant. So I was not surprised when, almost thirty years later, I read that the severe food shortage in Germany after the second World War had been aggravated by the refusal of the German peasants to share their hoarded provisions with the townspeople.

Fortunately we contrived to obtain some food from other farmers in the neighborhood—at a price, of course. I vividly remember one of these expeditions, when Mother and I returned with two shopping bags containing butter, eggs and sausage. On our way through the forest we suddenly caught sight of a policeman in the distance. We were just passing fir trees with branches reaching down to the ground. "Quick," said Mother, "let's hide the bags." In a moment we had dropped them behind the branches and continued on our way, bidding a smiling "Good afternoon" to the policeman as we passed him. Had he noticed anything? We walked slowly on; when he was out of sight we returned to the spot where we had hidden the bags. To our great relief they were still there, and, feeling like thieves who had eluded the coppers, we carried our treasures home in safety.

In November the war came at last to an end. We had been longing for it. The knowledge of the interminable bloodshed, the food shortage that was getting worse and worse, the fear of yet another winter without enough coal and clothes to keep us warm, penetrated deeply even into the lives of us children. For some time large placards, issued by the government, had been displayed everywhere. They showed two children biting into thick slices of bread and butter, or rather margarine, with the caption: *Wir lassen uns nicht aushungern*—We will not let ourselves be starved. Yet starved we were, without milk, meat, fats, sugar or white bread for years. I remember once, when our botany mistress mentioned the cocoa bean, the whole form broke out into a chorus of "Ahs," our imagination filled with haunting memories of cups of hot, sweet cocoa.

Nevertheless, when the end came, we felt as if our world was tumbling down around us. Special issues of the papers appeared several times a day with the catastrophic news. The sailors were revolting at Hamburg. The Kaiser had abdicated in favor of Prince Max von Baden. Germany had been proclaimed a republic. An armistice had been signed. The war was lost.

The war was lost and the Kaiser was gone. He had been part of my universe, as had been the notion that Germany could never lose the war. I was almost twelve now, and war years count double even in the life of a child. Though I probably did not express it to myself in quite these words, I was well aware that something had come to an end; that things would never be quite the same as they had been before. The word "republic" seemed strange to me, the word "revolution" full of terror. Yet it all seemed also somehow adventurous. I was a sufficiently authentic Berlin child to be filled with curiosity to see how it was all going to work out.

3. *A Girl in Revolt*

LIFE began to be very exciting as well as rather disorganized. There were constant strikes and revolts of one kind or another. One day we had no gas, the other no electricity, the third no water, or, worse, in the case of a general strike, none of these commodities. I did not like being alone in the flat in the evening, when Mother was out, with only a candle to throw an uncertain light on the table, leaving the rest of the room dark and threatening to my imagination, filled with tales of burglars and murderers.

But these fears would vanish in the broad light of day which found me all agog for new adventures. Our school was in a district where revolutionary outbreaks occurred quite frequently, and often we were sent home early to avoid possible dangers. Some of us did, indeed, obey the strict injunctions from both teachers and parents to go straight home on these occasions. But for my friends and myself these were opportunities far too good to be missed. Going home, when there were political orators getting on soap boxes making exciting speeches? When we could stand in the midst of a jostling crowd, swaying backwards and forwards, caught in its intoxicating rhythm, screaming with all the others our

"Hurrah!" or "Down, down with the traitors!"? This was better by far than the most thrilling adventure story. This was real life, history in the making, and we were there, in the very midst of it—while our mamas were cooking our dinners, and our papas were in their boring offices, imagining their small daughters safe at school.

There was danger, too, to add a further spice. Not that we were courting it, though. We soon developed a keen sense for *dicke Luft*, as it was called in the Berlin slang which we quickly picked up. When we saw some of the foremost shouters feel in their pockets, and the policemen reach for their truncheons, we would disentangle ourselves from the crowd as fast as we could. Nevertheless we were extremely proud when we read in the evening papers that shooting had actually occurred at the place where we had been only a short while before it started.

Though we were only children, we were already feeling ourselves a new generation, living in a new and exciting age. By this time I had quite forgotten the Kaiser, who had once waved to me from his car. Instead, the names of the Social Democrat leaders Ebert and Noske became household words for us. They had just caused great merriment to the German public, because a photograph of them showing their none too slim figures in bathing costumes had been circulating in the press. At the end of the year and in the beginning of 1919 they had great difficulties with the leftwing fanatics of their party, known as *Spartakisten,* whom they suppressed by force. There was frequent streetfighting, and we listened more eagerly than ever to the respective orators and joined the revolutionary mob in their favorite song: "Lights out! Knives out! Noske throws his handgrenades. Noske in his bathing costume shoots us dead, for freedom, peace and bread; for freedom, peace and bread."

On January 15th Karl Liebknecht and Rosa Luxemburg, leaders of the Spartakists, were brutally murdered by army officers, and their bodies thrown into the Landwehrkanal. To the horror of our parents we came home one day singing at the top of our voices: "A corpse is lying in the Landwehr-kanal; pass it on to me, but don't press it too hard. If no-body claims it, throw it in again."

I was then not quite twelve years old; my schoolmates were thirteen or more. When our mothers had been our age, they had been chirping sentimental songs of the boy who picked a rose, or "A maiden's prayer." And here were their daughters, singing of knives, corpses and politicians, and evi-dently thinking it immense fun. My mother felt it her duty to tell me that my behavior in general and these songs in par-ticular were quite unsuitable for a young girl.

But I did not want to be a "young girl." I thoroughly de-spised those of my schoolfellows who answered to this type. Not that I was a tomboy; but a "young girl" seemed to me a revoltingly insipid creature, disgustingly well-behaved, de-void of serious interests, in a word, intolerably dull. I was a "Berliner" and proud of it, and began to display most of the traits associated with the inhabitants of my native city: lack of reverence, a certain type of sarcastic humor, and a marked dislike of anything savoring of sentimentality. My conduct reports, which had hitherto invariably received the highest marks, deteriorated considerably; my attention was con-stantly flagging, for unless we had teachers who could make their lessons interesting I was simply bored and showed it. The outside world was so much more exciting than school, especially at the time of general and local elections, when we would go about distributing leaflets which we obtained from canvassers of one of the parties of which our parents ap-proved. These we would conscientiously offer to every passer-by. It was highly exciting to watch their reactions: some would disappointingly cast just one glance at them and throw them aside, whereas others would give us intense satisfaction by reading them from beginning to end.

It was perhaps just as well for our education that, though elections of one kind or another were frequent, there were nevertheless long periods without major political excitements. We were also getting more food now. The name of the Quakers will always remain associated in my memory with delicious white buns and hot, thick chocolate soup. As soon as a teacher came in at recess calling out: "Down children, to the Quakerspeisung!" we would all seize our bowls and spoons and almost fall over each other in our rush for the groundfloor room, where this great treat was awaiting us.

Despite my utter lack of faith I had retained a lively interest in religion, and invariably had high Scripture marks. Besides, I liked English which we had just begun to learn, since I could manage the pronunciation better than most of the others, and our teacher used modern methods involving the playing of gramophone records which I loved to imitate. My first theatrical experience, a matinee of Schiller's *Wilhelm Tell*, made a deep impression and gave me a taste for plays, though I never wanted to be an actress. Music, too, entered my life at this period; I started piano lessons and practised a good deal, which led to constant complaints from the people in the flat below.

As my mother was still teaching, I had to help her in the house. I quite liked domestic work, except dusting. This was a very tiresome task, for we had much handcarved furniture which my grandfather had designed himself. Woe betide if Mother still found a speck of dust on the elaborate ornaments of the immense sideboard or the writing desk, which had to be carefully brushed from all sides, or on the five highly complicated legs of the dining table, under which I had to creep with great difficulty to restore them to their normal highly polished glory. As I found it incredibly boring, I took to learning poems by heart while doing it; Hamlet's monologue, Sophocles' hymns to Eros and to Helios, and many other immortal pieces of literature were thus memorized, duster in hand.

At Easter 1919 I changed from the ordinary girls school section of the Augustaschule to the *Studienanstalt,* so that my early ambition of learning Latin and Greek could be fulfilled.

We started with six Latin lessons a week, given us by a master who had only recently returned from the war, and whose methods still savored unmistakably of the German army. Herr Schiering tolerated no nonsense; he drilled the Latin declensions and verbs into us as if we were his recruits, and mercilessly made us construe sentences, punctuating our diffident ventures with his "Nonsense," "Rubbish," "Please parse the verb." I cannot say I enjoyed this; nevertheless I was taught Latin so effectively that I never had any difficulty in reading it. Though I did not like memorizing irregular verbs and rules of syntax, I am not aware that these enforced activities had any undesirable psychological effects either on myself or on my schoolfellows. Indeed, the Latin lessons are the only ones which stand out in my memory; everything else is buried in a mist of indifference or boredom. We had a form mistress, on whom many of us had a "crush"; I think they even made poems on her. I could not understand this and thought it rather comic, but it seemed to provide a great thrill for those infected with it.

At this time Mother wanted me to be confirmed. All the other girls were starting their confirmation lessons, which took place twice a week, I think, immediately after school at the end of the morning. I objected violently. I had no beliefs whatever, how could I possibly be confirmed? Though Mother had always enjoined on me the duty to be absolutely truthful, she seemed to think it quite in order for me to give solemn promises and undertakings which I neither intended, nor was able, to keep. But her insistence on truthfulness went together with a good deal of utilitarianism; she was afraid it might cause me some detriment professionally if I were not confirmed, so she wanted me to conform to what she evidently considered no more than a meaningless ceremony. This kind of argumentation went counter to all my convictions; but Mother was very strong-willed, so I had to submit.

Pfarrer Mauff, to whom I went for instructions, was on the staff of one of the most fashionable Berlin churches, the Kaiser-Wilhelm-Gedaechtniskirche in the Tauentzienstrasse. We were a large class of girls from different schools, and the instructions he gave us were more boring and even less religious than our Scripture lessons at school. I remember he constantly repeated that a child experienced first the circle of the family, then the wider circle of the school, and finally that of the nation. This is as far as I got; for after a few weeks the instructions came to a premature end, at least as far as I was concerned.

One morning the Pfarrer had started a few minutes earlier, therefore a large number of girls, including myself, were slightly late. By way of punishment for what was not our fault at all, he made us latecomers stand in a corner for about three quarters of an hour. When I told my mother about it she was furious and decided that I need not go to these instructions any more, nor did she ever return to the subject of my confirmation. A few weeks later, when I was alone at home one afternoon, the front door bell rang. I cautiously opened the door without removing the safety chain, a very necessary precaution in Berlin. There was Pfarrer Mauff, asking why I was no longer coming to the instructions. Without removing the chain I snapped: "Because I don't believe in anything." He asked me to let him come in to discuss the matter. "There is nothing to discuss—I don't believe, and nothing will make me." I slammed the door in his face.

If he had behaved outrageously, so had I, though I was very satisfied with myself, and when I told my mother about it, she did not seem to mind either. But if my behavior could hardly be excused, it expressed in some way my attitude toward the German Protestant Church at that time. I had never so far met any believing Protestants save two; the one was Frau Kirschner, whose rather melancholy attitude failed to recommend her religion to me, the other was my grandmother, but she came into the category of "old people," for whom religion apparently had its uses. All others were just nominal Christians and did not seem to hold any definite beliefs of any kind. In these circumstances what was called the Evangelical Church seemed to me to have no *raison d'être* whatever. I thought its ministers hypocrites, because I could not understand why they should have taken up their profession. Pfarrer Mauff in particular had never been able to gain my respect. After all, I was in the period of puberty, and like many other girls and boys of my age, reacted violently against accepted opinions and conventions, and their representatives. I had no use for Christianity in the form it was known to me, as something irrational and sentimental. The image of Christ Himself, invariably presented as 'meek and mild,' to which I was expected to conform myself, was utterly abhorrent to me.

Some time after my scene with the Pfarrer, who to my great relief never made another attempt to bring back the stray sheep, I was on holiday at Marburg, in the house of a friend of my father, Geheimrat H., a professor of mathematics. Frau H. and I had a conversation during which she said that we must only love, never hate, I flashed back, with all the vigor of my fourteen years: "If we cannot hate properly, we also cannot love properly." Frau H. was shocked; but my remark was just another reaction against the prevalent milk-and-water version of Christianity, and against a correspondingly distorted conception of Christian love.

When, many years later, I read in Catholic papers about the "leakage" problem among teen-agers I remembered my own revolt from all religion at that time of my life. I am not sure whether I should have revolted so violently against a true presentation of Christianity. I quite possibly might have. It seems a natural thing that the soul, too, should rebel at a time when the body passes through a period of crisis, and if such be the case, the worst educational policy would be to enforce external conformity. On the other hand, a presentation of Christianity as it really is, as supra-rational, though not at all irrational, as a religion satisfying all human needs, more especially also the youthful instinct of hero-worship, might well have attracted rather than repelled me. The trouble in my case, and, I am sure, in innumerable others, not least in a certain kind of convent school education, was that, after I had lost my child's faith, Christianity had never been presented to me as a "grown-up" religion. Everything else grew and developed, my literary and artistic tastes and understanding, my knowledge of languages and science and history— only Christianity was just a sentimental story with some incredible miracles attached. That many of the greatest human minds had not only believed, but found their complete contentment in it, remained entirely unknown to me.

4. *Formative Years*

AT EASTER 1921, when I was just fourteen, I began at last
to learn Greek, as I had wanted to so much ever since I had
been six. When I actually started, however, I did so with considerably less zest than might have been expected. The reason
was that we had a teacher who was very kind and scholarly,
but quite incapable of keeping a crowd of lively young girls
in order.

A class of schoolchildren seem to have an uncanny kind
of collective instinct for the disciplinary gifts or otherwise
of a teacher. Poor Frau Loeschcke, the widow of a well-
known classical scholar, was completely powerless from the
first moment. She gave us eight Greek and six Latin lessons a
week, and we, who had only a few weeks ago presented a
most edifying picture of industrious young girls, their heads
demurely bent over the pages of Caesar's *Bellum Gallicum*,
were now transformed into a roaring, seething mass of hooli-
gans against whose noise Frau Loeschcke could hardly make
herself heard. Her untidy grey hair was gathered into a bun
which would periodically shed one pin after another with a
slight clink, till it finally came down on her shoulders in a
gentle cascade. "There you have it, children; one really ought
not to wash one's hair," was her invariable comment.

She was so nervous that she would often utter the most amazing nonsense. "Frau Loeschcke, can I ask you something?"

"Yes, but without speaking."

"How am I to do that?"

"Be quiet!"

"Please may I leave the room?"

"Yes, but go only before the door and attend to what is most necessary and that at once."

"Leaving the room" was, in fact, one of our favorite pastimes. As we were of an age when occasional sudden indisposition was to be expected, a certain license was granted us in this matter. In Frau Loeschcke's lessons some of us, including myself, happened to be permanent sufferers. The general noise was such that she could not hear in any case what ground of excuse we gave for walking out, and so we normally contented ourselves with murmuring: "Brummel-brummel sick" or "Brummel-brummel leave the room". She was probably quite glad when I thus removed myself, for I used to cause all manner of disturbances besides being impertinent. Once, as I was sitting on a radiator for the double advantage of being warm and near a friend to whom I was chatting, she told me to go back to my seat.

"It is much too cold over there," I replied.

"But think what our German soldiers had to endure during the war."

"But I am not a German soldier"—and I refused to budge.

As we had the agreeable rule that, when leaving the room, we had to be accompanied by another girl to assist in case of necessity, we generally contrived to take one of our best friends with us. So it might happen that two, three, or even four pairs were promenading in the corridors, exchanging all the latest news, discussing their various "crushes," but also more highbrow subjects.

My literary interests had become even more intense in

these years of puberty. My great love then and for a long time was Goethe. It is difficult for anyone not brought up in the circles of the unbelieving German bourgeoisie of the nineteenth and early twentieth centuries to realize just what Goethe meant to us. He was not simply one of the world's greatest poets, as Shakespeare is to the English and Dante to the Italians. He was at the same time a sage, a prophet whose words were full of wisdom, whose life was a marvel of achievement, whose Weltanschauung was to become part of ourselves, whose very weaknesses were, in him, virtues, since he was a "genius," bound by no moral law. If Goethe made love to an innocent girl and then left her (we had to know all his many love affairs in detail, because they had inspired so much of his poetry), she was really to consider herself supremely honored. Which of us would not have wanted to be kissed by Goethe and immortalized in one of his poems? If he carried on an intrigue with a married woman—Charlotte von Stein was a household name to us—surely the husband must realize that a Goethe could not be expected to suppress a passion "necessary" for his poetical development?

I am not exaggerating. This was the attitude implied in Goethe's own writings, and taken up by those who taught us. I accepted it unquestioningly, and immersed myself in Goethe almost to intoxication. At the age of fourteen I had read most of his works except the scientific ones, the *Iphigenie* alone no less than seven times; for the musical beauty of its language enchanted me. I knew much of his poetry by heart, and though my views on him have changed considerably since those early days, the perfect simplicity of his lyrics has remained for me an ideal unsurpassed by the complicated effusions of modern authors needing a running commentary to be intelligible.

Nevertheless, it is at least arguable that the totally uncritical cult of Goethe not only as a poet but as a man and a thinker has had a harmful influence on many generations

of German youth. He was known to us as the "great pagan."
In one of his most famous ballads, *Die Braut von Korinth*, he
mourns the passing of the gay sensuality of pagan Greece,
and the advent of the sombre creed of Christianity, with its
"unheard-of human sacrifice" (*Menschenopfer unerhoert*)
of virgins dedicated to Christ. My first idea of Rome and
Italy came from his *Italienische Reise*. He understood and
presented Rome entirely in classical and Renaissance terms,
and his lascivious *Roemische Elegien* completed my lopsided
picture of it as a city of past artistic greatness and present
sensual enjoyment.

Goethe's amoral influence was ably seconded by our German master. Dr. Kesseler was an unusual type: lively, temperamental, totally uninterested in us as human beings, but
nearly always rousing us to argument and discussion. Though
he was only in his mid-thirties, he looked much older, being
bald and rather fat. He everlastingly complained about the
cold. He usually appeared slightly late, with his hat and coat
on, and after consulting the thermometer in the class room,
decided that we must have had the windows open during
break for more than the exactly two minutes he conceded
us. After a long peroration on our disobedience in this particular and our bad behavior in general (though we were
really exemplary in his lessons), he would proceed to discuss
the play we were just then reading.

Grillparzer's *Medea* provided matter for interminable arguments between him and us. The main theme of it is the
unfaithfulness of Jason, the Greek hero, to Medea, his bar-
barian wife whom he abandons mercilessly for a girl of his
own culture. We were all on the side of Medea, Kesseler on
that of Jason. His argument was that Jason, being "a Greek
and a civilized man," had every right to forsake Medea when
he had tired of her foreign ways. We took the view that,
quite on the contrary, precisely because he was supposed to
be so much superior to her, he had the greater responsibility

and ought to have made allowances. Kesseler also gave Scripture lessons—indeed he was a licentiate of theology—but it never seems to have struck him that the views he defended before a class of impressionable young girls were simply immoral. The "double morality" which forbade to women what was allowed to men, had eaten deeply into the whole moral fabric of the German bourgeoisie and had evidently become part of his whole outlook. We also read Schiller's *Wallenstein* with him; and he would generally sum up the bad actions of the various characters of this and other plays as "psychologically understandable, though ethically to be rejected," implying that there could be no ultimate decision between right and wrong.

I had by now a circle of friends with similar interests. The most unusual of them was Marianne von den Steinen. She was the daughter of an explorer, and like me of mixed "Aryan-Jewish" parentage, the youngest of eight brothers and sisters, all very gifted. She wore her hair short, which was then still quite extraordinary, and in addition she had a string of beads around her forehead which gave her a rather theatrical appearance. But as she had fine, almost classical features, she carried it off without inviting ridicule.

She was slightly *exaltée,* and our views on literature and art were sufficiently different to make conversation interesting. She shared my admiration for Goethe. It was on the subject of modern literature that our tastes clashed. Her great favorite was Stefan George, "austere and beautiful," qualities which she considered essential for art to the exclusion of much else I felt necessary. His poems were written in a very artificial language expressing rarified emotions and appreciations quite foreign to me. He further irritated me by having them printed in special type resembling Greek on handmade paper, so as to distinguish himself and his work as far as possible from the vulgar crowd. As a final touch he used to recite his poetry by candle light, wrapped in a purple cloak.

All this seemed to me simply escapism from the realities of life, whereas I was quite consciously living in my time, in this world here and now, in the seething hodge-podge of a Berlin just beginning to go mad with the inflation. I read the papers and took a lively interest in politics and social questions, concerns which were far removed from the onesidedly aesthetic outlook of George and his followers. Moreover, whereas Marianne had ambitions of becoming an actress—only classical plays, of course—I wanted to be a journalist, and even occasionally produced handwritten 'newspapers' for the instruction of my school friends, complete with reports of Lloyd George's speeches in the Commons, a murder story, the installment of a novel and advertisements.

The poems I made at this time, typical puberty products, showed unmistakably the influence of Goethe. They expressed the desire for a purely human perfection, love of nature and the beauty of a spring day; they were written in a book carrying on its fly-leaf the words from Faust: "Him who strives without ceasing we can redeem."

At Easter we had a festivity to celebrate our transfer to the "upper school," the most thrilling feature of which was that we would no longer be called by our Christian names but *Fräulein,* followed by our surname. On this occasion 1 produced a special journal which among other contributions, contained a long poem ridiculing the classical authors we had been reading during that year, Cicero, Caesar and Xenophon, in the style of Heinrich Heine. Beside Goethe he was one of my favorite writers which he remained for several years to come; not only on account of his fine lyrical poetry, but even more because of his insolent travesties, which appealed to a trait in my own character. In the journal we were each given a verse, produced in collaboration, describing our salient characteristics. My verse was: "Can a dog bite worse than Hiltgunde's sarcasms?" I could not deny the truth of it.

There had been some discussion whether I should stay at

school and go on to the university, or whether, in view of my
journalistic leanings, it might not be better to leave now,
learn shorthand and typing and take some job in an editor's
office. I did not like the idea; but as owing to the inflation
our financial situation was deteriorating, I agreed that I
would myself earn my pocket money by coaching. At the
same time another question arose: English was now no longer
a compulsory subject. I quite enjoyed it, but I never liked
working more than absolutely necessary except for my favorite subject of German literature, and so I told my mother I
was going to drop English. She protested, but I objected that
we were allowed to decide this for ourselves, and I had quite
enough to do with Latin, Greek and mathematics. This pro-
voked a storm of the first magnitude. As long as I was living
in her house, my mother thundered, I was to do as she told
me. English was the world language, far more important
than my Latin and Greek. I must continue the lessons. She
added, prophetically, that I would one day thank her for
insisting. As I was still grumbling under my breath, repeating
that we were allowed to make our own decision, she worked
herself up into a real rage, so that there was nothing left for
me but to succumb. I have never regretted it.

I had it firmly implanted in my mind that I was entirely
lacking in any understanding of mathematics, for no other
reason than that my father had always been bad at it. It was
actually a pose which I felt justified in taking up, since my
other achievements were sufficient to keep me normally in
the fourth place. This fully satisfied my ambition, while not
making inordinate demands on the time devoted to my homework. Dr. Frohn, our mathematics master, who was now also
our form master, liked me and was always trying to rouse me
from my mathematical torpor. I can still hear him arguing
with me in his nasal voice: "But, Fräulein Graef, you have
quite enough intelligence to manage the mathematics required
at school—why don't you pull yourself together!" But I

failed to respond to his blandishments. He sometimes liked to tease us with cryptic remarks. When one of us asked him what electricity actually was he replied: "Do you know the Mona Lisa?" And, in answer to the vacant expression on the face of the enquirer. "Yes, that is electricity." No further elucidation was forthcoming.

For Greek we now had the oddest master imaginable. His name was Hartstein, and he liked to pun on it: "Beware of me, I am hard-as-stone—Hart-Stein." He was of Gargantuan dimensions and fond of using swearwords; indeed, his demeanor was more suited to the barracks than to a girls school. His achievements as a disciplinarian were in inverse ratio to his size and the immense volume of his voice. When we had infuriated him, as happened only too frequently, it would rise to such roars as to bring in the teacher from the adjacent classroom imploring him to moderate its vigor. We ceased even to pretend to do any work for him, and relied exclusively on cribs.

I was now evolving a religion of my own, resembling agnostic humanism. In a somewhat pretentious iambic poem I stated that religion should be perfectly free, untrammelled by dogma, because no religion had the whole truth. "Man bears what is highest in his own heart, no priest can give or take it, and no formula can wholly contain it. Why then all these ceremonies, why hosts, chalices, incense boats? Freely the human soul swings itself up to the sun and adores in its own pure light." I doubt whether I knew myself exactly what this was supposed to mean. But, in retrospect, it seems very odd that I, a Protestant, should have mentioned hosts and chalices as the first symbols of religion.

Yet despite this agnostic bravado I would sometimes lie awake at night a long time, tortured by a fear which today would be called existential. I was desperately afraid of death, because it meant nonexistence. It was agony to think that this ego that was I, this consciousness which returned to life every morning, should one day, however far off, simply cease to be. Belief in eternal life was surely no more than a wish-dream of those fearing to face death, as I was now trying to do, though my whole being revolted against it. So I was lying in the dark with my heart beating audibly, trying to imagine the unimaginable, that the world would go on and my consciousness, which knew it, would be wiped out. At last, when I could bear it no longer, I would forcibly put the thought out of my mind and go to sleep.

The literary expression of this fear was an odd, half-expressionistic poem called "Time." "I walked through a dark forest, farther and farther through the frightening night; my light step sounded gruesome as if a spirit were laughing at the Godhead. I came to a dim lake, its black surface smooth as a mirror, all human pain that earth has ever seen is lying in this lake. I heard a murmuring spring, but its water was full of grey sand—no sacrificial death will ever make it clear, the water that springs from the rock. I saw a quick-rushing river flowing into sorrowful depths; may its water never touch your foot—the river is everyman's grave. The river will destroy worlds and suns, it flows into the unfathomable; its water is bitter and salt, the name of the river is Time."

This instinctive fear of being imprisoned in the inexorable flux of time which would finally carry me to destruction was increased by my reading. I had turned from the serene world of the German classical authors to the sombre, gripping excitement of Ibsen and Strindberg, of Tolstoy and Dostoevsky. Germany was now in the midst of the inflation. I was earning some pocket money by giving private lessons, especially Latin, which were paid at the rate of a loaf of bread each, because it was quite impossible to fix a price in terms of the money that was losing its value from one day to the other, later even hour by hour. So I simply bought books as soon as I received my pay. I reduced my homework to the absolutely necessary minimum and read, read, read . . . *The Idiot*, with the enigmatic figure of Prince Myshkin made an immense impression on me; Raskolnikov, *The Possessed*, opened up a new world, not a real world, but the haunting world of Dostoevsky's imagination that was holding me captive till the small hours of the morning, regardless of my mother's protests. Gogol, too, enchanted me with his cossacks and his *Lost Souls*. And then I discovered Strindberg, with his black pessimism nourished on absinth, and became myself intoxicated with his bitter *Dance of Death, Miss Julie, Damascus*. This was reality—desperate, violent, amoral. And so I immersed myself, vicariously as it were, in a world of heady *fin-de-siècle* decadence that did me no harm, because, despite my nocturnal fears, I was really, as a slightly neurotic friend once expressed it, "disgustingly healthy."

At the same time my circle of friends began to develop a veritable craze for the theater. The *Deutsches Theater* and the *Grosses Schauspielhaus*, the latter recently founded by Max Reinhardt, became our favorite haunts. We had just enough pocket money to buy tickets for the gallery, where there were only about four seats from which one could see the stage properly; so we used to queue up many hours before the play started, and then made a dash for the gallery door as soon as the outer doors were opened. There was more queuing before the gallery itself, and eventually, about half an hour before the curtain went up, we had secured our seats. I do not think I have ever in later life enjoyed the theater so much as in these early years, when every play was an adventure of the spirit, and the actors were invested in our imagination with a splendor that seemed not quite of this world.

The general craze of the moment was Alexander Moissi, who expressed perfectly the neurotic, highly emotional atmosphere in which we were all living. His languid manner and singsong inflexion ("He has a voice like expensive chocolates" said Frohn to our horror) was the same whether he was playing Hamlet or Oswald in Ibsen's *Ghosts*; it certainly fitted best Tolstoy's *Living Corpse*, which completely knocked us out. My own predilection, however, was neither Moissi nor his younger imitator Ernst Deutsch, but the more masculine Werner Krauss, whose King Lear remained unforgettable, especially in the scenes after the blinding. Shaw was then the favorite author of the Berlin public, and Krauss' interpretation of Professor Higgins in *Pygmalion* and of Caesar in *Caesar and Cleopatra* were delight to my penchant for irony and debunking.

We preferred to go to first nights, because we enjoyed the atmosphere of general excitement and liked to compare the impressions of the reviewers next morning with our own. Naturally our theater-going habits made us rather late, for usually the performance was not over till after eleven; on the first night of *King Lear* it was even well after midnight when I got home, finding my mother standing in the hall weeping, because she was afraid I had met with an accident. There was quite a scene, while I was explaining that first nights always took longer, and that I could not possibly be expected to leave until Werner Krauss had made his last appearance before the curtain.

Not only my mother was upset, however, but also our teachers, because our work naturally suffered from this theater craze; nor did they consider Ibsen's and Tolstoy's marriage plays very suitable for us sixteen and seventeen year olds. We, however, would chant with gusto the popular strikers' song: "And if they put caviar on the soles of our shoes, we will not, no we will not be tempted to work."

We could work, however, and quite hard, when it was a question of acting ourselves. Our class was generally considered outstanding in four things: intelligence, laziness, noisiness, and theatrical ability. Our most ambitious venture was a performance, in French, of Molière's *Précieuses ridicules*, for which we even produced our own costumes. I had to play the long part of Mascarille, so no one could really expect me to do much else besides; this was at least my own opinion.

In Latin we had a highly boring mistress at the time, Dr. Tangl, whose lessons I would spend either in the corridor, or corresponding with my cronies under the table. She had a craze for old inscriptions, and this gave me the idea to play a prank on her. On the morning of April 1st, a few days before the end of the school year, I displayed a most unusual interest in her lesson. I told her that I had come across a journal in which some newly discovered Latin verse inscriptions had been published, which I had copied out for her. At once she was all agog, and I had to read them out, first from my place, then again from the teacher's platform. She was quite enchanted with them, praising the wonderful archaic rhythm and the simplicity of the language. She then took the paper from me and began to analyze the archaic forms for our benefit both etymologically and grammatically. At last she gave me back the paper, asking in which journal I had found these masterpieces. "April fool!—Made them myself last night!"

Poor Dr. Tangl stood thunderstruck. When she had recovered a little she began to laugh hysterically (she always laughed like a boy whose voice is just breaking) and finally moaned: "And my brother did warn me only this morning to beware of the 1st of April!" Alas, she could escape the fatal date no more than Caesar the Ides of March.

We were, indeed, fairly demoralized. But so was everyone else; for the year was 1923, Germany was in the last stages of the inflation, the atmosphere, particularly in Berlin, resembled a madhouse. My mother received her normally monthly salary every other day; as soon as she came home from school at lunchtime she would put some notes in my hand—hundred thousand marks or millions, as the case might be—and tell me to rush down to the grocer to get some butter and cheese, because at night the prices were bound to be up by at least fifty per cent. The shops changed their price tickets twice a day, sometimes even three times; news vendors called out no other headings but: the Dollar . . . a hundred-thousand marks . . . the Dollar . . . five-hundred-thousand marks . . . a million, ten million . . . a milliard . . . twenty-five milliards . . . a billion!!

Our heads were reeling; we felt it would go on like this forever, and were quietly preparing ourselves for trillions and quadrillions. Berlin was teeming with foreigners living in the best hotels for about a shilling a day, buying all they could. I myself earned a little extra money by acting as interpreter for an Anglo-Indian family with whom I went to the smartest shops where they bought the most expensive dresses, laughing at the absurdly low prices they had to pay for them. So why should we not spend our last millions on the theater? Surely that was better than putting them in the wastepaper basket a week later, which would then be all they were fit for.

In the midst of this hurlyburly of inflation, theater going and riotous reading, another influence entered my life. At Easter 1923 a new Scripture master made his appearance. Studienrat Schlemmer was a colorful personality. Coming from the youth movement, by religious conviction a liberal Lutheran, philosophically an ardent Neo-Kantian of the Marburg school of Cohen and Natorp, he used the modern methods of *Arbeitsunterricht* and had almost all of us keenly interested and breathlessly attentive from the first minute of his lessons to the last. He treated us as grownups, discussing all sorts of questions—in fact he told us that everything ought first to become a problem to us. Soon he was so popular that even some of our Jewish girls attended his lessons. He made a deep impression on me, which actually went far beyond the ordinary school girl's "crush," though I was afflicted with all its usual symptoms. Naturally I was quickly teeming with problems which had to be taken to him for discussion at all times in and out of lessons—nor was I the only one. He was usually to be seen during breaks deep in conversation with some girl or other. The German youth movement greatly emphasized the "Führer-principle" so dear to the German character, the young people choosing an older person, whether teacher or student, as their guide to whom they brought all the questions of their life for advice and decision. Though I did not belong to the youth movement and had no intention of joining it—shapeless dresses and sentimental guitar-playing have always repelled me—I soon asked Schlemmer to become my "leader," an office which he graciously accepted, though I was not prepared to fall in with all his views.

What puzzled me most was that he was a practising Lutheran who went to church every Sunday with his wife (they had no children) and yet, in all philosophical matters, fully accepted the Neo-Kantian agnosticism. When we had found out his philosophical interests we asked him to give us some extra philosophical conferences, which most of us attended. We read with him Kant's *Metaphysics of Morals* and later Nietzsche. In my summer holidays that year I went once more to Brunshaupten, and there, mostly sitting on a seat in the forest, I performed the prodigious feat of reading through the entire *Critique of Pure Reason*. It is quite incomprehensible to me today how I brought it off—without my intense devotion to Schlemmer I should never have dreamt of doing it. Though I could have understood it only very partially, the mental effort of trying to grasp Kant's closely reasoned arguments by which he attempted to define the scope of human knowledge was a fine training in logical thinking; so I have never regretted this strange holiday "recreation."

Later in the year Schlemmer also took us over in German, where I had no difficulty in playing first fiddle. My cousin Werner had introduced me to Rembrandt, some of whose best paintings were in the Kaiser Friedrich Museum. I was

immediately attracted by the extraordinary spiritual penetra-
tion of his portraits as well as by his inimitable chiaroscuro.
So when my turn came to give a talk, a novelty Schlemmer
had introduced into the German lessons, I chose as my subject: "Goethe and Rembrandt." The two had really not much
in common; but I was trying to show how both of them
lived true to their genius, and expressed, each in his own way
and medium, what is highest in man. This "highest thing in
man" was one of my favorite subjects in those days, when my
atheism had reached a note of defiance that was the echo of
Nietzsche, whose *Thus Spake Zarathustra* my friends and I
were eagerly discussing.

It is almost impossible to understand the extraordinary
influence of Nietzsche unless he be read in German, for much
of his attraction is due to the intoxicating beauty and rhythm
of his language. His influence was powerfully seconded by
our onesidedly classical education. We were now reading
Horace in an unexpurgated edition (as soon as Herr Schiering
left out a poem we would pounce on it at home) as well as
the Greek lyrics, Mimnermos and Sappho among them; and
I amused myself with making metrical translations of some
of their poems. My own poetical efforts of this time faithfully reflect the mixture of Nietzsche and the classics: "Enjoy life, for death will come soon; live for the day, for there
is no God. You, men, are yourselves measure and end, therefore vanquish the iron 'must' of fate. . . . Yet joy can only
come from what is noble and pure. We mortals judge, for we
are the measure, in us there is love and reverence and hate.
All-vanquishing death will soon snatch us away—therefore
live your life, for there is no God."

Much of this was no doubt "literature"; the classical
"Man is the measure of all things" had taken hold of me, as
had the equally classical concept of inescapable fate as rul-
ing man's destiny. Yet there was something more to it than
mere external influences. I wanted unity. About the same

time I wrote another poem with this as its title, asking my
senses to cling to the earth, their home, and my soul to rise
upwards to the light; "The body nourished by the soil, the
spirit by light, so let us be one and not separate ourselves."
I could not accept the religion offered me at school, because
it rent the unity which I desired, the unity between body and
soul on the one hand—for Protestantism has no use for the
senses except the ear—and between intellect and feelings on
the other, because even my ideal, Schlemmer, was capable of
believing one thing as a philosopher and quite another as a
churchgoer.

It was at this stage that he discovered that I had not been
confirmed. He told me he must speak to me about it, and
when we had both for some reason or other a free period he
took me into the large school hall, the only room free at the
moment, and there we sat talking, arguing, he persuading, I
resisting. Though I had asked him to be my "leader," he was
having a difficult time with me. I cannot remember all his
arguments; one of them I thought particularly fatuous: he
pointed out that I should not be able to be married in church
unless I were confirmed. As I knew that, owing to my father's
objections, my parents had been married only in a registry
office, I could see no reason why I should not do the same—
quite apart from the fact that marriage was very far from
my thoughts at that time. Schlemmer knew of course my
utter lack of belief, which did not seem to worry him, and
realized that any religious arguments would be even more
useless than his practical suggestions. Finally he asked me
whether I would let myself be confirmed if he found me a
pastor prepared to accept only some quite vague promises,
such as that I would try to live as a Christian—whatever that
might mean in the case of someone who did not even believe
in God!—and that even if I ceased to be one I would not
publicly turn against Christianity. I have never quite understood why he was so extraordinarily anxious to see me con-

firmed; but as he seemed to set such great store by it, I was prepared to submit to the ceremony on the terms he had suggested, and he told me that a friend of his, a brother of the author Georg Kaiser, whose play *Gas* I had just been reading with great interest, would probably consent to confirm me with all these safeguards to my conscience.

In the spring of 1924, therefore, I went for several weeks to Pfarrer Kaiser for instructions. He was a very broadminded and cultivated man, and I enjoyed our talks, though religion did not come in at all, as far as I can remember. He never asked me to go to church, and it never occurred to me to do so. At least not to a Protestant church. But in the beginning of May, Schlemmer, who treated Catholicism very objectively (he even explained Indulgences and the Infallibility of the Pope quite correctly), told us we ought to go into a Catholic church at this time, because they were having beautiful May devotions with plenty of flowers and candles. This seemed interesting, so one evening I went into the Ludwigskirche which was quite near us.

I had hardly entered, genuflecting, as I saw everyone else doing, and which seemed to me quite natural, when I felt extraordinarily happy and experienced a strange attraction from somewhere, which I could not explain at all. I knew nothing, of course, of the Blessed Sacrament, much less of what actually happened at Mass, though in Church History we had discussed the question of Transubstantiation. I only realized, to my intense surprise, that I liked being in this church, whereas I greatly disliked being in a Protestant church on the rare occasions when I was forced to go there with my school. The attraction was so strong that I went again the next day. Then I thought it might be a good idea to go to Mass on Sunday, as I knew this was the principal Catholic service. This bowled me over completely. It was a Low Mass, with no external ceremonies that might have accounted for the attraction. Yet at the ringing of the bell my whole being was simply thrilling in response to I knew not what. When I came out of the church that morning I said to myself: If I go inside a Catholic church even once again I shall become a Catholic—and I do not even believe in God! This of course is ridiculous. Whatever this queer attraction may be that I feel every time I go inside that church I am not going to give way to it. And so, as I was not prepared to let what I took to be mere emotion get the better of my reason, I made up my mind then and there never to go inside a Catholic church again. I was seventeen at the time, and I kept my resolution for just about another seventeen years.

I told neither Schlemmer nor anyone else of this strange experience in the Ludwigskirche, for I was rather ashamed of it. I hated being carried away by feelings. My confirmation was to take place towards the end of June. Schlemmer told me I ought really to go to church at least once before being confirmed; on June 23rd there was going to be a special "Johannisnacht" service conducted by Pfarrer Kaiser with lights and hymns. I went and sat through the service, but though it was rather "romantic" I had no desire to repeat the experience.

On the day of the confirmation I was in my most defiant mood. I did not wear a black dress, as is usual in the German Protestant Church, but a white summer frock. Then, giving way to some strange urge, I put a red rose in my belt. Mother was aghast.

"Are you quite crazy? Take that rose out of your belt. You are not going to your wedding, are you?"

"I am going to keep that rose, I want it."

"You can't. They won't confirm you in that get-up."

"They will confirm me, and I will have that rose."

"You are mad."

"Never mind."

I had my way, and the rose. I could not say now, and I could not have explained it at the time, why this rose in my belt suddenly assumed such importance, despite my normal dislike of anything smacking of the theatrical. I think I seized on it as a symbol, meant to signify the world, the excitement of life I was feeling so keenly at this time, as opposed to the black, or rather grey dullness which I associated with the Protestant Church and Christianity in general. For I never regarded the strange "thrill" which had electrified me so disturbingly in the Catholic church as connected with any religious experience.

I had invited a number of my school friends to the ceremony. I do not remember much of the service, except that I made my promises, which even some of my Jewish friends who were present considered not particularly Christian, and then received communion together with my mother. I carefully prevented any emotion that might arise in me during this act by deliberately watching a fly that was creeping along on the black gown of the Pfarrer.

If I had been a believer I might have thought it providential that I should have been confirmed at a time when I urgently needed support. For just then Schlemmer told us that he was going to leave after the summer vacation, as he had been made headmaster at a school at Frankfurt-on-the-Oder. I realized only then how much this relationship had meant to me. I managed to keep a hold on myself in school that morning; but when I came home and told my mother, I dissolved into a flood of tears. All through dinner I kept sobbing, so that Mother got very impatient. "Don't be so ridiculous. You couldn't have married the man anyway, so why on earth are you carrying on like this." I could not make her understand that Schlemmer and marriage were two incompatible ideas, even if he had not been married already, and that my relationship with him was on a totally different plane. "Eat your dinner and stop this nonsense." I gulped down my food and decided that the only person who would understand was my aunt Sabine. I would go to her.

Sabine Lepsius was a portrait painter by profession, but also very musical, widely read, of outstanding intelligence, besides a shrewd businesswoman who kept a fairly large household going mostly by her own work. She had been very beautiful as a girl, with a large circle of admirers. Now, when she was about sixty, she was an imposing figure, of great feminine charm as well as dignity. She and her husband, Reinhold Lepsius, also a portrait painter, had been intimate friends of Stefan George, who would from time to time read his poems in their house. But by the time I was old enough to be invited to her parties, the friendship had come to an end. I never discovered the reason, but she tried to interest me in his work and lent me his poems, which I now read more carefully, but still disliked as heartily as ever.

Sabine was also an excellent hostess. At the parties she gave her guests quickly formed themselves into small groups; as soon as she saw the conversation flagging in one of them, she would go and by some actually very carefully chosen, but seemingly chance remark stir up a lively discussion. When this was in full swing she would go to another group which she saw needed a spark. She was not above some play-acting in order to produce "atmosphere." I was sometimes invited to a meal with the family (she had three daughters, all considerably older than I) before the party started. Then I had an opportunity to observe one of her favorite devices. Having been busy getting everything ready till the very last moment, she would suddenly make a dash for the grand-piano and begin to play in the dimly lit drawing room a few seconds before the first visitors were expected to ring. When the maid opened the door to usher them in she would go on playing, with a far-away look in her eyes, until a sufficient number had arrived. Then she suddenly seemed to come to, and, her arms spread out in welcome to the guests who had reverently stopped near the door, she greeted them effusively: "Oh dearest, I am so sorry I did not notice you had come in

—but I do get so few opportunities for playing nowadays." It was a superbly acted scene. The visitors were quick to take their cue urging her to carry on, which she of course refused, and soon the conversation was in full swing. I could not help smiling, having watched how hastily she had arranged herself before the piano in the nick of time, but I did appreciate the art in what, to the others, seemed perfectly natural.

When, on that June day in 1924, I came to her to pour out my sorrow, she took me up into her small study which I liked particularly, because it had an atmosphere of intimacy inviting confidential talks. Though she might sometimes appear cool and courting effect, Sabine was really a warm hearted and courageous woman, who had deeply suffered when she lost her only son, Stefan, in the war. She was the first person to mention to me the names of the medieval German mystics, and showed me a book by Henry Suso, though I did not take notice of it then.

She understood my relationship with Schlemmer and the shock his loss gave me far better than my mother; and after having poured out my heart to her I felt considerably relieved. Yet, though I loved and admired her and liked to be with her, the *l'art pour l'art* attitude which she and her circle represented were far removed from my own aspirations. About this time I noted down my impressions of the world for which she stood:

"There is a strange air in the Lepsius' house. When I go there, I always have the feeling as if there were no twentieth century with its problems, its social questions, its expressionism, its youth movement. Dusty nineteenth century, outworn impressionism, feminism, all these give me a feeling of suffocation when I am there. There is no youth. But I want expressionism, I want the sun-intoxicated figures of Pechstein, the vigorous masculine beings of Franz Marc; I want the passion-rent poems of Werfel, Kaiser's accusing social plays. I want wireless and traffic lights, skyscrapers and factories, I want ardent, autonomous youth. I want the struggle for expression, for religion. I want reforms—I want everything that comes to me warm, living, and strong in this glorious age. But it must be true and great—only untruthfulness and meanness are evil."

I loved my time; I loved Berlin, this most modern and rootless of European capitals. I loved nature, too, but as a city-dweller, without any nostalgic desire for going "back to the land." At this time I wrote a short essay on the desires of youth, expressing my own ideas on the relations between industrialization and "nature"—one of the very few subjects on which my views have never changed, and which became relevant to me in a new way about twenty years later. "They, (the young people I was describing) were city youth; yet despite their great love of nature they said Yes to the city, for they realized that it is impossible to put back the clock, and to abolish the achievements of the machine age in order to get rid of the misery which industry and the large cities have brought in their wake. They knew there were frightening abysses, but they wanted to look also into the depths when the time had come. For they were not allowed to close their eyes to vice and filth, to the repulsive things of the world, which do, indeed, exist—for they wanted to help."

The social problems agitated me much in this last school year. I was reading all the most recent German literature in which they played a central part; besides the writers already mentioned, I read Wassermann, Alfred Doeblin, Erich Maria Remarque. Yet I saw clearly the difficulties of the position of intellectuals like myself. A few months later I wrote: "Christ once said: They have eyes to see and they see not. But it is worse even to see and yet not to act. This is the fault of most people: cowardice. They see, but they fail to act accordingly. We all see the misery of the unemployed, of underpaid workers. We feel, we recognize that something ought to be done to better their lot. We are fully conscious of our own responsibility and even uneasy about it—yet, are we doing anything at all about it? No. We people of the twentieth century are far too easy-going and weak to change our mode of life. We talk and talk—but we fail to draw the consequences. We all ought to be ashamed of ourselves. And yet—would things get better if we would all suddenly give up our present way of life and devote ourselves to the poor? No; then we should be poor ourselves, we would have to do mechanical work and neglect our education, and finally be in the same state as those whom we wanted to help. The whole thing is a terrible muddle. I think only state intervention from above could bring real help. But we should at least endeavor to see the problem in its distressing reality, and help find a solution as far as in us lies. It is shameful to shut one's eyes to it completely, as does the circle round Stefan George."

Beyond longing for the welfare state and discussing the matter with my friends, I felt I could do nothing. It would never have occurred to me to live with the workers, like a Simone Weil, partly, I suppose, from cowardice, as I wrote myself, but partly also because my common-sense told me that it would only make me miserable without helping anyone else.

These manifold interests helped me to get over the shock of Schlemmer's departure. Besides, he was still accessible, for Frankfurt-on-the-Oder was only about an hour's train ride from Berlin where he had to go quite often; so I still met him fairly frequently and then he would take me out to a restaurant, so that I had the additional thrill of discussing my problems with him over lunch or a cup of coffee.

The summer vacation this year was not much of a holiday. For early in 1925 I was to take my final examination—and all these last years I had really only been working for the subjects I liked. Now the *Abitur* consisted of two parts, one written, the other oral. One might be excused the latter if he had high marks in at least two of the four written papers, and nothing less than satisfactory in the other two. I knew I should easily get high marks in German and Latin, but in mathematics I was the last in the class. On the other hand, if I should have to do the oral examination, there was almost bound to be a catastrophe because of my perennial laziness in the subsidiary subjects. The only thing to do was to drop all my pretences to finding mathematics unintelligible and get down to do some work on that in order to achieve a satisfactory and thus dispensation.

So in the summer holidays I went to my mother's birthplace, Weener on the Ems, near the Dutch frontier, to have a quiet four weeks of bracing air and hard cramming with the family of my mother's eldest brother. With a case full of mathematical books I settled down to make myself at last acquainted with the mysteries of parabolas and hyperbolas, sines and cosines, Cavallieri's principle and many other subjects I ought to have learned long ago. I was greatly relieved, though not altogether astonished, to find that I did understand mathematics when I tried to. Soon after my return I caused an uproar when my next mathematics paper turned out to be the best in the class, to the great satisfaction of Dr. Frohn who repeated over and over again: "I've always said it—you can do mathematics if you take the trouble."

At this time Scripture was taught us by a rather sentimental young mistress, Fräulein Kranold, who had a knack of talking about "the wonderful sobriety of St. Paul" with her eyes ecstatically raised to the ceiling and her fingers dug in her palms. She brought out all my worst instincts, and I made myself a perfect nuisance by continually arguing with her; for I had soon discovered that she simply could not give any reasons for her beliefs. When I pressed her, asking how one could believe that what she said was true, seeing it went right against reason, she had no other answer but: "You must have experienced it."

"But I haven't—so what?"

"Then I can't help you."

One day I had the idea to outrage her by reading aloud in class one of Heine's most blasphemous poems, *Disputation*, in which a Jew was made to sputter insults against Christ and His Mother. Heine himself had at one time become a Catholic, but then renounced Christianity; the poem in question belonged to this latter period. Fräulein Kranold was rightly shocked, but quite incapable of pointing out Heine's errors, and so the poet and I had the last word.

Yet for all my impertinent bravado the religious problem was still one of my main preoccupations, and despite the approaching examination I found time for elaborating my religious ideas in writing. My chief concerns were the existence of evil and the mystery of the Ego. As these notes are the last evidence of my interest in these matters for many years to come, I may perhaps be permitted to cite a few passages from them. In January 1925 I wrote:

"Evil may also be considered as something purely negative, that is as the not-being-there of the good. (As far as I remember this view of evil could not have come to me from any scholastic sources, as will be seen from the following). If we take this view of evil two consequences result for our conception of God: one either imagines God as a being that radiates good, but whose rays do not penetrate the world completely; or we shall arrive at the view that God is not wholly good, that He is a complex containing also other qualities, sending diverse radiations into the world." I illustrated my meaning by drawings, representing God and the world by two circles, and continued: "Both these views present God as an extramundane force sending out rays; they are far removed from any pantheism. They also contain the concepts of omnipresence and eternity, but not those of omniscience and omnipotence, which would presuppose a personal God, whereas a force can never be personal."

If I found the existence of evil puzzling, my own self

seemed even more mysterious, and I was keenly feeling its limitations. A few weeks later I wrote: "To me the concept of the Ego is one of the most problematical phenomena. It causes exultation and despair at the same time. *I think, I live, I do—* what wonderful words. This complex of the Ego, one body and one mind; one mind, which is capable of receiving and giving out, which can discover and invent new things. It is the talent entrusted to us that we may and ought to use according to a mysterious third, the will. This, too, is a strange faculty, just as inexplicable as the concept of the Ego. One can indeed describe it by words and metaphors, but one cannot really know what it is. Certainly, the consciousness of one's Ego causes elation. But it is also depressing, for it limits our being. If we could transcend the Ego-concept, we should be able to recognize objective truth and the thing-in-itself. But now we have a limited sphere in which we live, which is the Ego. And because of this Ego there can never be a total union of two human beings, for no man can penetrate completely through his Ego to the Thou. Even if we would perfectly mortify our Ego like the Indians, we could not do it. For it is I who mortify my Ego. Now I can mortify my Ego only when I will to do it, hence I still have a will, hence my Ego is still alive; and never will a man be able to transcend the Ego by any means, whether spiritual or physical. Yet every spiritual religion tries to do precisely this, which proves that men consider ridding themselves of self and becoming Ego-less the highest achievement. And thus I come to the concept of God as the non-Ego. God may not, He cannot say, "I am the Lord thy God," for He has no Ego. According to this conception God is either the Ego-less 'thing in itself' over against the I, or He is the totality of the world with the universality of its being. At the moment I am still undecided between these two possibilities."

I might well be. While writing these abstruse speculations which were, of course, largely influenced by Kant, I

nevertheless proclaimed aloud that I was totally uninterested
in philosophy and had no mind for it, in fact hated it. This
was an emotional reaction to my cousin Werner, who had
first studied medicine and then philosophy, the only subject
in which he was really interested. He worked especially on
Nietzsche, on whom he later wrote his doctor's thesis, and
during these years, when he was in his mid-twenties, he was
a rather unprepossessing embodiment of a superman. He
seemed to consider most human beings (except, I suppose,
Jaspers and Heidegger, whose disciple he became) far beneath
him, and if anyone else ventured an opinion in his presence
on any subject whatsoever an indulgent smile would say more
eloquently than words: "Poor little fool!" I had a particular
grouse at this time; for I remembered that six years ago,
when he had been preparing for the *Abitur* as I was now
doing, the atmosphere in his home had been permanently replete with awe. Hardly had the maid opened the door when
I came to see my uncle or aunt, when the latter would appear
at the back of the hall with her finger on her lips: "Sh, Werner is working." Now I was in the same position—but no
one took the slightest notice of whether I was working or
not. That I had nevertheless a sneaking admiration for him—
though heaven forbid that I should ever take work as seriously as he—did not improve matters. Yet my intense dislike of modern philosophy has been for the greater part due
to the picture of a philosopher he presented to me.

Our last months at school were greatly enlivened by a
romance that might have come straight out of a film. Among
the best in our class was Elly Holl, the elder daughter of the
well-known Lutheran theologian. She was a very attractive
girl with ash-blond hair and dark brown, almond-shaped eyes.
She was usually rather quiet, but could be very witty. She
had always been punctual; yet recently she had often been
late in the morning. We were wondering what had befallen
our conscientious Elly, when the rumor began to spread that

every morning, on her way to school, she met the son of our headmaster. Director Lenschau was a very clever and cultivated man much inclined to sarcasm. I liked him, though with reservations; his lessons were not vivacious, like those of Schlemmer, but, like himself, highly civilized and interspersed with funny stories. He had no qualms occasionally to joke with us at the expense of his own staff. Once he came into our classroom asking: "What is Scylla and Charybdis?" answering himself: "When I have safely passed the door of the ladies' staffroom I fall into the hands of Frau Oberstudienraetin"—his second in command, who was a perfect specimen of the authoritative spinster.

Naturally we were all agog at the news of Elly's meetings with Director Lenschau's son. When we found that the rumor was a fact, the whole class followed developments with bated breath. Though they met so often, letters, too, were exchanged. One morning, in a lesson given by none other than the headmaster himself, Elly could not prevent herself from once more reading Eric's latest billet-doux under the table. Suddenly Director Lenschau's glance fell on her bowed head. He kept looking at her, while the whole class were on tenterhooks wondering what would happen next; but Elly was far too engrossed to notice anything. At last the headmaster took a few steps forward: "How does he sign himself—yours lovingly?" There was a fearful commotion under Elly's table while she was trying to hide the note; then she looked up— her face as red as the reddest of poppies. Seeing this utter confusion the headmaster was too tactful to pursue the matter further—he never guessed that it was a letter from his own son that had thrown Elly into such a state. Like every true romance this one, too, had its complications. When the young couple decided to get engaged, Professor Holl was far from pleased. He was just about to be made Rector of Berlin University, and envisaged a brilliant young professor for his pretty daughter. Elly was in tears, but not to be swerved from her determination to have her Eric. We accompanied these vicissitudes with ardent sympathy for our romantic lovers, whose faithful devotion eventually broke down the resistance of the famous theologian—but this did not happen until after we had left school.

Early in February 1925 we sat for our written examination. Everything seemed to have gone well with me, even mathematics, so I was confident I was going to be excused the oral. I therefore had the impertinence to dispense myself from the sports examination. I had always hated gymnastics, though I liked games; and I was not going to produce myself in front of our sarcastic headmaster and the other male staff in our absurd gym bloomers, trying to heave my reluctant frame over horses and parallel bars. Instead I sat down on one of the former, consuming large quantities of fruit salad provided, according to custom, by the Lower Sixth, and grinning defiance at the alternate threats and blandishments of our gymnastics mistress, Fräulein Friese of the "legs like overturned champagne bottles," as we uncharitably described them.

This defiance no doubt gained me a special sermon from the headmaster when he announced who was going to be excused the oral. "Fräulein Graef, I am sorry to say we had to dispense you in accordance with regulations; but I am bound to tell you that we all are agreed that you have not really deserved it, because you have never taken enough trouble. Nevertheless, you have been dispensed."

This was meant to be a reproach, but as he was looking at me disapprovingly from behind his golden pince-nez, I felt my mouth extending to the broadest of grins. This, surely, was the crowning glory of my school career, to have achieved dispensation with a minimum of effort despite the reluctance of the headmaster and his staff. While the others were preparing for the oral examination, I gave vent to my political views in a highly emotional poem entitled "War and Fatherland," which ended thus: "Why all this murder? For the fatherland. What is that? Red lines on the map, denoting frontiers. Red lines—red with blood? This, fatherland? This, our highest good? In the fatherland all speak the same language. Then the whole world is my fatherland. The cries of the women in labor are everywhere the same, the groans of the dying are everywhere alike. Fatherland? I want to be united to all men, I want my hands pure from blood. I know states—may they exist without war. But above all states I want the world to be my fatherland."

It was my early reaction to the narrow Prusso-German nationalism I saw round me, and which I hated, because I realized even at that time its incompatibility with a truly human life.

I left school with an acute sense of frustration, which found its expression in a letter to the then influential *Vossische Zeitung*, in reply to an article which had extolled life in a school of the same type as the one at which I had been educated. I pointed out that the old conception of Greek classical culture as reflecting only simplicity and greatness, still taught at school but disproved by modern scholarship, held no attraction for modern youth, living in the age of expressionism. "Perhaps it would really be better to prepare our youth for the demands life will make on them. What, for example, is more profitable for our nation, whose future is in the hands of youth, learning Latin odes by heart or being taught our constitution? Might it not be advisable to devote one or two of the eight Greek lessons a week to contemporary history, to inculcate respect for our republic, of which there is unfortunately far too little at present? . . . . And if we cannot do without classical ideals, we ought to give them that of the self-sacrificing citizen of old Rome."

Only a few years later, the majority of the German university students turned out to be the most ardent supporters of Hitler. A one-sidedly intellectual school education such as

I was criticizing as soon as I had completed it was, perhaps, not altogether innocent of this. When we received the vote, a year or two after we left school, the great majority of us were certainly quite incapable of understanding any political issues that might confront us.

5. *Studies, Fashions and Flirtations*

BEFORE I entered on my studies our financial situation had to be clarified. During my last school years it had become apparent that my view on how much money I could reasonably be expected to spend on clothes differed considerably from Mother's. She had not much sense for dress, whereas mine had developed to such an extent that my dream was to become a fashion journalist. Therefore we were often at loggerheads when I wanted a new frock or hat. So we agreed that I should pay for clothes, holiday travel and other controversial items, whereas Mother would continue to be responsible for my home and food. This arrangement left me with sufficient financial burdens for a girl of eighteen, the greater part of whose time was to be devoted to study. I proposed to pay my way by means of coaching, which I had already started at school, only now it had to be on a much larger scale. After my first term I also had no longer to pay university fees, for, following a general means test, I passed a private examination by one of my professors at the end of each term, who then gave me a testimonial stating that my achievements were sufficient to warrant a scholarship.

In Germany the difference between school and university

is far greater than in the United States of America. At school all our work had been mapped out for us; we knew exactly what we had to do at any given time. When I had registered at Berlin University—studying anywhere else, as I should have liked to do, was out of the question for financial reasons —I was handed a closely printed book, the *Vorlesungsverzeichnis*, containing all the lectures, practices and "seminars" in all the four faculties, that is to say their titles and the names of the professors giving them. No further guidance was available, beyond an occasional indication in the catalogue "for beginners" or "for advanced students," but even these were rare. From this highly confusing document, I was expected to compose a timetable by my own unaided lights. This would have been difficult enough without any special snags; but I soon discovered that the times of the lectures were arranged on the assumption that English and French went together, and hence must not collide, as did also German and history; moreover, theology, being a faculty in itself and not belonging to philosophy, seemed to clash with everything else all round. But I had chosen German and theology as my principal subjects and English as a subsidiary, so to concoct an adequate timetable of lectures and seminars from this hodgepodge seemed beyond my powers of organization. Besides, I had also to study philosophy for the first four terms, when an examination in this redoubtable subject was enjoined on all students belonging to the Philosophical Faculty, and, to add a touch of perfect craziness, I had decided to attend some mathematical lectures—just to convince myself that mathematics were not altogether beyond my power of comprehension, after all.

All this was exciting enough. But university life had another than the merely intellectual side to it. It is true, I had attended dancing lessons when I was about fourteen, and had gone to balls in the houses of my friends, but men had so far played a negligible part in my life; though, owing to my promiscuous reading, there was little about the relationship of the sexes that I did not know. I think I must have been about fifteen or sixteen when my mother had the idea formally to forbid me two books, the Abbé Prévost's *Manon Lescaut* and Murger's *Bohème*. This sufficed to make me want to read them at once. As I had not seen them on our book shelves, I concluded that Mother must keep them locked up in her desk, the keys of which were in a basket on top of it. So one afternoon when she was not in, I opened the desk and took them out. Now I had derived part of my instruction on sex matters from a volume of seventeenth-century poems in my father's library which contained some very lascivious material bordering on the pornographic. Besides, my modern reading consisted of an assorted diet of Erich Maria Remarque, Doeblin, Ernst Juenger, Tolstoy, including his *Kreutzer Sonata* and his son's *Prelude by Chopin*. After this *Manon Lescaut* and *Bohème* seemed singularly tame; indeed disappointingly so, seeing they had been so strictly forbidden. Having read both from cover to cover without finding anything to warrant the maternal fears, I came to the conclusion that Mother had no idea of "modern youth" and that her innocence had better not be outraged by informing her that what she thought risqué seemed very stale to me.

Kant once wrote that innocence is a good thing, but unfortunately easily spoilt. In the absence of all sound moral teaching—the only reason for keeping chaste ever presented to me was that the consequences of the reverse might be very undesirable—it was perhaps just as well that I had sufficient knowledge not to run headlong into the more obvious dangers that existed in the all too free and easy life of Berlin University in the twenties. After a major war followed by revolution and inflation, the young men, unhampered by any religious sanctions, took their pleasure where they found it, and the women students, unless totally unattractive feminists, were the obvious targets on which to try their young mascu-

line charms. One started working together *à deux,* and after
an hour or so found oneself, without quite knowing how it
had happened, having soberly begun with Anglo-Saxon verbs,
in a highly flirtatious conversation.

Casta est quae non rogatur, we were told, with all the
authority Latin citations inevitably convey. While pretending to translate *Beowulf* together I remember once interrupt-
ing the flow of persuasive arguments on the part of one of
my fellow students, myself continuing his peroration for another five minutes. He looked at me, a mixture of pain, surprise, and acute stupidity in his normally not very expressive
china blue eyes.

"But how did you know? That is exactly what I was
going to say."

"Heard it too often, know it all by heart," came the cal-
lous reply. Needless to say, our collaboration came to an
abrupt end.

However, we did not only flirt. In those days Berlin had
a reputation for being a "working university," not a romantic
playground like Heidelberg. After my first outburst of
mathematics and Hebrew, required for Scripture as a principal subject, I assessed possibilities in a sobered frame of mind.
The German system of dispensing with tutors and leaving the
young students to their own devices certainly involves a considerable loss of time—the first and often also the second
term are almost wholly spent on finding one's way through
the maze of lectures and seminars—but it does encourage independent work. When, many years later, I began to study
in England, I found I could make myself acquainted with a
subject far more quickly than even the older English students, simply because I was used to doing my own research.

After my first exploratory term at Berlin I changed my
subjects round. I did not like to learn Hebrew, after all.
"Can't get my eyes to read from right to left," I said; so I
took Scripture as my subsidiary and English as my principal
subject.

The professor for modern English was Wilhelm Dibelius, a brother of the superintendent, later Bishop Dibelius. He was a short, spare man with a neatly trimmed grey beard and lively eyes. His special subject was the nineteenth century; his lectures on it were highly stimulating. If I later came to England with a greater understanding of English ways than most Continentals, I owe it very largely to his teaching. "The German university professor has lost the (first) World War," he used to tell us, "because the German students were never taught to grasp the English character. England is slow to anger. She will go on looking at things for a long time without doing anything at all, so that the others are deceived into thinking her hopelessly weak, with no energy left. But then, suddenly, a point will have been reached beyond which England is not prepared to go. Then she will spring into action, swift, decisive, efficient . . . Whether it be a matter of foreign affairs or internal reforms, things will be delayed and delayed again, until action is absolutely necessary, but then it will, indeed, come. This is the English way, it is extremely deceptive. But you must know it, you must realize it." At this point a note of urgency would creep into his voice which I have never forgotten, "You, the future leaders of Germany must fully grasp it, or you will be deceived yet again, and there will be another catastrophe."

While he was thus imploring us to understand England, a young Austrian paperhanger had just completed a two-year political prison term and was once more free to continue his activities. The professorial voice of Dibelius was crying in a political wilderness.

Because he thought a true understanding of England so essential, he would divide his lectures on the nineteenth century into a political and a literary part. Poor Laws and Enclosure Act, Catholic Emancipation and Reform of Parliament were subjects we had to know thoroughly; Disraeli and Gladstone became familiar figures to us, and the fundamental continuity of British policy whether conducted by Conserva-

tives or Liberals was impressed on us, and greatly impressed
at least one of his hearers. I do not think Dibelius actually
liked England, though he had a profound respect for it, and
for this reason one remark of his remained engraven on my
memory. "It is strange," he said, "England is almost always
on the side of right. Not out of sheer virtue, oh no—but it
simply so happens that in most modern political conflicts she
has supported the side of justice; no doubt because it coin-
cided with her advantage—but this in itself is remarkable."

The Church of England, too, received much attention in
his lectures, and he did his best to unravel to us the almost
incomprehensible intricacies of High, Low, and Broad, together with the religious as well as the political roles of the
Free Churches. On the literary side his favorite was Dickens.
In one of my periodic examinations for remission of fees he
asked me whom I liked better, Dickens or Thackeray. I had
no hesitation. For me Becky Sharp far outshone Little Nell,
and though I appreciated Dickens as a writer, his sentimentality got on my nerves. "Thackeray," I replied bravely,
knowing that he himself preferred Dickens.

"Why is that?"

"I like his irony."

Dibelius laughed. "Are you a Berliner?"

"Yes."

"Ah, that accounts for it."

We had practically no contact with English people at
Berlin University. Even the courses in advanced English syn-
tax, pronunciation and so forth were given us by a German,
Julius Freund, who had, however, lived in England and the
United States for many years. So we were all agog when
a lecture was announced by no less a personage than John
Galsworthy. He was introduced by our senior professor, Dr.
Aloys Brandl. Brandl was an expert in Anglo-Saxon—he re-
vealed to us the mysteries of Beowulf—besides a typical Ty-
rolese with a luxuriant beard. He spoke English with a most

remarkable Tyrolese accent, and the contrast between the strange language of his introductory remarks and the English in which Galsworthy delivered his lecture was truly extraordinary. I do not remember his subject, only our unanimous reaction to his personality: "Today we have seen an English gentleman."

German was, on the whole, less inspiring. Julius Petersen, the professor for modern literature, indulged in multitudes of names and dates and was altogether lacking in the verve and topicality that attracted me so much in Dibelius. He held seminars on Hoelderlin and on Heine; after reading a paper on my favorite subject, "Irony in Heine's lyrics," I was admitted to his advanced course.

My two principal subjects took up all my time, and Scripture was completely neglected. In my first two terms I still went to Harnack, but his lectures at that time were more in the nature of social gatherings, with a large admixture of ladies wanting to see and hear the famous man rather than to be instructed in the foundations of liberal Protestantism.

The words "all my time" are perhaps not quite correct. What I mean is "all my working time," apart from my coaching activities. I have never approved of the feminine habit of throwing oneself entirely into one activity to the exclusion of everything else. When I began to study I had no intention of becoming a blue-stocking, badly dressed and spending her entire time poring over learned tomes, a type I had ample opportunity to observe in our various seminars. One of my favorite recreations was window-shopping, for which the magnificently decorated windows of the fashion houses on the Kurfuerstendamm offered ample opportunity. Besides, I succumbed only too frequently to the temptation of cheap student tickets for fancy dress balls arranged by the Academy of Arts and similar institutions. These dances could be very wild affairs for anyone who chose to avail himself of the opportunities offered by those responsible for their management. Once, as I was wandering around the various rooms looking at the decorations, I came across one that was totally dark, with mattresses conveniently spread on the floor. . . .

On Sundays Mother and I would often go with relatives or friends for excursions into the very beautiful surroundings of Berlin. One of our favorite haunts was a tiny village by a large lake, the Schwielowsee. It was much beloved by artists, and the red and purple sunsets over the lake are among my unforgettable experiences of natural beauty. We usually reached our village after over an hour's walk through a magnificent forest. In autumn it took us much longer, because we used to pick mushrooms on our way. The forest was then full of them. We knew most of the edible kinds: the yolk-colored chanterelles, the sturdy, dark-capped boletus, and its slender variety that grows only near birchtrees and imitates the silver and black coloring of the trees on its own graceful stem. Besides fungi of all sorts, the forest was full of bilberries, and we would arrive at the house of a peasant family that was our destination laden with the principal ingredients of a meal which tasted all the more delicious for having been provided and prepared mostly by ourselves.

Another frequent goal of our *wanderlust* was a hamlet near Spandau, where we knew an open-air restaurant, the *Schwanenkrug*. There we could sit under dark old fir trees and consume our homemade cakes. This restaurant belonged to the type that allowed its customers to provide their own meal, only supplying for a very modest sum the boiling water and milk for the drink. Such establishments carried on their sign-board the legend *Hier koennen Familien Kaffee kochen* (Here families can make their coffee). Though I liked these excursions up to a point, I really preferred more fashionable outings. So whenever there was an opportunity I would slip away from the family and join friends for a *thé dansant* at Wannsee or at the Kroll restaurant in the Tiergarten.

After two years of university life I felt sufficiently in

favor with my professors to allow my lighter side to show itself in public. We were going to have a Christmas party at the "English Seminar," and I offered to be responsible for part of the entertainment by singing the latest rags, most of which I knew by heart, with a slightly changed text adapted to university events.

Dibelius was smiling benignly from his front row seat, while I was informing my professor that I would not be in the seminar tonight, as I was going with my sweetheart into a little bar, and, in another song, proclaimed that women's university studies were no good unless accompanied by dancing and flirting. The most popular item of the program, however, was one poking fun at historical grammar. Everyone was singing at that time: "When and where shall I see you again?" which I adapted to "When and where has â changed into ê?" It evidently greatly amused Dibelius; more than two years later, after my final examination, he said smilingly: "Now you may forget all the whens and wheres."

After the official part of the entertainment was over, the professors left and we started dancing. My partner was most of the time the son of a professor of Frankfurt University, Herbert K., a very intelligent young man, tall, fair and blue-eyed, with just enough of the unusual about him to be more attractive to me than the ordinary run of students. We had begun working together, and gradually fallen in love with each other, and I was vaguely wondering whether it would really be possible for me to spend a lifetime with him— though whenever I indulged in such speculations the remedy of the divorce courts was never entirely absent from my thoughts. In the imagination of the circle to which I belonged a divorced woman was, indeed, invested with a certain glamor —most famous actresses and film stars were divorced, and in one's own family and among our friends marriage was no longer viewed as an indissoluble union.

When matters between Herbert and myself had come to

a head, he suddenly informed me, to my complete surprise, that he had a mistress, a little post-office girl, his equal neither in intelligence nor in social standing, whom he had meant to give up . . . but he had got himself involved in a situation which made it morally impossible for him to leave her.

Fortunately I had plenty of work to do to take my mind off him; besides, life was too varied and too interesting, and at twenty-one I had no intention to let myself be made miserable for long by a young man's vagaries.

Shortly after this I became friendly with Margaret B., who was several years older than I and just preparing for her doctor's examination in German. She was an interesting person, to me particularly, because she was a fashion journalist, a career I was still hoping one day to embrace. One fine June morning she suggested we should play truant, and instead of letting ourselves be bored by Professor Petersen rather go to the Havel, where one of her friends had a sailing boat. I was only too ready, and this was the first of many delightful river parties.

Kurt Gamrath, the owner of the boat, was a painter, a short, rather silent man with a weather-beaten face. His boat *Fuechschen* (little fox) was just the right size for the Havel, though he had also been in the Baltic with it. It had no motor, because Gamrath considered such an instrument an abomination. This prejudice of his would sometimes land us in unpleasant situations, since the winds would not always fall in with our plans. One Sunday evening they absolutely refused to blow. We were well out on the Havel, a good distance from Berlin. It was six o'clock, still swelteringly hot, when there suddenly descended an absolute calm. No ripple on the water, not the slightest movement in the air. We were in the middle of the river, its wooded banks half concealing a fair-sized tower, the Kaiser-Wilhelm-Turm, at which we began to stare apprehensively. One sailing boat after another was dashing past us, gaily carried along by its humming motor. Margaret and I were making remarks under our breath about people with silly prejudices which Gamrath pretended not to hear. We began to consult our watches every five minutes. Seven. Half-past seven, after what seemed an eternity. We lit one cigarette after another, hoping against hope that the smoke might at last decide not to rise in an angle of exactly ninety degrees. From time to time we looked at the Kaiser-Wilhelm-Turm that seemed to mock us, because we were as immovable as itself. At eight o'clock we made ourselves some supper, from the remains of our lunch which Margaret and I had cooked on the oil stove. I was beginning to get very restive, as I knew Mother would imagine me drowned at the bottom of the Havel if I were not back by eleven at the latest. At nine, when we were already resigning ourselves to the prospect of having to spend the night in the tiny cabin, a slight breeze at last roused our *Fuechschen* from its torpor. Gradually the Kaiser-Wilhelm-Turm, which neither Margaret nor I ever wanted to see again, receded into the background, as we were setting all our sails to catch whatever wind we could. I arrived home at one o'clock in the morning, and, dead tired as I was, now had to face Mother, who had already been crying for her lost daughter. Far from being overjoyed to see me back alive, her previous sorrow immediately changed into fury, which none of my explanations about lack of winds and motors could alleviate.

Another of Margaret's friends was Willi S., a lawyer, whose great attraction was not a sailing boat, but a cottage in Werder, a picturesque village on the Havel famous for its cherry blossoms in spring and its heady fruit wine later in the year. There we would lie in deckchairs sunbathing, after dipping into the river, and recuperate from our philological exertions.

Margaret liked working at night; and she would often ask me to her rooms to have supper with her, after which we would go through Petersen's lectures point by point and ask each other questions, consuming as we went along, numerous plates of sandwiches and even more cups of strong black coffee. She was a night worker, and I am not—after ten o'clock my brain normally refuses to function, and no amount of coffee will make it. Though I tried to keep my eyes open and respond in tolerably intelligent manner, about midnight Margaret, still as fit as a fiddle, would tell me I was looking like a sheet and ought to go home—though I was quite capable of dancing till six o'clock in the morning without turning a hair.

I had told Margaret about my ambition to become a fashion journalist like her, so she introduced me to dress shows. I thoroughly enjoyed watching the models slowly coming on to the stage presenting the latest trends from Paris, and would dearly have loved to report them for some paper. But as it was very unlikely that any editor would consider ordinary fashion articles from an outsider, I conceived the idea to make poems about them, and great was my delight when a provincial paper began to accept them. Though my mother had insisted that I should prepare myself for a "safe" school career, one day she showed me an advertisement inviting application for the post of junior fashion editor on the staff of an international magazine, knowledge of English essential. I applied at once, enclosing some of my published poems, and was summoned for an interview. Two somewhat formidable ladies confronted me, talking volubly in English. To my intense mortification I understood hardly a word of what they said, but I gathered they were representing the American edition of *Vogue* and intended to bring out a German one. As I simply did not understand the questions they asked me my replies were very vague and unsatisfactory. I was puzzled that I found it so difficult, seeing I had been able to follow Galsworthy's lecture quite easily, until it dawned on me that they were, of course, speaking with a strong American accent! Two days later I received a polite refusal; they were sorry they could not engage me, as my English was not sufficient.

I was now in my eighth term (in Germany there are only two terms of about three and a half months each to the academic year), the earliest moment when we were allowed to take out examination papers. In Berlin most students waited till the ninth or tenth term, but my professor assured me I could safely risk it now. So in the spring of 1929 I took my courage in both hands and applied to be admitted to the examination in the following January.

I had to write two theses. As Petersen had given me as my subject "The night in German seventeenth-century lyrics," Dibelius gave me a kindred subject, "Predecessors of Young in seventeenth-century England." For the next eight months, while I was engaged on this work, both professors and fellow students would rarely fail to greet me with "What's your night doing?" instead of "How are you?" I was now generally working by myself, as Margaret had finished her examinations, and we had drifted apart.

Instead, I was seeing a good deal of her friend Willi, with whom I used to go to cafés or for walks in the Gruenewald. At that time homosexuality, not only among men but also among women, was rife in Berlin. It was common knowledge that one of the most famous actresses was Lesbian, and Willi told me there were certain cafés catering especially to such women, and should I like to explore one of them under his protection. I was sufficiently curious to agree, and so we went into what looked like an ordinary night club. The place was full of smart young men in evening dress and equally elegant women. There was the usual soft music and dancing, with couples flirting in alcoves. At first I could not make out why the atmosphere was so curiously oppressive; it was like a nightmarish dream, eerie, almost frightening, where nothing was real, everything different from what it appeared to be. I looked more closely at the dancing couples. Then I realized why everything seemed so queer—each one of the smart young men was a girl. To see this crowd of women making love to each other was a nauseating experience; and soon both Willi and I had the unpleasant feeling that we were attracting attention. This was not surprising, since he was such a pronouncedly masculine type that no one could possibly have mistaken him for a girl in disguise. "For heavens sake let's finish our drinks and leave here," he said under his breath, "these viragoes are already looking at us as if they wanted to kill me and carry you off."

As soon as we were outside, we instinctively shook ourselves like poodles coming out of the water. "Phew . . . let's go and have a cup of coffee in a normal place after that." As we were sitting in what seemed the superlatively wholesome atmosphere of an ordinary café, Willi said to me: "By the way, did you not know that Margaret is that way inclined?" I gasped. "Oh yes, and she told me she even tried on you, but you were so totally impervious to her advances that she gave it up." I was completely dumbfounded. I had never had the slightest suspicion of that, and I tried in vain to recall any occasion on which she could have manifested her strange predilections. Only many years later I remembered a conversation that had completely slipped my memory, in which she told me about some revolting practices of Lesbian women. I had listened, registering uninterested disgust, and then changed the subject, as the details on which she enlarged were sordid enough to make me sick. But by the time I remembered the incident, Margaret was already married to the most respectable of civil servants.

I was working quite hard by now, though practically never more than seven hours a day, my maximum capacity for purely intellectual work, and so I had time enough to write my fashion poems, which became a modest source of pocket money, and go to the pictures, to which I was then much addicted. Garbo and Marlene Dietrich were the rising stars of the moment, and I went to most of their films, though I preferred Marlene's sauciness to Garbo's languor.

Of my two theses, the one had to be written in English. Nearly all my colleagues wrote theirs first in German and then translated it; but as this procedure usually resulted in bad English, besides, an even weightier argument in my opinion, involving more work, I wrote mine in English from the start and found that I could do so without very much difficulty. My preparation for the examination included also the question of dress. After years of the knee-showing fashion, long afternoon and evening dresses were just making their appearance, and I was determined to be as fashionably attired for my examination as possible. I had a clever little dressmaker who would come to our house for two or three days at a time, and after long consultations on patterns and materials I eventually supplied her with yards of black silk and cream coloured lace, from which she produced my first long dress.

A fortnight before the oral examination I decided to have one last fling and went with some friends to a small restaurant on the Kurfuerstendamm, where we drank a concoction of porter and champagne and danced till three o'clock in the morning. When I arrived back about half-past, there was another of my late-arrival-scenes with Mother, who prophesied inevitable disaster at the examination. A fortnight before the fateful day, dancing till the small hours of the morning— I seemed to take nothing seriously at all. I assured her that there was not the remotest prospect of my failing, though I knew I had messed up my chance of getting a First by being too interested in other things beside my studies.

I also suddenly remembered that I had a subsidiary subject, for which I had done quite literally no work whatsoever. I had not the faintest idea what I was expected to know in theology, seeing there was no tutorial system in Germany, and so, about ten days before the examination, I just raced through all the more important books of the Bible, because I surmised that some scriptural knowledge would be required.

My first oral examination took place at seven o'clock in

the evening, the worst time of day for me, as I am a morning worker, so I was really grateful for the moral support afforded me by my new long dress, especially after having observed that all the other examinees were still wearing short ones. When I was ushered into the examination hall I was nearly knocked out by an atmosphere of thick smoke and an appalling noise. This was produced by about fifteen students sitting at as many tables, and their respective professors, many of whom were puffing large cigars. I was led to the table of Petersen, who began to question me in his normal very low voice. His neighbor at the next table was the temperamental professor for French, Eduard Wechssler, whom an ignorant candidate seemed to have roused to a pitch of excitement, for he was bellowing like a bull, and I constantly found myself listening to his questions rather than to those of my own examiner. The situation was aggravated by Petersen's irritating habit of changing the subject as soon as one showed oneself well-informed, and of probing deeper and deeper into one's ignorance as soon as he discovered a lacuna. This ordeal lasted for an hour, when I at last staggered out, and to my relief saw Willi with a large bunch of flowers ready to take me out for dinner to be restored to life.

My theological examination was really a farce. It was a wonder but I did answer a few questions, owing to my recent high-speed perusal of the Bible and some reminiscences from Schlemmer's lessons. When the half hour was up, there was a quick consultation between the examiner and his referee. I could pick up the words: "dearth of Scripture teachers" and "good results in her principal subjects," and so my totally inadequate performance was called satisfactory.

My university education was finished, and I was due for two years' educational training to fit me for teaching at secondary schools. In this I submitted to the wishes of my mother and the arguments of common sense; but I was still as determined as ever one day to become a journalist.

6. Teaching and Journalism

I HAD different ideas on education from most of my older colleagues, and soon began to voice my heretical opinions at meetings of teachers' organizations. I was militantly anti-feminist, because the tight-lipped spinsters who formed the overwhelming majority at these meetings repelled me, and I have always held that the primary vocation of women is marriage and motherhood. This does not rule out that many women are well fitted for academic and other professional careers and should be given every opportunity for embracing them; but it seemed to me that if they lost their femininity in the process this was too high a price to be paid. If I had once flippantly sung that women's university studies were no good unless accompanied by dancing and flirting, this had not been meant entirely as a joke. The serious idea behind it was that, unless women were capable of studying in such a way as to retain their capacity for love and all that this entails, their academic careers were a loss rather than an asset. I should have liked to see only those women admitted to the university who were sufficiently gifted to take their studies in their stride; for I had seen far too many who were using, or rather abusing, their feminine virtues of patience and industry to scrape through their examinations by sheer plodding. In consequence they had overstrained their capacities, lost their resilience, and finished up unsexed, defective human beings. I therefore opposed the current one-sidedly intellectual training for girls and advocated reforms designed to develop also their specifically feminine characteristics. As my views were anathema to the overwhelming majority of my older colleagues, I was soon involved in many disputes at these meetings.

Apart from these small skirmishes with the feminists, my first year of training was uneventful. The second, however, was far more lively. For this I had been assigned to a boys' school in the Western suburb of Charlottenburg. We were four *Studienreferendare*, the somewhat clumsy title of graduates training to become secondary school teachers, two men and two women. We had soon assorted ourselves in pairs, my charming and, like myself, non-feminist colleague Li von Hauff with Rudi K., a lively young man with slight Nazi leanings, and I with Dr. Joachim H. He was sedate and steady, rather stocky; he had decidedly serious intentions, which I did my best not to encourage too much, as he was not "my type." Our tutor was Dr. Kamitsch, a very understanding person of pleasant manners, our great standby in the difficulties Li and I had with the other members of the staff. These were due to the fact that we were the first women who had ever invaded the peaceful masculinity of the Werner-Siemens-Schule. Our colleagues were mostly men over fifty, and if they were younger they at least behaved as if, like the others, they had settled down to a middle-aged routine existence with fat, dutiful wives, large-sized mugs of dark beer, games of skittles, and stuffy featherbeds. I soon found myself at loggerheads with one of these worthies. The only mirror in the whole place was in the staffroom. So, one morning, as I was just going home, I was standing in front of it putting a pocket comb through my bobbed hair.

The old boy was glowering at me from a corner of the room. At last he could bear it no longer and broke out: "What would you say if I started shaving here?"

I, amiably: "But I'm not using any lather, am I?" This combination of logic and impertinence floored him, while Kamitsch grinned approvingly in the background.

Naturally we did cause some upheaval with the boys. Li had been given a lower fourth with forty-four of them, who had never before been taught by a woman. The effect was disastrous, and after several weeks of it poor Li, who was petite and not very robust, one morning rushed out of the class in tears. As neither of our male colleagues had English as his subject, I knew that they would be handed over to me. When I came in for the first time there was pandemonium. I looked at them with as much of a poker face as I could muster, and gradually the row subsided. I had them for three months, and I managed to keep a certain amount of discipline and even teach them some English, though to make German boys pronounce an English r and th is rather more than human effort can be expected to achieve, and by the end of each lesson I was invariably soaked in perspiration.

However, there were compensations. There can hardly be an experience more gratifying to a young woman than to teach the sixth form of a boys' school. Most of my sixth formers were between eighteen and nineteen, one of them even twenty-four—my own age. With this latter, however, it was quite impossible to work, for every time I called his name he would blush to the roots of his hair and simply not answer at all. When I dropped a pencil, the entire form would precipitate themselves onto the floor to pick it up. Their devotion reached its climax one day as I was going home at the end of the morning. When I opened the door of the staffroom, I saw them to my amazement lined up in two rows between the staffroom and the outer door, so that I had to walk out between them, each pair bowing low as I passed them. One or two of my older colleagues were watching this unheard-of spectacle from the distance, no doubt grumbling about this latest blow to the morale caused by the appearance of young women on the staff.

Since we were being trained, there were frequent visits not only from Dr. Kamitsch but from other colleagues and school inspectors during our lessons. One day when a large number of these were expected I was busy taking chairs into the classroom. My fourteen-year-olds were watching me with intense interest, wondering what was going to happen. At last one of them had an inspiration: "I know—relations coming!"

My time was not wholly taken up with teaching, however. I was now beginning to have some journalistic success. I felt I had achieved something when I had my first poem accepted by the Ullstein evening paper *Tempo*. The poem, called "Vintage 1910," reflected my own life, the experiences of war, revolution, inflation, unemployment, ending on a note of tough defiance: "But if everything breaks down, if they all sigh and groan, we alone shall stand firm. We are used to all this from childhood—Vintage 1910."

I was imitating a kind of poetry current at the time, which had been started by Erich Kästner and Bert Brecht and was called *Gebrauchslyrik*—utility lyrics. It was a form well suited to a time of despair. For in 1931 the army of the unemployed had swollen to steadily increasing millions, and the specter of a totally insufficient dole was haunting at least some member of almost every family in Germany. I myself was very doubtful if I should find a job once I had finished my training; the numbers of the workless, lolling about in the parks in summer, warming themselves in the public libraries in winter, were a constant reminder of Germany's plight. They would often spend their last mark on backing a horse. The betting offices were crowded with them, which produced another "utility poem" for the *Tempo*, as did the large empty windows of the shops up and down the most fashionable quarters carrying red notices "For Rent."

If the *Tempo* failed to accept my *Gebrauchslyrik*, there were the provincial newspapers which would take it, and so I kept myself in pocket money turning into verse the general depression, from which I, too, was suffering. I wrote prose articles, too; the *Tempo* printed a description of the last lesson I had given after my first year of training in a girls' school, discussing with the sixth form their own uncertain future—another reflection of the uneasy years before Hitler's advent to power.

With two or three million unemployed, Hitler was making rapid headway, at each election gaining more seats in the Reichstag. My mother's sister Leni, the widow of the gambler, had married a blond "Aryan" fifteen years younger than herself. Fritz T. was a rabid Nazi; my aunt, like most of her family, did not look Jewish at all; soon enough he introduced her to the "party," and she occupied herself with cooking for her "brown boys." She would cause me to explode with fury, raving about her wonderful "Führer," who was sure to wipe out the "disgrace of Versailles" and establish his Thousand Year Reich where everyone would live happily ever after.

I was a strong supporter of Bruening, and during his chancellorship voted for the Center Party and not, as I had done before, for the German Democrats, because I considered Bruening at that time the most likely man to stem the flood of Nazism, though, as it turned out, he unwittingly prepared for it by governing without the Reichstag by emergency orders. As I was reading the daily papers I realized only too keenly that Germans were in urgent need of political education in order not to fall a prey to the first demagogue promising them the stars. I still held that the failure began in the secondary schools, and I wrote an article on the subject for the *Vossische Zeitung* urging less philosophy and literature and more politics and economics. As my name was beginning to get known through these writings I was now occasionally asked to contribute articles on women's education, and I persistently urged nearness to contemporary life, to the needs and interests of our youth.

For our final examination we had to write a thesis, and I chose as my theme the treatment of the Storm and Stress period in boys' and girls' schools, as I had been teaching this period of literature at both. I took a little more trouble about this examination than I had done at the Staatsexamen, since I knew that unless I did well I should not have much chance of finding a job. We had to give two lessons in our principal subjects before a commission of two men and two women. Before our lessons the commission had a meeting which, we were told, would last about ten minutes, in order to agree on "preliminary marks," combined from the report on our two years training and the result of our thesis. The four of us were waiting for the commission to emerge from their deliberations, so that we could start our lessons. The "ten minutes" seemed rather long. After half an hour there was as yet no sign of the commission. We were beginning to wonder what could have happened. Was any of us such a doubtful candidate that the commission could not agree? Three-quarters of an hour had passed, an hour. The suspense was trying, indeed. What on earth could be the matter? After about an hour and a quarter they came out at last, flushed and obviously in a state of annoyed excitement. Kamitsch whispered to me: "It's you who has held us up—I'll tell you afterwards." I was very puzzled and decided that they must have been doubtful whether to give me "good" or "very good" as my preliminary mark—I could not envisage anything lower. So I gave my two lessons without any misgivings. The boys were extremely good, they knew what was at stake for me and followed my lead perfectly, both the fourth in English and the sixth in German.

Afterwards we were called in singly for a brief oral examination on educational theory. Then at last I realized what had been the matter. One of the two lady examiners began to discuss my thesis with me. In this I had voiced the opinion that the teacher must take account of the psychological differences between boys and girls and approach the same subject from different angles. I tried to show how this was to be done for the period in question, how the Storm and Stress should be treated from a more personal angle with the girls, from a more objective and "political" one with the boys. It seemed to me the most natural thing in the world, and I had not thought that even the most enraged feminist could take exception to it. Nevertheless the examining lady told me that I was wrong, that men and women were quite equal, equally objective, interested in the same things, that there were, in fact, no psychological differences between the sexes. I just had the sense not to ask—the question was almost on my lips —why, if this were so, they did not take it in turns to have babies. I did not want to mess up my examination completely, however, so I contented myself with saying in my opinion men and women were also psychologically different, and boys and girls should therefore be approached differently by their teachers. She prophesied that once I gained more experience of my own sex (I seemed to understand the other better!) I would change my views on the subject. But even now, almost twenty-five years later, this prophecy has not yet been fulfilled.

Later Kamitsch told me what had happened at the secret council of the commission. When they had to agree on preliminary marks, they were faced with the unusual situation that in their report on my two years training my tutors had accorded me the highest possible marks, whereas the two

ladies who had read my thesis had given it the very lowest—
totally unsatisfactory. Hence the long discussion, at the end
of which they found it impossible to agree on a common de-
nominator, and decided to suspend judgment until I had
given my lessons. These, the ladies reluctantly admitted, had
been satisfactory. Whereupon, so Kamitsch told me, the two
men had brought down their fists on the table saying they
should all be very glad if they had given such good lessons
themselves, the very least they could do was to mark the lessons, as well as the result of the whole examination "good,"
notwithstanding the thesis. The ladies, vanquished by this
display of male strength, had at last been forced to agree to
this, and so the battle of the sexes ended with an at least
partial victory of the stronger over what I hardly dare to call
either the weaker or the fairer.

This, however, was not quite the end as far as my thesis
was concerned. I really could not have had a more striking
proof of my view that, generally speaking, women are less
objective and more easily swayed by their emotions than men,
than the behavior of these two ladies on the commission who
gave the lowest possible marks to what seemed to me a perfectly good thesis, for no other reason than that they happened not to agree with the opinion expressed therein. By
this time Schlemmer was no longer headmaster at Frankfurt,
but had returned to Berlin as *Oberschulrat,* which corre-
sponds roughly to a director of education. I therefore went
to see him and told him of the row. When he had read my
thesis he shook his head. "These women are crazy. This is an
excellent paper. Abbreviate it a bit and send it to the *Deutsche
Mädchenbildung,* which is an influential educational periodical. You can mention my name to the editor." So I made
my thesis into an article. It was immediately accepted, and
with great glee I sent an offprint to the lady who had so
nearly wrecked my examination on its account. She sent me

a bitter-sweet reply, regretting that my deplorable views had now found their way even into print.

I followed up the article with a letter to the *Vossische Zeitung*, in which I further elaborated my ideas. Notwithstanding the debt of gratitude we owed to the feminists for making higher education accessible to us, I wrote that "The point of departure as well as the aim of women's education is to prepare them for motherhood, by which we mean not only the physical process, but which we see as a gift and an obligation for which the girls must be made ready." I should have been much surprised had I been told that the view which I was instinctively defending so vigorously was just about this time being proclaimed by Pope Pius XI as the traditional teaching of the Catholic Church.

Luckily Schlemmer helped me to find a job. It was part time teaching, but better than nothing at this time of general unemployment. The school was far from my home, in a slum district of East Berlin. It was one of the few private Evangelical Church schools, and I was to take most of the Scripture teaching except in the top form, where it was given by the Pfarrer, and in addition a few English and German lessons. Besides, I was to take school prayers every Saturday morning—the Pfarrer did this on Monday—which involved not only hymn singing but an address. So, before I knew quite how it had happened, I found myself up to my eyes in religious teaching, and an understudy of the Pfarrer. I had a slight attack of stage fright when I ascended for the first time the rostrum in the school hall to give a religious talk to the school, including the headmistress. However, it went off well, and though I still did not even believe in the existence of God, it seemed I was able to say the things that were expected of me. The girls, too, liked my lessons, and I was on excellent terms with the charming headmistress, Frau Dr. Christ, and all my colleagues—except the Pfarrer who, I think, found me too flippant for a Scripture mistress, as indeed I was, but just this gave me perhaps a greater influence on the girls than a more "pious" teacher would have had. Naturally I stressed particularly the ethical element in Christianity, and explained all the miracles on rationalist lines; but as this was quite acceptable to a large section of the German Evangelical Church, no one minded it.

One embarrassing experience remains engraved on my memory, though I did not see its implications at the time. I was teaching the Ten Commandments in a class of twelve to thirteen year old girls. When I came to the Sixth, I simply read it out, having no intention to discuss it, as I did the others, because the children were really too young for that. As I was just going on to the Seventh a girl in the last bench put up her hand and waved it so vigorously that I could not overlook it. I called her name, and she said calmly: "But I think you have got to do that if you want a divorce." I simply did not know what to say to that. In the divorce courts adultery was, indeed, the most easily accepted reason for dissolving a marriage. To the best of my knowledge the Protestant Church in Germany had no very definite views on divorce; besides, and this was the most embarrassing point for me, the girl could hardly have known about adultery being a reason for divorce if her own parents had not discussed the matter—for all I knew they might at this moment be trying to get divorced. If I said, whether divorce or not, adultery was always a sin against the Commandments, it meant telling the girl in so many words that her own parents were gravely offending God, which might cause fearful conflicts in her just at her most difficult age. Besides I myself, despite my view of marriage as the principal vocation of women, very illogically accepted divorce as a necessary part of the institution. All this went through my mind in the split of a second, while I was hesitating to give the child an answer. At last I could do no better than mumble that, though adultery was, indeed, required for a divorce, it was nevertheless forbidden by the Commandments. With this dusty answer the girl had to be content, while I was hastily going on to teach them, with less embarrassment and greater conviction, that it is wrong to steal.

In the second year of my educational training I had met again, I forget how, my childhood friend Heinz Kirschner. He had grown into a tall, fair young man; and as he was much interested in literature and experimented with play writing, we had a great deal in common and were soon gently flirting with each other. Though he was then still studying at Cologne, I saw him from time to time, usually when he came to Berlin; but once I also went for a week to Goslar, where his mother was then living, and from where we made excursions into the Harz mountains. Lately we had also begun to discuss politics, but on this subject our views were diametrically opposed. Heinz had formerly entertained Nazi leanings, but was now a fervent adherent of Communism, keen to convert me to his views. But fanaticism, whether of the right or of the left, has always been foreign to my outlook on life, and I could see no advantages whatsoever in a dictatorship of the proletariat. We had endless discussions, and I discovered that Heinz, though very intelligent, was simply a starry-eyed idealist and completely muddleheaded where politics were concerned. To him the workers were a company of saints, wronged and down-trodden by the wicked bourgeoisie. Once their native rights had been restored to them the millennium was sure to break. When all his arguments had failed he persuaded me to see his new evangel in action and go with him to a Communist meeting.

We set out one Sunday early in the afternoon. I cannot remember how it happened, but for some reason or other we had not had lunch. I wanted to go to a restaurant first and have something to eat, but Heinz said there was no time for such bourgeois activities, and very reluctantly I gave way, and we took an underground train to Spandau, where the meeting was to be held in some garden restaurant. I have always found it difficult to go without regular meals; the hungry feeling gives me not only a bad headache, but an even worse temper. Perhaps Heinz thought hunger would teach me more sympathy with the "starving masses," but if so he was mistaken. All the way to the meeting I kept grumbling that I had had nothing to eat, and that I wasn't interested in these darned Communists anyway. "Wait till we get there, and you will see how wonderful they are," said Heinz, adding soothingly: "And perhaps they may have some bread and sausage for you there." This thought cheered me considerably, but unfortunately turned out to be a chimera.

Finally, after a lengthy journey and some wanderings, we reached the place of the meeting. There was beer enough, but no food. We sat down at one of the painted iron tables. Heinz seemed to be in his element and embarked on yet another of his explanations of the Communist creed, while I was looking round to see what kind of people they were. They looked not in the least like revolutionaries; they were, indeed, quite different from the seething crowds I had liked to watch when I was a child, during the revolution. These were rather disgruntled but otherwise quite peaceful citizens; workers and lower middle-class families, looking very dull, drinking, and eating—how I envied them!—the cake and sandwiches they had brought with them. From time to time they shouted appropriate slogans when a speaker mounted a table to address them. A less inspiring crowd could hardly be imagined, and I was getting more bored and hungry every minute. When the meeting had at long last come to an end, Heinz and I had what I think was our last row on our way home.

"You are a hopeless bourgeoise," he sneered.

"I suppose I am—and proud of it," I retorted.

When, several months later, Hitler had seized power, I

wondered what had become of him. He had probably either been shot as a Communist or turned Nazi—"beefsteak" as we called it, red within, brown outside. I wrote to find out. I had a card back with a swastika stamp on it: he was attending a course at a training camp for National-Socialist leaders. I have never heard of him again.

In the summer of 1932 I went to Austria for a holiday. Teaching at the boys' school and the following examination, together with the political anxieties, had left me rather worn-out, and I had developed a kind of nervous reaction, so that I could not go to sleep at night if I had to get up early next morning to go to school. It was the only period in my life when I suffered from the modern complaint of insomnia, and I hoped the Alpine air would restore me. It was a glorious summer, and at Zell-am-See I could combine swimming in the superb lake with going for long walks in the mountains. I have always loved mountains, though I have never done any actual climbing. A fairly leisurely walk is enough for me, preferably above the thousand metres line, where the air is light and one can walk on without feeling tired, dipping one's hands and arms into the cooling snow, while the sun is scorching one's face. On other days I would just go for a morning's swim in the lake and lie lazily in the sun, looking at the snow-capped mountains that were reflected in the water. I quickly made friends with other young people, and at night we would go and have a cheap supper of delicious brawn and red country wine at some inn, and afterwards go to a dance. After about a fortnight I had to interrupt this idyllic life to cross the frontier into Germany; for there were General Elections, and I felt it my bounden duty to cast my vote against Hitler, who was daily gaining ground.

In the autumn Schlemmer found me other part time work in addition to what I had already; it was teaching Scripture at the Lettehaus, a well-known domestic science school in West Berlin. The two jobs together gave me enough

to live fairly comfortably. Yet there was a feeling of inse-
curity all round.

The ubiquitous Nazis were marching and shouting,
marching and shouting. They were singing their Horst-
Wessel-Song in the streets and in the backyards of our blocks
of flats, they were screaming their slogans *Deutschland er-
wache! Juda verrecke!* Once I met several of these brown-
shirts dragging the black-red-and-gold flag of the republic
through the mud. It was difficult to control one's temper in
the face of such outrages, but nobody dared to intervene.
Bruening fell, and the all-too-versatile von Papen took his
place. We knew Hindenburg disliked Hitler—but what could
the old man do against that rapidly rising meteor?

"Hitler will give us either husbands or jobs," said one of
my colleagues at the Evangelical School hopefully. Though I
felt sure he would do neither for me, seeing I had been too
imprudent in the choice of my grandmother, I did not think
the prospect of being supplied with a husband by Hitler very
appealing even for an Aryan without blemish. But the remark showed me the gullibility of even the educated German
public, especially of the women, among whom Hitler found
many of his most ardent supporters.

Most of my non-Nazi friends were frankly appalled by
the prospect of yet another winter, with now between six
and seven million unemployed. Besides providing spinsters
with husbands, Hitler was expected to abolish unemployment; this and his antisemitism were his chief attractions.

About this time one of the girls at the Evangelical School
surprised me with the question: "Why are there more Jews
in the world than Christians?"

"More Jews than Christians? Certainly there are far fewer
Jews than Christians—how did you get that idea into your
head?"

"My daddy says the Jews are everywhere."

Then I understood. It was the well-worn complaint that

the Jews were occupying the best positions, whether in industry, or medicine, in law or in the arts—"the Jews are everywhere."

Now as I have suffered myself on account of my partly Jewish origin, and members of my family have been detained and killed in concentration camps, I hope I shall not be misunderstood if I say there was a certain truth in these complaints. Germany had received the bulk of the Jewish refugees from the East, especially from Poland. These Jews, unlike the "Western" Jews who had come from Spain and other countries centuries ago, were not particularly cultured and often quite unscrupulous moneymakers. Moreover, they were very ostentatious, especially their womenfolk. During the worst time of unemployment and general poverty, they could be seen strutting up and down the fashionable Kurfuerstendamm in mink coats and silver fox stoles, parading rows upon rows of pearls and diamonds on their enormous bosoms, while their husbands indulged in shady and highly lucrative transactions on the stock market. These women were quite a feature of the Kurfuerstendamm, to which they seemed to belong as much as the film stars belong to Hollywood; but by their vulgar display they aroused a hatred quite disproportionate to its cause. I do not mean to imply that they were responsible for Hitler's atrocities, but they certainly had their share in preparing the ground to nourish the evil seed.

"The Jews are everywhere." The girl had asked me her question in perfectly good faith; I knew there was a certain foundation in the general accusations. But I also knew that there were millions of excellent, generous, kind-hearted, highly cultivated Jews (my doctor uncle was one of them) who, though quite innocent, were held responsible for the vices and bad behavior of the few. I would explain to the girls, as long as I was still free to do so, why the Jews could be so frequently met in the "moneymaking" professions. I therefore told them about the medieval ghettoes, about the ban formerly placed on every other Jewish activity except money lending, so that they simply had no choice but had to devote all their energies to this kind of occupation. "But then the Jews have been treated very unjustly!" came the immediate response from the girls.

"Yes, they have been treated unjustly—there is no doubt about that."

It was as easy as that. You could tell these children the truth, make it all quite clear to them, and they would accept it, especially if they trusted the person who explained it to them. For the first time I was brought face to face with the almost frightening influence a teacher can have—for good or ill.

7. *Life in the Third Reich*

ON THE thirtieth of January 1933 the long-dreaded event happened: Hitler became Reichskanzler. If we had been wondering whether he would really carry out his threats against the Jews, we were quickly disabused of any illusions. Placards went up in restaurants, in shops, even at the entrance of towns and villages: *Juden unerwuenscht* (Jews not desired). The SA were marching and singing more vigorously than ever, the sinister black-uniformed SS, tall young men with hard, set faces were strutting through the streets, looking a perfect illustration of the aggressive Nazi song: "For today Germany belongs to us, and tomorrow the whole world." Streets changed their names, Adolf-Hitler-streets and -squares cropped up everywhere overnight, like mushrooms after the rain. Even the interval sign on the wireless was transformed into the opening bars of a Nazi song *Volk ans Gewehr* (People to the Guns). The Jews, witty as always, even, or rather especially, in adversity, were quick on their part to change the folksong *Alles neu macht der Mai* (May makes everything new) into *Alles neu macht der Goi,* goi being the Hebrew word for Gentile.

Soon jokes became the only secret weapon left us to de-

fend ourselves against the mounting terror. For Hitler began
to set up his concentration camps, and we knew, however
much incredulous surprise Germany may have officially displayed after the war, that horrible things were going on in
these camps. A butcher, a Social Democrat, had disappeared
from our neighborhood. A few weeks later his family found
an urn filled with ashes bearing his name on their doorstep
one morning. "They have to burn them," we reflected, "because they have been so terribly mutilated." We knew, though
there were many who did not want to know. If we had not
known, why did the very word "concentration camp" strike
terror into us—and by us I mean all Germans, whether Jews
or Gentiles. But refusal to face unpleasant facts is a common
human failing, and the Germans can hardly be blamed very
much that they should have conveniently overlooked, and
then forgotten, what they knew to be true.

In my Scripture lessons now I used to stress increasingly
the duty of Christians, especially of Christian women, to love,
to love not only one's friends, but one's enemies. My own
class was the upper third, girls between fourteen and fifteen
years of age, most of whom knew well enough why I was
constantly talking about love, while wireless, newspapers,
books and cinemas were fast being turned into one grand
orchestra for Goebbels' concert of hate and lies.

For some time now he had been advertising new laws that
were to purify Germany from all Jewish influence, and first
of all its civil service, to which the teaching profession belonged. In April 1933 these laws were to be promulgated.
In the evening of the appointed day Mother and I were listening to the wireless. There was a pandemonium of military
music and speeches, marches, singing, speeches again; interruptions by the announcer that the laws would now be read
—but then again only music. The suspense was nerve-racking. We knew the laws would not only affect Jews but also
non-Aryans, but we were not quite certain how far back

they would trace the non-Aryan contamination, and what kind of penalties would be inflicted. At long last the dreaded moment came when the fate of millions, including my own, was being decided. No doubt was possible, the civil service was being purged of all who had any traceable Jewish blood in their veins, certainly up to the grandparents, but if there should be any doubt about these, the great-grandparents, too, would be investigated. My school career was at an end.

I did not think it necessary to tell anyone yet; I was quite uncertain what to do next, for of course a journalistic career would be closed to me, too. I decided to go on teaching at the Evangelical School until I received the questionnaire that was to be sent to all civil servants in the Reich.

A few days later my headmistress took me aside. We had one master called Wolf, which is also, but not necessarily, a Jewish surname. Frau Christ asked me anxiously whether I thought he was of Jewish origin. It would be dreadful if he had to leave. I calmed her; he had not given any signs of being upset, I really thought he was Aryan. It was a most ironic situation. "If you knew," I thought, "who is the non-Aryan here"—but my name was so hundred per cent Teutonic that nobody could have possibly suspected me.

We had to learn new manners now, too. So far the children had greeted me with the customary curtsy, which I answered with a nod or smile. Now we had to combine this with stretching out our right arm and saying *Heil Hitler*. I contented myself with the merest shadow of the gesture, which I never used on any other occasion, but while I was still teaching it was impossible not to conform. The most comic situation always arose on Saturday mornings, when the headmistress and I behind her would march into the school hall for prayers, both with our right arm stretched out, passing through a forest of outstretched arms on either side of us. I felt we ought to be accompanied by a band and perform a real goose-step; it seemed very much like comic opera.

On the first of May there was to be a mass meeting of schoolchildren in the Lustgarten, before the former imperial palace. I could not avoid it; so I had to set out about five o'clock in the morning, before the first underground left the station near my home, and by a combination of walking, bus and finally underground reached the school in time to collect my class and start marching. Fortunately it was a perfect day—"Hitler-weather!" Everything was organized to perfection, and soon we met columns upon columns of schoolchildren and their teachers all walking in the direction of the Lustgarten. When we had arrived, after over an hour's marching, we were competently directed to the place allotted to us. The whole Lustgarten was swarming with boys and girls. So far everything had run smoothly, but now we had to wait for about two hours till the speeches were due to start. It is true, aeroplanes kept circling over our heads throwing leaflets, but this was not enough to entertain the many thousands of children and young people between ten and eighteen. Suddenly I heard several of my girls squealing behind me. I made my way with some difficulty through the closely packed ranks to see what was the matter.

"The little boys are sticking us," the girls complained.

"Sticking you? What with?"

"There you can see them, they take the pins off their swastika badges and stick us with them." I gave the boys a dressing down, and there was peace for a few minutes, until the game started again. Eventually I had to confiscate the pins which had been put to such unworthy use on this solemn occasion, and then, to my great relief, all the loudspeakers began to blare. Baldur von Schirach was making his speech.

A few weeks later I received the forms to fill out, which would reveal my objectionable ancestry. German thoroughness had surpassed itself. There it was all neatly set out: we had to give our present and, if it applied, our previous religion. Then came father's (and previous, as before) religion, mother's maiden name and religion, mother's father's, mother's mother's, father's father's and father's mother's religion, together with all the names, previous names if any, maiden names . . . and great-grandparents, to be sure, should the grandparents' names or religious professions leave any room for doubt anywhere. Having conscientiously filled up this document, I went to Bavaria for a holiday to recuperate.

Soon after my return home I received a printed notice informing me that, according to paragraph three of the law concerning the restoration of the civil service I was to retire. As I had been a teacher only for not quite eighteen months and had held no full-time post, I had no claim to any compensation. I immediately went to my headmistress to ask her whether I should leave at once or stay on till the end of term. She was greatly distressed, for she had never suspected me to be affected by the new laws; she asked me to stay on till the end of term. The principal of the Lettehaus was equally upset and at once offered that, if I wanted to take a course in any practical subject taught at her institute, I could do so without having to pay any fees.

On my last day at the Evangelical School, I gave out the reports to my class as usual. Then I told them I was going to leave. They asked why, for they were very attached to me, and I gave them the true reason. "But can't we ask the minister of education to let you carry on?" I told them this was impossible, the decision was irrevocable. Then one or two of them put their heads on the table and started sobbing, and in a few seconds all of them were crying, and I had to comfort them as best I could. The headmistress paid me an additional month's salary, apologizing that she could do no more, for being a private church school, they were very poor. I said goodbye to my colleagues, who were all very sympathetic, and went home with a strange sense of elation, because my school career, which I had never liked very much, had come to an end, and life, if difficult, had also become adventurous.

During the following fortnight of autumn holidays something unexpected happened. The day after they had begun our front door bell rang. There were two of my girls with an enormous bunch of flowers and a box of chocolates. They wanted to say goodbye. I was greatly touched, and even more so when this was repeated every day, so that at the end of the holidays the whole class had been to see me, our flat had been transformed into a flower garden, and I had a chocolate supply sufficient to open a sweet shop. Much later one of my former colleagues told me that Nazism had made remarkably little progress in my class, only four or five had joined the Nazi girls organization *Bund deutscher Mädchen*.

I had been wondering what to do next. I had no connections abroad, so I decided to avail myself of the offer of the Lettehaus and take a course in advanced cookery, as I had always liked cooking, and this would be an asset everywhere. The course took three months. We had a wonderful mistress who might have come straight out of a film: large, redfaced, wearing high boots no doubt on account of her varicose veins, with a voice like a Prussian N.C.O., and very efficient. I did very well, and at the end of the course the Lettehaus employment agency found me a job with a widower with two sons. I had a good maid, plenty of time, and was supposed to help the boys with their homework besides doing some cooking. Nevertheless my life was a perfect nightmare, for the master of the house was a very queer man, and he obviously drank more than was good for him. He would come home at night with several bottles of spirits under his arm in a not too steady condition. The maid told me the former "housekeeper" had been his mistress, and this seemed to be one of the "duties" that went with the job. So I locked and barricaded my room every night, for he was a strongly built man who might easily have forced the door. After ten days of dodging him whenever he was in, I could stand the situation no longer, packed my case and went home.

Soon after my return my mother came back from shopping one afternoon in a great state of excitement. "Do you know, I have just seen Hitler, standing in an open car—he has really a most charming smile!"

"Mother—you? Don't tell me *you* have fallen for that man?"

"Certainly, I hate him as much as ever—but I can't help it, he *has* a most wonderful smile."

I have never seen Hitler myself; but once, as I was standing with a friend at a window of the German Foreign Office in the Wilhelmstrasse I saw a crowd cheering him, though I could not see him. I have never again seen such a display of mass hysteria. They were roaring, screaming, throwing their arms into the air, rolling their eyes. At that moment none of them was normal. Had Hitler ordered them to murder their own mothers or throw themselves into the flames, they would have done so without an instant's hesitation. As I could not see him from where I was standing, I do not know whether he would have had the same effect on me—his sight had certainly been enough momentarily to bewitch my mother; but I began to understand that the astounding influence he had on people was partly due to some uncanny charm of his personality which appealed to the irrational instincts—as did his politics. For he was no great man, in the sense of a Napoleon or a Bismarck. He was rather a little man, a frustrated, quite incomplete personality, but he had a hypnotic attraction that caused people simply to succumb to him.

In the spring of 1934 Frau H., the wife of my father's friend, the mathematics professor at Marburg, wrote to me that their lady housekeeper was leaving, and would I come to take her place. Frau H. was a née Hahn. One of her nephews was Dr. Kurt Hahn, who had just transferred his school "Salem" from the Lake of Constance to Scotland, where his most famous pupil was the future Duke of Edinburgh.

Marburg is an enchanting town, replete with a charming

scenery and theological and philosophical fame. Here the stern Conrad of Marburg had once lived, the confessor of St. Elizabeth of Thuringia; here Luther had had his famous conversation with Zwingli on the reality of the sacramental presence; here was the home of Neo-Kantianism, and at present the University was counting the Protestant theologians Rudolf Otto and Martin Bultmann among its most distinguished members. The city is dominated by the fine Gothic Elisabethkirche, in front of which the peasant girls in their picturesque costumes would parade up and down on Sunday mornings.

The house of Geheimrat H. stood in a magnificent position in a lovely garden at the top of a hill, surrounded by park-like woods. When I arrived, the old housekeeper, Fräulein Mohrmann, was still there to instruct me in my duties. These were not particularly onerous. About half-past nine in the morning I was expected to have a conference with Frau Geheimrat on meals and other domestic subjects and do a little dusting. After that I was to go down the hill into the town to do the shopping. "I never come back until just before lunch, about one o'clock, in time to set the table, even if the shopping does not take me all the time. I advise you to do the same. If you have finished earlier, just have a cup of coffee somewhere or a chat with a friend." I was not slow to take this hint, having no intention either to compromise the excellent Fräulein Mohrmann or to overwork myself. After lunch I could rest till tea time, when I had again to set the table, and, when there were guests, pour out the tea. The same happened at supper.

Apart from these lighter duties there were the great battle days of washing, fruit preserving and parties. In most German families the washing is done every four weeks. The ritual in the H. household was awe-inspiring. Two washerwomen would appear very early in the morning, dressed in their black Hessian costumes, and would be hard at it for two full days. During this time both Herr and Frau Geheimrat were reduced to a state of complete subservience to their staff. The dinner had to be of the simplest kind, else Frau Becker, the cook, would have given notice straightaway. She had the typical temper of her profession; the last half-hour before dinner no one dared to come near her. She was very short, and though she ate remarkably little, everything about her was round. Her arms were of the shape of two reddish balls mysteriously joined together, and her fingers might easily be mistaken for Wieners. She was generally amiable, except when she had one of her tantrums. In such situations, Fräulein Mohrmann had told me, the best way of subduing her was to suggest that there might be a thunderstorm tonight. She was terrified of thunderstorms. At the first grumbling she would cover all the cutlery with teatowels and then betake herself to the darkest corner of the kitchen, where she would remain, her face buried in her hands, moaning and sobbing, till the calamity had passed. So when she became too intractable I would gently tell her I had a headache, which was a pretty sure sign that there was thunder in the air, and she would immediately become as docile as a lamb. Unfortunately this device could not be applied in winter, though it was very useful at almost any other time of the year.

Though Frau Becker had very little to do with the washing except giving the women their food, it was understood that she must be treated with even more than usual consideration during these trying days. Almost as soon as the women had finished, however, I became the temporary heroine who had to be humored, for I had to do the ironing. I was helped by Gretchen, the charming housemaid. She was a real treasure; neat and pretty in her attractive light-blue or pink Hessian costume, she was always good tempered. When the washing was dry we would take it down from the loft in large baskets, stretch it, put it through the mangle, and finally iron it. This latter usually took two, sometimes even three afternoons from two to seven, and was fairly back-breaking. Nevertheless I enjoyed it. Instead of tea in state in the dining room, I had coffee and enormous quantities of rolls, jam and butter or cake with Frau Becker and Gretchen in the kitchen, though the hierarchical order was preserved, I being enthroned at a separate table by the window. I did need sustenance—for dozens of enormous sheets and table cloths, about fifty large napkins and innumerable quantities of towels and handkerchiefs were no joke; and of course, it being a superior German household, they had all to be ironed just so, with the initials properly pressed out and no edges protruding anywhere.

When I came up to supper after such an afternoon, Frau Geheimrat would ask apprehensively: "How is it going? Shall you be finished tomorrow?" And Herr Geheimrat would commiserate with me as if I had just survived a major operation.

The most exciting events were the parties. These necessitated endless discussions beforehand, for the dinners had to be arranged in accordance with the social standing of the guests. There was then, and presumably still is, in Germany a strict social distinction between the senior professors of the universities and the junior lecturers, the *Privatdozenten,* whereas school teachers or business-people, unless the latter were very rich, were altogether below our horizon. Once I was discussing the dinner with Frau Geheimrat for a party of rather junior university people. We had at long last hit on venison, but now the difficulty was what to serve with it. I suggested red currant jelly. "No," quoth Frau Geheimrat, "this is really too elaborate for these people."

"Well, what about red cabbage then."

"Ah no, that would be *too* vulgar."

I was at my wits end. What would be the right mean between refinement and vulgarity suitable for *Privatdozenten* and their wives? Frau Geheimrat herself solved the problem: it was to be curly kale.

It took me quite some time till I had grasped the mysteries of setting the table for these parties. It was a law of the Medes and Persians that sugar and salt must always have stars impressed on them by means of two crystal milk jugs, one big (for the sugar), the other small (for the salt), the bottoms of which, decorated with such a design, had to be pressed on sugar and salt respectively. The making of the after dinner coffee was usually my duty. As this took place while the guests were having the dessert, Frau Becker would save me a plateful in the kitchen so that I should not miss it: "Eat it here," she would tell me, "so that you can behave like a lady upstairs."

In summer meals were even more complicated than in winter, for they were then served not only in the dining room, but, according to the temperature which Frau Geheimrat would ascertain with a thermometer about half an hour before, either on the veranda, on the terrace in front of the house, under the oak tree, or, terror of terrors, in the ravine. The ravine was the coolest part of the garden, very far from the house, and in summer Gretchen and I would tremble if, on the day of a tea party, the weather became stiflingly hot, for then Frau Geheimrat would mercilessly order the party there, which meant carrying basketsful of china and cutlery across the whole length of the garden.

The visits of Professor Rudolf Otto, "der heilige Otto" as we used to call him because of his famous book *Das Heilige* (The Numinous), used to present us with a special problem. For the tall, handsome professor, whose white hair provided a kind of halo for his impressive face, insisted on being accompanied by a minute terrier. Naturally there was no question of this animal, however superior, being admitted into Frau Geheimrat's drawing room, and so we had a busy time— in addition to our other duties—pacifying the barking creature who had to stay behind in the hall, tied to a bannister.

In fact we were carrying on as if there were no Hitler

and no Aryan Laws. It was perhaps a kind of self-defense, for
the family had been cruelly hit. Their only son had taken his
life soon after Hitler had seized power, leaving a widow with
two boys, who often came to see us. This brave woman, herself an Aryan, was known to help Jews to escape, until, some
time after I had left Marburg, she, too, took her life when she
had been caught and put in prison.

We had many visitors, especially in summer; among them
was Frau du Bois-Raymond, a sister of Herr Geheimrat. She
was a very cultured and witty woman, lame and ailing at the
time. One night at supper we were discussing the latest news:
people who were suspect of being opposed to the Führer were
having their telephones tapped, so that the conversations in
the room could be overheard by the Nazi authorities. When
I came into the dining room next morning I saw Frau du
Bois-Raymond sitting stiff like a statue at the breakfast table,
staring with wide-open, terrified eyes in the direction of the
telephone. I followed her glance: there was a young man
busying himself with the receiver. From that time we always
put a tea cozy over it when the conversation took a political
turn at meals, as it only too often did. It was also unsafe to
trust the housemaid, charming and devoted though she was;
and so, whenever she came in to serve while we were talking
about the Nazis, Herr Geheimrat would immediately change
the subject to a beautiful tree in the garden which he could
see from his seat. "The Tree" became the danger signal, at
which we would at once begin to discuss the beauties of
nature.

Unless one has actually lived under a ruthless dictatorship
it is difficult to imagine how the awareness of danger gradually permeates one's whole conscious and subconscious being,
so that one develops quite instinctive reactions for warding
it off. Once as I was sitting with two American students in
a garden restaurant, I was going to tell them the latest joke
about Hitler; but first I quickly looked behind me to see

whether anyone was listening. The Americans laughed. "That's the 'German movement,' " they said. It was difficult always to avoid giving the Hitler salute. Sometimes, when I was shopping in the town, an SA company would come marching along bearing the Swastika flag, then I would quickly escape into a side street, or else turn my back on them to stare at some shop window.

At one time during my stay at Marburg there was an "election." At a previous one, when I was still in Berlin, I had resolutely voted with the invariable two percent who were allowed to oppose Hitler, to the horror of my none too courageous aunt Hermine, the doctor's wife, who voted for the "Führer" and even listened to his speeches on the wireless. But in Marburg, which is quite a small town, voting against him would be even more dangerous. In order to get out of it (at that time non-Aryans still had the vote), I thought I was being very clever in applying for a form entitling me to vote away from my place of residence under pretext that I was going for a weekend. I duly received the necessary forms. Then, two days before the elections, it was announced that a particularly strict watch would be kept on those who voted away from their home, and that the authorities would ascertain whether these people had actually cast their vote. So the fat was in the fire. If it came out that I had neither voted nor left Marburg, things would look fishy, indeed, and a spell in a concentration camp might be considered necessary, especially as I was racially contaminated.

With a heavy heart I went to the polling station with my forms and, having duly said "Heil Hitler," explained that I had not gone away, after all. The official smiled amiably, gave me the ballot paper, and I withdrew into the box. I reflected that my vacillations about going away must have aroused suspicion, that my vote would not make the slightest difference as the result of the election was a foregone conclusion, and that the whole thing was really not worth going to a concentration camp. So I put my cross in the appointed place expressing my confidence in the Führer; nevertheless this act of cowardice troubled me for a long time; I felt I had betrayed my deepest convictions.

In more normal times I should probably never have started on a crazy affair of the heart, if it can be called that, as the heart was not really involved overmuch. Arranging meals in the H. household was further complicated by the fact that we also fed "the Professor," who had a delicate stomach and had generally to be given something special. "Now what on earth are we to give Professor Frank?" Frau Geheimrat would sigh at least five times a week, "He is sure not to be able to eat all this fried stuff. You had better go over and ask him what he would like."

Professor Erich Frank was a philosopher, who lived a very retired life in a cottage on the grounds of the villa. It was the most romantic house imaginable. Half hidden by bushes, its wooden panelwork was decorated on the outside with painted ornaments, so that it looked exactly like the witch's house in Grimm's fairy tale "Hansel and Gretel." It was a perfect setting for its quiet inhabitant, who was then just over fifty. He was an Austrian, a Jew by race but a Catholic by religion, though he did not practise at all, and, as far as I could make out, seemed to hold some vague beliefs about God that might be compatible with almost any kind of faith. He was a great friend of Bultmann, the form critic, with whom he would go for long walks at six o'clock in the morning, discussing philosophical problems as a pre-prandial exercise. Frank had a nineteen-year-old daily maid, "Professor's Emma," as we called her, to whom he was very attached on account of what he termed "her wonderful character," though the domestic staff of Villa H. were none too fond of her, because she used to be very cheeky when she came over to us to fetch her master's food.

As I had to go to see him very often to enquire what he

would like for his dinner, our conversations gradually shifted from purely culinary matters to other subjects. He first introduced me to Kierkegaard, of whom I had heard much, but whom I had never read, and lent me many of his works. These impressed me and were partly responsible for making the idea of a personal God more acceptable to me than it had hitherto been. Frank himself talked much about God, though, as I have said, in a rather vague way. He would bring Him in sometimes when he was disgusted with my flippancy and superficiality, which had increased steadily ever since I had left school. But I had not given Scripture lessons for nothing and once disconcerted him by quoting: "Judge not, that you may not be judged." For about this time I began to have a vague feeling that, if God did exist, and if He wanted me to believe in Him, He would make it clear to me; however, so far He had not done so, and I was not going to let myself be lectured by a philosophy professor.

Frank also made me acquainted with Kafka, whom he had known as a young man, and for whom he had a great admiration. I read *The Castle* and several others of his works, including a short story in which a man is changed into an insect, which haunted me for some time. I thought Kafka a very powerful writer; but he had a diseased mind, and his distorted world, ruled by a malignant power that delighted in man's sufferings without redeeming him, was quite foreign to my naturally gay and optimistic temperament.

Neither Kierkegaard nor Kafka, however, could prevent me from starting a flirtation with the professor, from which he, being an Austrian, showed himself by no means averse. In the summer of 1935 this romance was in full swing; my visits to the witch's house became longer and more frequent, and in the autumn we were actually beginning to discuss getting married.

We were certainly a rather ill-assorted couple, not only in age, but especially in temperament, and we both knew it, though I was trying my best to hide it from myself, since by that time life in Germany had become so hopeless, the future looked so black, that I simply wanted someone to lean on, however ephemeral his support might be. At the end of November, after endless discussions and hesitations, we eventually decided to become engaged. I rang up my mother to tell her the happy news. She did not sound nearly as pleased as mothers normally are when their daughters announce the prospect of marriage. After a long silence she said at last in a very diffident tone: "Well, I hope you'll be happy." It sounded not particularly encouraging.

The few weeks of our engagement were rather stormy. He had misgivings from the beginning, not only about our characters being suited to each other; he also doubted whether it was wise to marry at this juncture, when everything was so utterly uncertain, especially as he was a hundred per cent non-Aryan. I knew quite well that he was right and that the whole thing was really preposterous, but I did not like to admit it, because I did not know what else I could do, and I did not cherish the idea of remaining "lady housekeeper," ironing sheets and setting tables for the rest of my life. After unending arguments, scenes and tears, we at last decided to break it off. I once more rang up my mother, who this time heaved a sigh of relief. I would go to Berlin the next day to talk things over, and then come back for a few days till the H.'s, who were most helpful and understanding had made other arrangements.

As I was sitting in the train back to Berlin I felt at the end of my tether. I had had enough of everything, especially of Nazism and all its works. As I had been crying a good deal the last days, and had been altogether too listless to powder my face, I must have been a somewhat distressing sight, for a man sitting opposite me in the compartment said seriously, and indeed mournfully, that I must be very ill, he was sure I had not much longer to live! Though I did not quite share his opinion, I was certain I had a nervous breakdown. So, after a heart to heart talk with Mother and a good night's rest I went to my doctor uncle, who was a nerve specialist, to have myself examined.

He put me through the usual interrogation: "I suppose you cannot sleep?"

"Oh no, I am far too exhausted *not* to sleep."

"Smoke a lot?"

"No taste for cigarettes at the moment—I only seem to want milk, eggs and fruit."

"I certainly could not have prescribed a better diet. Let's take your reflexes."

So he knocked against my feet and my fingers and went all over me to find indications of a nervous complaint. At last he looked at me with a broad smile. "My dear child, there's nothing whatever the matter with you. Nerves in perfect condition. Just take it easy for a few days, and you will be perfectly all right." I seemed, indeed, to be "disgustingly healthy."

I went back to Marburg feeling very much better. Frank had fortunately gone to Austria, and I had a peaceful few days arranging things and saying goodbye to several people. Among these was Fräulein Ditzen, a charming elderly maiden lady who coached students in English conversation. I told her I wanted to go abroad now, though I did not quite know how to set about it. "If you ever go to England," she said, "be sure to call on Miss Agatha Norman, who is a friend of mine; I will give you her address and will write to her about you."

Back in Berlin I now began to cast about for possibilities to go abroad. My mother's sister in Vienna was in touch with some well-to-do relatives in Holland. She asked them to invite me, and soon enough Lizzy de Kadt, a cousin of my mother, asked me to visit them.

8. *Goodbye Germany*

I ARRIVED at Haarlem one dark February night in 1936. I was met at the station by an alarmingly superior chauffeur who stowed away my luggage, while I was reclining in the cushions of an expensive Buick, wondering what kind of a reception the "poor cousin" would be given on her arrival. Knowing the circles in which my aunt Charlotte liked to move, I had misgivings which proved fully justified the moment I got out of the car. My hostess, a very pretty blonde, petite and doll-like, came into the hall, and after saying "How do you do," her first question was: "Do you play bridge?" Alas, bridge had unfortunately had no place in my curriculum. When I confessed my ignorance she made the shattering comment: "This is a serious lack in your education." She then informed me that her husband hated Germans because of Hitler, and that he did not speak German on principle. It evidently made no difference to him whether one belonged to the persecutors or the persecuted. When I went in to dinner I was prepared for the worst.

It was perhaps fortunate that in the presence of Lizzy's husband everyone spoke only Dutch, for so I was absolved from taking part in the conversation. This would have been difficult in any case; for as soon as we entered the dining room the son, who was in his father's business, turned on the wireless, which subsequently everyone tried to shout down in order to make himself heard. So I could give my full attention to the food, which was excellent, and try to grapple with my profound uneasiness as best I could. After supper the daughter, Rosemarie, took me up to her room and we talked awhile. She was not nearly as pretty as her mother, but of a more intellectual type and interested in writing.

When I was at last allowed to retire I sank exhausted into a luxurious bed, from which at least I need not fear that the Gestapo might arouse me in the middle of the night. About nine o'clock in the morning there appeared instead a very neat and charming housemaid (in fact I soon came to like the staff better than the family, who seemed to be entirely devoid of any human kindness and sympathy). She carried a tray with wonderful coffee, butter, honey and so many various kinds of bread as I had never seen before. I was profoundly thankful to have at least this meal in peace.

I came down into the sitting room about eleven, as I had been given to understand that this was the hour when the feminine part of the household began their day, father and son having gone to their office much earlier. I found the formidable Lizzy ready to depart to the hairdresser; and Rosemarie suggested that I should accompany her to the golf course, as it was a fine, crisp spring morning. While she was kicking her ball about I had sufficient time to think over my situation. It did not look as if I should ever be able to gain the sympathy of this family, seeing I had none of the accomplishments they thought essential for life. Nevertheless I would try to make myself as agreeable as possible and cast about for a job. How this was to be done I did not know.

After lunch, which was more pleasant than the dinner last night, because the men were not there and we could speak German, the two ladies retired for a short rest, and later I went with them to a bridge party. These bridge parties took place several times a week. They began about three in the afternoon and lasted till one or two o'clock in the morning, interrupted only by magnificent refreshments and by the arrival of the men in the evening. I duly watched the players, because I was expected at least to try to pick up the mysteries of the game as best I could; but I certainly did not give it my undivided attention. I was feeling too poignantly the contrast between the life of perpetual fear that I had left behind, and this society of men and women who appeared to be interested in nothing but their bank accounts, their hairdos, dress, golf, and bridge. They were playing bridge on a volcano—but their eyes were held, and had anyone told them that only four years hence they themselves would share the fate of their German brethren, they would have laughed and calmly carried on: "Your bid next."

Bridge at that time seemed to be omnipresent. My old colleague Li von Hauff had given me the address of a Dutch aunt of hers, who might be of help to me. When I rang her up the maid came to the telephone and informed me that Madam was just at the bridge table, would I ring up another day. I was beginning to feel as much persecuted by that game as by the Nazis themselves.

When there was no bridge we went to the pictures, usually to Amsterdam. Once I went there in the morning to look at the city and go to the Rijksmuseum. I have rarely been so depressed in my life as during this time in the lap of luxury at Haarlem, and this visit to Amsterdam was the first ray of light in the "encircling gloom." The *grachten*, the canals of this Venice of the north enchanted me; I have always loved to wander about aimlessly in old cities, and Amsterdam's blend of old-world leisure and new-world vibration was particularly attractive. In the Rijksmuseum I made straight for Rembrandt, to gaze at the "Night Watch" and the "Jew's Bride." I have never understood why some people feel they ought to look at every single picture in a museum; it only confuses the mind, and when one comes out one's eyes are so tired of a surfeit of impressions that the memory retains hardly anything, or at best a confused welter of forms and colors. Rubens was too fleshy for me, Frans Hals, though I appreciated his superb workmanship, I found a trifle commonplace, Vermeer was charming and I feasted my eyes for a short while on his colors—but Rembrandt touched a chord in my own being that responded immediately. I could, and still can, stand before a picture of his and by simply looking at it become recollected and understand a little more of human life, of its sufferings and its joys. Rembrandt's old Jews, their lined, bearded faces expressing their age-old sorrow and their unshakable faith in the God of Abraham, Isaac and Jacob; his women, naïve as Hendrikje or wistful as Saskia, his self-portraits reflecting a certain sensuality necessary for the artist, yet behind it, especially in the later ones, an awareness of another world beyond the real one of sense experience . . . they all held me captive, though I did not realize then just what it was that made such a deep impression on me. As I was on the point of leaving, I noticed another picture. I think it was by Memling: a small Madonna with Child, standing in a church flooded by sunlight. It did not attract me by its subject matter, but by a most extraordinary peace that seemed to flow out from it and into me. I stood looking at it for a long time, and as I walked out into the street again a ray of its peace seemed to accompany me.

I needed it. For I had now been almost three weeks with the de Kadts, and Lizzy told me in so many words it was time I went back to Germany. However, a faint hope of being able to stay on in Holland had now appeared. My mother had forwarded a letter from a Jewish girl, Alice Hirschfeld, whom I had once coached in Latin in my student days, and with whom I had remained in contact. To my utter surprise she wrote from Scheveningen. I replied immediately, and she was as pleased as I that we had found each other in Holland. She was a most generous person; nothing was ever too much for her to help with. As it was now the beginning of April, we went together to see the tulips and hyacinths in bloom in the famous nurseries around Haarlem. We both had imagined large fields of tulips waving like cornfields, and were rather disappointed when we saw instead a carpet of flowers neatly divided into innumerable small squares. Nevertheless, it was a magnificent display of brilliant color, lit up by an already warm spring sun.

Alice had not met me only to look at the tulips. I told her about my unfortunate experience with the de Kadts. "Of course you cannot go back to Germany. I know a German Jewish family in Scheveningen; he is a lawyer at the International Court at the Hague. I am sure they will be able to do something for you." So she arranged an interview with the wife of Dr. Melchior. She was a very charming and forceful personality, with the fullest understanding for my predicament. She persuaded her husband that I could be useful to him as a help for his secretary. I could come and live with them at once.

I was profoundly grateful to be able to leave the de Kadts. Though Lizzy had shown me unmistakably that the sooner I went the better, she seemed actually annoyed that, instead of going back to Nazi Germany, I had found another place in Holland. I still had a pair of shoes with her shoemaker at Haarlem to be resoled, which I asked her to forward to my new address, when they would be ready. A few days later the shoes arrived at Scheveningen. She had not only failed to pay for the repair, but even sent them on without postage, which I now had to pay from the ten German marks my mother was allowed to send me each month.

With the Melchiors I was to my great relief in a far more congenial atmosphere. Though I did not know shorthand I managed to take down German letters for Dr. Melchior, as he dictated rather slowly; I typed out manuscripts, collected documents at the International Court, and generally made myself useful. I received no salary, which I did not expect, as board and lodging were really sufficient remuneration for the little work I did. Alice was living quite near, and we were much together. She was a great standby for me in these difficult days; it was due to her initiative that I at last decided to leave Holland. "You will never find anything worth while here; the country is too small to absorb immigrants. You ought to go to England, especially as you speak the language."

I was only too ready to go there—but how should I be able to achieve that, with all those immigration difficulties? Alice, who had been in and out of England several times during the last three years knew all about that. "You put an advertisement for an *au pair* job as nursery governess or mother's help in one of the London papers. You are sure to get replies; then you fix up with a family and get into the country on a visitor's permit. Once you have a family who want you, I will tell you how to deal with the immigration officer."

It sounded attractive enough—but where should I find the money for the advertisement, and, even more important, for the journey? I had just been spending over half of the ten Marks mother had been able to send me in April on having a wisdom tooth extracted. That had been another of my misfortunes in Holland. I had suddenly developed a violent toothache; Frau Melchior had recommended a refugee dentist in the Hague. When I went to see him he told me he could not possibly extract a wisdom tooth without first taking an X-ray. I asked how much this would be; he named a sum that was more than double all the money I possessed. It seemed not to occur to him that in such a case of need he might take an X-ray free of charge; instead it greatly troubled his conscience to pull a wisdom tooth without one. At last I persuaded him to do so, paid him half my month's allowance for this favor, and was thankful when after a fortnight's bad pains no further complications developed.

Having now only about ten shillings left, I could not see how I was to get to England except as a stowaway. A few days after my visit to the dentist, having still a swollen face and frayed nerves, I found beside my breakfast cup a Dutch money order for the equivalent of about fifteen pounds. The sender was unknown to me, but he had written after his name: "On behalf of Professor Frank." The explanation came the next day. Erich, who had written to me once or twice after our parting, knew I was penniless in Holland and had paid several bills for a Dutch friend of his who had spent a short time in Germany, so that this friend should send me some money. A few days later came a second installment. So now I had about thirty pounds, which seemed a fortune, certainly sufficient to take me to England and even leave me a little over "against a rainy day."

Alice set to work at once. She put an advertisement for an *au pair* job in the *Daily Telegraph,* and to my surprise there were eleven answers. We selected one from the wife of a director of education with two small children in Wiltshire. The lady agreed to send me a formal invitation, so that I could enter the country as a visitor; for at that time foreigners were not even allowed to take domestic *au pair* jobs without a permit from the Home Office that was extremely difficult to obtain.

Alice did everything for me; she even asked a friend of hers to meet me at the station in London. I wrote to Miss Norman, the friend of Fräulein Ditzen, that I was coming to England. I had a letter from her by return post asking me to call her up when I should be in London. Alice accompanied me to Rotterdam, where she gave me the final instructions on how to cope with the immigration officer: "Above all, never contradict yourself. You must stick exactly to your original replies, because he will cross-question you. Now remember:

you got to know that family during a holiday in Austria. They have two children and a maid. You are going there only to improve your English."

In my case this was particularly plausible, as I still had my original profession of secondary school teacher in my passport. We were discussing this as we were walking about in Rotterdam, and though my mind was almost entirely occupied with the formidable immigration officer, I had just enough interest left to observe that Rotterdam was not nearly as attractive as Amsterdam, that it was much more of an ordinary port, with little distinction about it. Alice accompanied me to the boat, hoped I would not get seasick, and left me after a final warning about being consistent in my replies on landing.

I went to my cabin, lay down and kept repeating my replies to all the possible questions the immigration officer might ask, until I fell sound asleep.

9. *How Do You Do, England*

DESPITE my excitement I slept like a log, and when we arrived at Gravesend about seven in the morning, I felt strong enough to be a match even for the sternest immigration officer. It was just as well I did, for it was every whit as bad as Alice had foretold, and I hardly think I could have weathered the interview without her coaching. How I envied the thrice lucky people who could sail through the barrier marked "British Passports" reserved for the "sheep," while I had to wait with the hapless foreign "goats" to be delivered over to a cross-examination that would have done honor in its thoroughness even to my own countrymen.

"Do you want an interpreter?"

"No, thank you."

"Where are you going?"

"To Mrs. So-and-So. She invited me. Here is her letter."

"How many children do they have?"

"Two."

"They have no maid, I suppose?"

"Oh yes, they have a maid."

"Where did you get to know them?"

"In Austria, at Innsbruck."

"How many children did you say they have? Did you say they had a maid? Why did you come to this country? Only to improve your English? Where did you get to know these people? How much money do you have?"

At last I scored. My fifteen pounds reassured him sufficiently to put a stamp in my passport by which I was "Permitted to land at London on 15th May, 1936, on condition that the holder does not remain in the United Kingdom longer than two months and does not enter any employment paid or unpaid." Two months was not much—but Alice had said that once I was in the country it would be quite easy to obtain an extension. I boarded the boat train to London with a deep sigh of relief—I was in England, at last.

At Liverpool Street Station I was met by Alice's friend. As I was staying in London till the next day, she took me to a large hotel in Bloomsbury, where one could have a room for five and six a night. As soon as I had booked there I staggered my kind guide with the request to take me to a telephone box, since I wanted to ring up Miss Norman. She was at home, and when she heard that I was going to Wiltshire the following day, she asked me to come to tea with her the same afternoon. When I put down the receiver I asked the German girl could she direct me to Kensington later in the day, as I had to go to tea with Miss Norman. I had not expected that this simple request would call forth a reaction of utter surprise mingled with awe: "What, you have hardly arrived here and you have already an invitation to go to tea with an English lady? This is more than I have achieved in the three years I have been here. You will go far."

I thought it the most natural thing in the world to go to tea with English people when one was in England, and only realized later, when I had seen more of my fellow refugees, that this was not so usual as I had imagined. Guided by my escort who insisted on accompanying me to the door, I found my hostess in a romantic looking cottage near Nottinghill Gate.

This first tea party in an English home shattered very pleasantly all my preconceived ideas. For I had come to this country with considerable misgivings. I had been told in Germany over and over again that the English were cold and stiff, that, though they were polite, a foreigner could practically never make friends with them. I had found the few Dutch people I had met rather stiff—if the English were stiffer still, heaven help me. Miss Norman was anything but stiff. She was kind, understanding, sympathetic. She assured me that I could always count on her help, and I knew at once that these were no mere empty words, that she meant everything she said. When I left her I knew I should feel at home in England.

Next morning I had a surprise of a different kind. I had learned at school that English people always talk about the weather, but I had never believed it. It surely was one of those exaggerated tales people were telling of other countries. Now when I came down in the lift for breakfast the lift boy greeted me. "Nice morning, Miss, isn't it." I was staggered. It was really true, they *did* talk about the weather like that without, to my mind, any provocation. I think I was too much taken aback to make an appropriate response; though I learned soon enough to talk as volubly about the vagaries of the British climate as if I had been brought up in it.

Fortified by an unaccustomed breakfast of bacon and eggs, I went to Paddington station to set out on my journey to my first English job. What I had told the immigration officer was true: the family to whom I went had two small children and a maid. The latter, however, told me at once that she was leaving next day—nobody could stand it there, I should soon enough see for myself.

It certainly was not easy. I was expected to get up at

seven, and from that time till eleven at night I was constantly on the go, with about half an hour's break after lunch. I was not used to small children, whom I was expected to teach German, though they showed not the slightest desire to learn that language, for which I did not blame them. The little boy, aged about two, showed his resentment by throwing himself on the floor and kicking in all directions. "You must coax him," said Madam; but nothing I—or she, for that matter—might say made the slightest difference. His sister, who was several years older, showed no more interest, and in the end I was learning more English from them than they German from me. In the meantime the maid left, and my mistress discovered that I could cook, so to my relief I was let off the children from time to time to do the cooking.

After a week of hard work I thought it time I had my ten shillings pocket money which she had agreed to pay me. So I gently suggested that this was now due. I had not expected that my reasonable request would be met with an outburst of abuse. According to her, nobody in this country ever asked for pay; it was an impertinence that I should do so. I must have made my feelings pretty clear, for next morning she said appreciatively: "You were not short of your English last night." We agreed that it would be better for me to look out for another job.

I once more tried the *Daily Telegraph,* and my second advertisement brought several answers which seemed suitable. I had made up my mind to take a job in London this time, as there would be more opportunities for building up a career of some sort. When I told my mistress I wanted to go to town for an interview, she did not like the idea. I had done so well these last weeks (I think they had never had so tasty food before; they liked my Continental dishes), she was quite ready to keep me. However, I had decided to change, and so I went for my interviews.

The first address I had was at Bromley. When I called,

late in the morning, the lady of the house opened herself, heavily made up and wearing a very low-cut dress. The atmosphere seemed decidedly odd. She was overwhelmingly amiable, too amiable, I thought. When she said in the course of the conversation that her husband was a most charming man, I decided that it was better not to try this particular job; and to her obvious regret I told her I had still someone else to see and would let her know.

My next interview was in Hampstead. There it was the exact opposite. Mrs. Fawcett was a most respectable clergy-man's widow with one grown-up son and two daughters. She wanted me to help in their flat with light housework; I should have to cook the breakfast for her children who all went out to their jobs in the morning, make one or two beds, set the table, do the washing up, but otherwise there would be plenty of spare time for me. It would be quite all right with the Home Office, too, she told me—for of course, I should have to undergo another cross-examination for changing my abode.

Life with Mrs. Fawcett and her son and daughters was pleasant enough. I soon became an adept at frying bacon and eggs for breakfast; by eleven o'clock my morning's work was generally finished, and then Mrs. Fawcett and one of her daughters would often go out in the car, taking me with them, for a picnic lunch in Hyde Park. As there was not much to do in the afternoons either, I was sent out to look at the sights of London; the Houses of Parliament and the Tower, Marble Arch and the Embankment soon became familiar. I found London an enchanting city, so different from my native Berlin. I thought it both far more imposing and far more homely. At first I was rather disgusted by the dirt and untidiness. In Berlin I could have eaten my dinner off the floor of the subway, it was so spotless; and if one dared to drop a ticket in a bus or streetcar, the conductor would come and make one pick it up. In London everybody seemed to throw about whatever he fancied, tickets and banana peels, old newspapers and cigarette butts. And the soot and grime everywhere—my clothes were black in no time. Yet life was so much more pleasant. I was quite surprised at the amazing number of small houses with gardens in the capital of the British Empire. In Berlin there were only large blocks of flats, except in some very fashionable suburbs where the millionaires had their villas. But in London you might go round the corner of one of the main roads and find yourself in what might be a village street. In Berlin the fashionable quarters were strictly separated from the poorer ones, actual slums were nonexistent. In London everything was mixed up in very democratic confusion; there were slum houses in Mayfair and Kensington and stately mansions in Lambeth, though W.1 was a first-class address and E.5 no address at all. It was most intriguingly bewildering.

Yet Berlin, for all its ostentation (one of my pre-Nazi poems, published in a Frankfurt paper, was called *Berlin renommiert*—Berlin boasts) appeared incredibly provincial, compared with London. India and South Africa, New Zealand and Canada seemed only a stone's throw away; their names appeared everywhere, on the signboards of banks and business houses, on the wrappings of food or in the conversation of people who were either going there or just returning from a trip to one of these, to me, fantastically distant parts of the world. It was exhilarating to walk through the London streets and just become part of their life, which, though hurried and businesslike, yet had a quality of leisure and friendliness conspicuously absent from Berlin. I was amazed when I first saw people helping themselves to their evening paper, putting their pennies on the unattended pile, while the news vendor was having his tea in a neighboring pub; when I saw full milk bottles, sometimes even with sixpences or shillings on top of them, standing peacefully outside the houses; but, most astonishing of all, when drivers were slow-ing down before me and actually waving me to pass. When this first happened to me I wondered what could be the reason; it dawned on me only gradually that this was simply the polite concern of British car drivers for their pedestrian fellowmen. In Berlin I had to run for my life, because the car could kill me, but not I the car; and if I dared to cross the road against the red lights even if there was no traffic far and wide to be seen, I would be fined a mark. London was, indeed, an extraordinarily human city; and not the least of its human features was the cats sitting well-fed, well-groomed, and altogether comfortable on the proverbial mats before the front doors.

Only one endearing feature of Continental cities was then sadly absent from London, missed keenly especially by the homeless stranger: the cosy small café, where one could sit for hours before a cup of coffee or a glass of wine, reading the papers that were hanging in wooden frames on the wall. It was bad enough to be without them in the afternoon—the teashops were no equivalent, for you had just to sit down, have your meal and run off again—but at night, after supper, there was simply nowhere to sit other than home, unless one had sufficient money and energy to go to the West End. Sundays were even worse, I had never quite believed what Dibelius had told us about the strength of the Puritan tradition. Sunday in the largest city of the world without theaters, cinemas, dances, and with most of the cafés and restaurants closed seemed utterly preposterous; yet now I experienced it myself and disliked it intensely. Instead Mrs. Fawcett would send me off to church on Sunday morning. She and her family went to a high church; but as I was supposed to be a Lutheran she thought I would prefer a low church, and so she suggested Matins at a church on Finchley Road. I duly went there the first time; and it touched me greatly that they were praying for the persecuted Jews in Germany. On the following Sundays, however, the weather was too lovely for me to resist the temptation to play truant and go for a walk on Hampstead Heath instead. Fortunately Mrs. Fawcett would not ask me what the sermon had been on!

I could not help being depressed sometimes. I was certainly never homesick; I liked England far too much for that; but my position was too insecure not to be worried. It must have been during one of these moods, as I was sitting in my room one afternoon, that I suddenly wished I could pour out my troubles to a Catholic priest. I do not know how this idea came into my mind; it was simply there as a keen regret that this could not be. For I had as yet got no further than a rather vague belief in a personal God; and I discarded the absurd thought almost as quickly as it had entered my head.

The idea to do something about my position came from Mrs. Fawcett herself. "You are really far too well educated" she told me one day, "to go on doing housework. You ought to find some job at a school." I thought myself this would be better, despite my dislike of teaching. But how was I to set about it?

I might, of course, have got in touch with the refugee center at Woburn, later at Bloomsbury House, which helped Jewish and also Christian refugees from Central Europe. Both Alice and her friend, who had met me on my arrival, had told me about it. The latter had once used the expression: "If one lives in the emigration." I had reacted immediately: "But I am not living in the emigration; I am living in England." I had no intention to become the perpetual exile, living in a narrow circle of fellow refugees. I liked England and English ways, and was determined from the start to assimilate myself as much as I could, and to make friends with English people. It was perhaps due to this determination that I have never experienced the coldness for which the English are renowned on the Continent, but have always met with kindness, understanding and friendship. I felt that once I began to rely on refugee organizations I should be drawn too much into the limited sphere of a little Germany situated in Hampstead, which would considerably retard, if not actually stultify, the process of my Anglicization.

I was particularly fortunate in having Miss Norman as a resourceful adviser, so that I could dispense with Bloomsbury House. When I mentioned Mrs. Fawcett's suggestion to her, she thought it a very good idea and immediately got in touch with the head of a large scholastic agency she knew. Within a few days I received the notice of a vacancy for a German mistress on the staff of a small private school at Taplow, near Maidenhead. My application was answered by return of post, and the principal arranged that I should meet her at the agency in London.

Miss R. was a rather formidable, red-faced lady in her sixties. I do not think she had any intellectual qualifications to fit her for her post, and her account of the duties connected with my position as German mistress was none too reassuring. They included teaching the three R's in the kindergarten (she considered my English quite good enough for that), washing the girl's hair, seeing the small day-children across the road, and giving a few private German lessons to some of the older girls. My remuneration would be thirty pounds a year, and I should have to make my own arrangements about the holidays. The point that decided me to accept this hardly attractive offer was that Miss R. assured me there would be no difficulty about getting a labor permit for me, since she had always had a German "Fräulein"—pronounced Frolleen. I had been working illegally for several months now, and was in a very precarious position, as there was no guarantee that my permit of residence would be renewed again and again if I was still pretending to be a "visitor." A proper labor permit would make all the difference, and once I had been in this country for longer, other possibilities might emerge.

There was one last snag. As I had come here on a visitor's

permit, this could not be changed into a labor permit while I was in England. I had to leave the country while a new application was being made, and come back when it had been granted. As the Olympic Games were just then taking place in Berlin, I thought it quite safe to go back for a few weeks while awaiting the permit.

Germany presented a more cheerful picture on my return in July 1936 than when I had left in February. The formalities at the frontier were reduced to a minimum in order not to discourage foreign visitors; Berlin had donned its gayest attire, beflagged and more spotlessly clean than ever; even the police were remarkably lenient and polite when I came into collision with them when crossing the road against the red lights, as I had been wont to do in London when no vehicles were in sight. When I informed the policeman who stopped me that I came from England he refrained from fining me.

I had told my mother about the extraordinary consideration with which British car drivers treated pedestrians, which she could hardly credit. One morning, as we were crossing a busy thoroughfare, we waited to let a large, smart car pass. To our utter surprise the driver slowed down and motioned us to cross in front of him.

"Look, Mother," I said, "this is exactly what the cars do in London." Instinctively I looked at the number plate. It had GB on it. "There you are! I knew no German car driver would ever have behaved like that."

I enjoyed my brief, and so far my last, stay in my native city, which for all its cleanliness and decoration seemed already to belong to another existence. There was just a slight fear at first that something might go wrong with the permit; but when this had duly arrived I felt free to have a last fling, take final leave of all my friends, sit for the last time in the front gardens of the cafés, eating *Torte* with whipped cream, and go shopping in the Leipziger Strasse to lay in an adequate supply of clothes, as these were the only possessions I was allowed to take out of the country.

Two days before my departure I did a dreadful thing. Mother and I were having lunch with a friend of ours, himself an opponent of Hitler, and his two nieces, Sudeten Germans, whom I had not known before. When the conversation turned to Hitler I gaily remarked, no doubt intoxicated with my past five months of freedom and the prospect of a speedy return to England. "That man ought to be hanged on the nearest lamp post." There was a shocked silence.

"But Hiltgunde, how can you say such a thing?"

I grinned innocently: "Why not, he deserves it, doesn't he?" The subject was hastily changed.

Afterwards I was told that the two nieces were ardent admirers of Hitler, like most of their countrymen. "It is high time you went back to England," remarked my mother, "if you stayed much longer you would bring us all into a concentration camp. You seem to have quite forgotten what it is like here." I had not forgotten, but the short spell of freedom had made it far more difficult than before to keep my mouth shut.

When I crossed the frontier forty-eight hours later, the Nazi official asked me what I had in my suitcase. "A million marks," I said laughing. He laughed, too, and bothered no further. Indeed, I should never have attempted to smuggle out anything; it would not have been worth the prospect of death by torture.

The channel was less kind to me on this occasion than the Nazi. I have never again been so seasick as I was then. The only alternative to being on *terra firma* that I could desire was immediate death. At last, when the steward told me that the uproar had ceased and land was in sight I staggered on deck. I do not know whether it was partly due to my weakness, but when I saw the English coast again tears came into my eyes. "Thank God, England."

It may seem strange, but it is a fact: there was no trace of regret that I had now finally left my own country, no suspicion of a desire to return, even should Hitler ever fall. I must have been fairly green in the face; for when the immigration officer had been told I had a teaching permit he let me pass at once, and the customs officer gave me just one look and chalked his cross on my luggage without asking any questions. I had come back to England to stay.

10. *A School Out of Dickens*

IT TOOK me three days of a tea and toast diet to get over the effects of my seasickness, and before I went to sleep the first night in London, my bed seemed to be rocking with me as if I were still on the storm-tossed channel. Mrs. Fawcett, with whom I was staying as a guest now, warned me that I should probably have to share a room with another mistress at the school to which I was going. I was glad she had prepared me for this, else I should have been even more shocked by conditions at S. House than I actually was.

The first sight of the school, however, gave me a pleasant surprise. It was evidently a converted manor house, standing in beautiful grounds near the main road; an imposing drive led up to it. Miss R. received me very amiably and went up with me to show me my room. Mrs. Fawcett had been right: I had to share it with the gym mistress. It was an attic with a small window, and contained two iron bedsteads covered with thin, bluish-grey blankets which looked as if they had been acquired at a sale of old army stocks. Beside each bed was a cane chair; the seat of mine was defective, so that it was a hazardous undertaking to sit down on it, and I decided that the only place to sit and type would be on the bed.

A row of hooks for clothes with a curtain in front and a small wooden chest of drawers with a wash basin and a carafe on top of it completed the furniture. "Is there anywhere to put my books?" I asked naïvely; for I had brought about a dozen from Germany, as well as my typewriter and a ream of paper. Miss R. looked at me as if I had asked her to place a lady's maid and a page boy at my disposal.

"Our staff have no books beside the Prayer Book and a spelling dictionary," she replied severely. "You will have to leave them in your suitcase."

"Yes, Miss R., thank you."

When she had left I quickly unpacked the most necessary things and then sat down on the bed to survey the situation. It would be grim, there was no doubt about that. It was the worst room I had so far occupied; and Miss R. was not likely to do much to make my sojourn in her house more pleasant. I wondered what my room-mate would be like.

I had not to wait long, for about half an hour after my arrival a boisterous young woman precipitated herself into the room together with an avalanche of suitcases, tennis rackets and knitting bags. She introduced herself as Sheila Cameron, and her pretty face with its fresh complexion and dark hair was as attractively Scottish as her name; her gaiety was a good tonic for my momentary depression. Gradually other staff members arrived. Next door were the junior English mistress, Gertrude Stephens, a very charming and friendly girl, and Miss Needham, the music mistress. Miss Goldsworthy, the senior English mistress, had a small room to herself in another part of the building; and "Mademoiselle," who had been with Miss R. for twenty years and also acted as her chauffeur, shared the principal's quarters. The staff seemed easy to get along with; and if they were able to stand things, surely I could do the same.

When I was shown the school I had another shock. The four classrooms were all on the ground floor; there was very little light, and the air seemed damp. The wooden forms must have seated many generations of pupils; they were very old-fashioned with uncomfortably straight backs, full of scratches and ink blots. I looked in vain for such, to my mind indispensable apparatus as maps, microscopes, models; instead, I was surprised to find that there was a magnificent swimming pool, several tennis courts and a large playing field. The staff room, on the other hand, was tiny, containing only a table, three chairs and a rickety old sofa. It was near the bathroom, which we had to share with Miss R., or "old Bobs" as we disrespectfully called her. We were allowed one bath a week; and even this was usually cut short because "Bobs" was having hers afterwards, and would shout outside the door for us to be quick.

Our day began at seven o'clock, when the housemaid rang the bell with sufficient vigor to waken the dead. I would jump out of bed at its sound; but Sheila generally turned over for another five minutes, while I was washing in the icy water. Soon the house would be filled with the most nerve-racking sounds: three girls were maltreating Schubert and Chopin, who were really far too difficult for them, on as many pianos; and while I was "taking prep" in another room I amused myself trying to decide whether the horrible dissonances reaching my ear were due to the fact that all three pianos were permanently out of tune or to the mistakes of the unfortunate pupils. My deliberations together with the noise were happily cut short by the eagerly awaited sound of the breakfast bell at eight o'clock.

Meals at S. House were one of the more penitential exercises for me. Until the food had made the journey from the secret regions of the kitchen which we were never allowed to penetrate, to the two drafty classrooms which at meal time were transformed into a dining hall, its temperature had reached a state of tepidity which made it even more unpalatable than it would have been otherwise. Breakfast consisted of the weakest tea ever, lumpy porridge, and infinitesimal slices of tough bacon occasionally replaced by uncommonly salty kippers which seemed to have an extraordinarily lavish supply of bones. Midday dinner varied according to the days of the week, its main course not being meat and vegetables, but pudding, more accurately suet pudding. This latter appeared with iron regularity every day except during the weekend, either as ginger, chocolate, or treacle pudding. The latter was the traditional fare on Monday, and it took me some weeks to discover why I was invariably feeling sick on Monday afternoons. This so called treacle pudding had the shape and weight of a greyish white cannon ball, needing stomachs trained from infancy to digest the food of ostriches. When I had found out that it was the pudding that upset me every Monday, I persuaded Miss Goldsworthy, who was privileged to dish out the dinner for our table, to give me only a teaspoonful of it, but discreetly, so as not to attract "old Bobs' " attention.

There was one feature about these school meals, however, that deeply impressed me. It was the perfect manner of the girls. I was quite staggered to watch even the ten-year-olds gravely serving each other, their eyes almost more attentively on the plate of their next door neighbor than on their own. On the rare occasions when a girl failed to notice that someone else wanted something, she was immediately reprimanded by the teacher at the head of the table. I rememberd how at birthday parties and school excursions our German girls used to grab their food, unblushingly taking the best pieces for themselves, and demanding whatever they wanted, which was indeed inevitable, for they were all looking only after themselves. Here everyone behaved with the greatest decorum; if anyone dared to raise her voice, a "don't shout" from the head of the table immediately reduced her to a whisper. In fact the poor things were supposed to speak French during meals, but this rule was not always rigidly enforced, since it limited the conversation to such interesting remarks at *Avez-vous un chat?* or *Avez-vous un chien?*

The early training in table manners impressed me deeply. Soon enough I was sitting on my bed, my typewriter on my knees, writing an article headed "An English Girls School" for a Swiss newspaper, in which I admiringly exclaimed: "These are indeed the future hostesses of England." This was perhaps somewhat exaggerated; for these girls did not belong to the top layer of society. Their parents were mostly officers, civil servants or businessmen in India or other parts of the Commonwealth, who could not afford to send their daughters to a better-class boarding school, and so entrusted their education to Bobs, who certainly did teach them manners and comportment (a dancing mistress came every week from London, and they were all adepts at Lacrosse), though not much else. Bobs herself took school prayers every morning, reading the collects and the verses from the Gospels in such a peremptory tone that Gertrude said of her: "She dictates to God."

After prayers the lessons would start. I was teaching the smallest children in one of the rooms which also served as a dining hall; at the table next to me Miss Tarrant, a nonresident mistress, took the slightly older girls and boys. She was a pleasant, quiet, middle-aged person, and though our tables were fairly close together we did not disturb each other. There was no question of modern methods; I taught them to read that the cat sat on the mat; to learn that twice two are four, and supervised their writing exercises. Matters would become difficult, however, when Mademoiselle appeared on the scene. She was a petite woman in her early forties, still very pretty and vivacious. We were all puzzled what could have induced her to spend the best twenty years of her life at this school, at the beck and call of tyrannous old Bobs; she seemed so obviously made for better things. Still, she did not appear to be unhappy, and she certainly had a privileged position in the school. She had achieved the feat, not uncommon among foreigners who have been living in this country for a long time, that she now spoke both English and her native language with an extraordinary accent, and gaily mixed up French and English words that sounded similar. When she entered the class to take the bigger children for French, I would give up even the pretence of going on with my own lessons. For soon would sound from the neighbouring table: *"Les petits bateaux, qui vont sur l'eau, ont-ils des jambes?"*

First softly sung by her, soon lustily, even if wrongly, parrotted by the children: *"Les petits bateaux . . ."*

"But no, darling, not tibato—*petit, pe, pe, pe . . . petit.* Once again, Patsy, now come on: *Les petits bateaus . . . ont-ils des jambes?"*

While this interesting discussion on the *petits bateaux* and their *jambes* or otherwise was going on, my own form were starting at pretty mademoiselle, fascinated by her increasing liveliness, until both forms finally joined in the chorus, and the whole school resounded to the question: *"Les petits bateaux, qui vont sur l'eau, ont-ils des jambes?"* At this point Bobs would sometimes poke in her head to see what was going on; but when she realized it was Mademoiselle engaged on imparting French polish to her charges she discreetly withdrew.

Both children and teachers stood in awe of the principal. She often was in a specially bad temper early in the morning, when she would boom through the house like a foghorn. Only the domestic staff were safe from her fury, because they were in a position to give notice at once. "You realize why she has these fits in the morning, don't you?" Gertrude said to me. I suspected the cause, but would not divulge my thoughts. "You look into the garage next time you see the door open," she suggested. I took the hint, and there was indeed the unmistakable evidence of an imposing array of empty brandy bottles.

I confess I could have done myself with a drop of something strong to warm me up. It was my first English winter, and though it was happily comparatively mild, I was in no way prepared for it, especially as I had to spend it in the most unfavorable conditions. It goes without saying that there were no heating arrangements of any kind in the bedrooms; we could not even fill a hot-water bottle, for there was practically no hot water on our side of the house, and no gas ring or other provision anywhere to provide it. The two hard, thin blankets on our beds gave no warmth; the mattresses would hardly have passed muster in the worst equipped youth hostel. I gave up turning mine after the first efforts, since it was so full of lumps that I was glad when I had managed to lay a tolerably comfortable hole into it after a week. We all took to going to bed attired in our dressing gowns, stockings and other garments not generally slept in. Conditions in the staff room were not much better; it had a minute radiator, on which one had to hold one's hands for a long time to ascertain whether it was cold or actually a little tepid. As Gertrude had wisely provided herself with her own eiderdown, she used to take it over to the staffroom, and so three or four of us would sit huddled against each other on the sofa, the eiderdown over our knees, trying to keep as warm as we could. Whenever we had an afternoon off we would go into Maidenhead into a café for the luxury of a really hot cup of tea and a crackling fire, or, if there was an interesting film on, to the pictures, where one could also get warm.

Nevertheless, I very nearly succumbed to the change of climate and the lack of proper woolen clothes which I had never before seen worn in such profusion, one on top of the other, as in this country. I started a cold in October, and this went on with insignificant interruptions till the following

May; though in order to prevent me from becoming too bored with it, it changed its symptoms like a chameleon its color; sometimes taking the form of a "streamer," at other times coming out as a cough, a sore throat, aching limbs and whatnot. There were days when I would sit on my bed in the morning with a swimming head that seemed to indicate a temperature, wondering whether I should be able to get through the day. However, the thought of Bobs' infallible method of curing colds and influenza would finally bring me to my feet: for the prospect of being confined to my icy bed on a diet of cold milk at odd intervals to the exclusion of all other food was an excellent pick-me-up. Every now and again my physical discomfort would produce slight depressions; but a dream I had several times during these first months at S. House served to disperse any black moods. I dreamt I was travelling in a train in Germany. I was saying things against Hitler, though I realized that a lady sitting opposite me was watching me; but I could not stop saying these things, though I knew all the time that she would get out at the next station to have me arrested and put in a concentration camp. At this point I would wake up, my heart still beating with the fear I had been feeling in my dream, and with a deep sigh of relief say to myself: "Thank God, I am in England. It can't happen here."

I had not been long at S. House when the abdication crisis became acute. The division of the country into the emotional sympathizers with "the poor King, why should he not marry the woman he loves," and the upholders of royal responsibility and the Christian indissolubility of marriage was faithfully reflected in the staff room. Only five years ago I should probably have been wholeheartedly on the side of Edward VIII and Mrs. Simpson. But since then I had seen the lawlessness and lack of tradition of the Weimar Republic clear the way for a brutal dictatorship; the very traditionalism of England seemed the best defence against those dark powers that had enslaved my own country and other parts of the continent of Europe. Romantic love that disregarded the moral strictures of society might perhaps be tolerated in private life; but I was beginning to realize that there were "values" that might rightly demand the sacrifice even of one's own personal happiness. English cant asserting itself once more? I had come to be less sure about cant and moral hypocrisy. Where there are definite moral principles, a certain measure of hypocrisy on the part of the not-so-sincere will be inevitable; but would it be better to sacrifice morality altogether in order to avoid cant? I read the accounts of the *démarches* of the Archbishop of Canterbury and Mr. Baldwin. I could well understand the heart searchings of all those who bore the responsibility for the ultimate decision. Though I was a foreigner, I was deeply concerned with the issues at stake, and took sides against the romantics in the staff room.

Probably because I was a foreigner, used to the bull-in-the-china-shop methods by which affairs were conducted in the country I came from, I was deeply impressed by the way in which this most difficult and delicate matter was handled here. I did not think that in any other country in the world such a crisis would have been solved without a major revolution. Here the king was politely exiled, even those opposed to his abdication acquiesced with hardly a murmur; his brother was proclaimed king in his place. A tremor had caused a minor agitation in the British Commonwealth, and the Crown emerged even more secure than before.

I have always considered it a privilege to have lived through this experience within the first year of my coming to this country, and in entirely English surroundings. It made me understand English ways and the English character better than I could otherwise have done. I saw for the first time that it is possible to discuss divergent political views amiably. I also realized the tremendous moral backbone of the country and the unifying power of the Crown which had to express it, even though the personal morality of a large number of its subjects might leave much to be desired. If this be cant, I would rather have it and the principles that lay behind it, than the sincerity that I had known and the moral confusion it was supposed to vindicate. When Hitler was told that homosexuality was rife among his storm troopers, he was reported to have replied: "My SA is not a kindergarten." Evidently moral licence was as compatible with political tyranny as moral respectability was with political freedom. I was beginning to appreciate the combination of the latter which I saw around me.

Some time before the end of term Miss R. asked at supper with an air of intense concern: "Does anyone know when Eton breaks up?" As none of us was quite sure of the date, one of the staff was set the task to find out for certain.

"What does it matter when Eton breaks up?" I asked Gertrude afterwards.

"Ah, my dear, you do not know us yet. However different S. House may be in other respects, it is a law of the Medes and Persians that we must at least begin term and break up on the same day as Eton—it is Bobs' special pride."

For the Christmas holidays I found a job with the family of a master at a public school at Malvern, whose two children I was to keep occupied and teach some German. They were very pleasant people; it was quite a different experience from the one I had in my first job of this kind in Wiltshire. The mere physical relief of being able to sit in front of a hot fire and get warmed through was bliss; the children were interested and easy to entertain, and I was almost as excited as they when I was told we were all going to London for the feast itself, where we would stay at a hotel and take the boy and girl to pantomimes.

So I spent my first Christmas in this country in a very traditional English manner, so different from the German way. In Germany the climax is Christmas Eve, the lighted

Christmas tree, the hymns, all very religious, the exchange of presents under the tree; it is very much a feast of the home and the family. Here the climax is Christmas Day, holly and mistletoe, the carols—scarcely religious and surprisingly gay—the turkey and the pudding (this, by the way, quite different from what I had imagined), the parties and the pantomimes. It was a mood I associated rather with New Year's Eve and with the Carnival; nevertheless I enjoyed it thoroughly, and London at its pre-war gayest prevented any feeling of homesickness that this first Christmas abroad might otherwise have aroused.

Next term's dreariness was interrupted by the Coronation. I could not go to London on the day itself, but went immediately afterwards to look at the decorations. There was still a feeling of excitement in the air that belied the Continental idea of the permanently phlegmatic and insensitive Englishman. As I was crossing the road I was nearly run over by a car dashing round a corner at top speed. "If that man doesn't drive like a darned foreigner," I said to my companion. I looked back and just caught the D for Deutschland beside the numberplate. The experience was the perfect complement to my previous one with a British car during the Olympic Games at Berlin. When I came to this country I had sadly made up my mind to abandon all thought of writing; for I imagined that one could not write for publication in any other than one's native language. Now, however, I was longing to express this odd twin-experience in print, and with the help of my friend Gertrude, who gave me some useful hints on English style, I produced an account of it, which I bravely sent to the *Evening Standard*. To my delighted surprise it was published under the title "A German Girl's Cure for Road Grumblers," just about a year after I had come to this country. I have rarely received a check with such elation as this guinea I had earned by my first English literary effort.

My outings to London were oases in the dreariness of my

school job. Gertrude and I had been talking about the various customs of our countries, and she confided that she had never had her hand kissed; it was an experience she had wanted to have for a long time. "Nothing easier than that," I said. "Next time we go to town again I'll ask a friend of mine, Dr. S., to come to Paddington station and perform the ceremony."

"Would you really? You think he'll do it?"

"Certainly, why shouldn't he? Quite a normal thing to do on the Continent." I duly notified Dr. S., could he meet us at Paddington and kiss a nice English girl's hand, a proposition he naturally accepted with alacrity.

In the train Gertrude was already showing signs of excitement which I found hard to understand, since my own first experience of a hand kiss dated back to my fourteenth year and remained engraven on my memory only because from that moment I no longer considered myself a child. When the train stopped at Paddington I wondered what would happen, since Gertrude seemed to think it terribly daring. I suppose she almost hoped Dr. S. might not have come. But there he was, quite ready to do what was expected of him if only the lady would let him. But Gertrude, seized by a sudden attack of coyness, kept her hands well out of his reach, while I had great difficulty carrying on a conversation without bursting into hysterics. Eventually Dr. S. said he had to go. It was now or never. With sudden determination Gertrude simply flung her right hand somewhere in the direction of his lips, while I averted my gaze so as not to lose my self-control altogether. He later told me that he had just about managed the kiss with great difficulty and without the grace this chivalrous gesture requires, as her desperate movement prevented him from bowing over her hand. However, Gertrude had had her thrill and was content.

When the summer vacation was nearing Miss Norman asked me whether I should not like to spend it with my mother. She herself was going away, and we could have her house in Kensington. So we spent four weeks together, and to my surprise Mother took to England as quickly as I had done. She was thrilled to find the milk bottles in the morning on the ivy-covered wall of the front garden, and she got on remarkably well with Miss Norman's daily, a real cockney, though she did not know much English at that time. When Miss Norman returned about the middle of August, Mother went back to Germany, and I found myself a small furnished room in Kensington High Street for the rest of the holidays, as I intended to do some work in the British Museum. I was reading old chronicles there with a view to finding material for articles in Swiss newspapers. I did not yet trust my English sufficiently to write it; besides I did not know the requirements of the English market, seeing English papers did not have a *feuilleton* like the Continental ones. As a result of my research I was able to place several articles in Switzerland, and so to replenish my infinitesimal post-office account.

Towards the end of the holidays I had a conversation with Miss Norman that was to have far-reaching consequences. In answer to a casual question about the kind of school I had attended in Germany, I told her I had learned Latin and Greek.

"Greek?" she exclaimed, "You actually know Greek?"

"Indeed I do."

"Look here, this gives me an idea. Would you like to study theology? Are you at all interested in it?"

"Certainly I am; Scripture was my subsidiary subject for my degree."

"This is marvelous. For, if you should like to take up theology and study for the Archbishop's Diploma, I could put you in touch with the authorities concerned and get you grants so that you could take the examination. What do you think?"

What did I think! I should have caught at a straw to get

me out of S. House—and here I was offered a most attractive prospect of a new career in this country, for Miss Norman held out hopes of a post as lecturer at an Anglican missionary college or something similar. I had no objection to joining the Church of England; I had been to several of its services and greatly preferred it to the Protestantism I had known in Germany, though my beliefs were still as hazy as ever. Miss Norman arranged that I should meet Miss Hippisley, the tutor of women theologians at King's College, London, under whom I was to study, and several other ladies connected with the Lambeth Diploma course. It was agreed that I should be allowed to take the three years' course in two years, as I knew Greek and was a graduate of Berlin University. I was provided with a grammar of New Testament Greek, so that I could brush up my Greek in the following months before beginning my studies next January.

I returned to S. House in high spirits. Though my naturally gay temperament had served me well in the difficulties of these last four years, I had sometimes found it hard to be allowed no scope for any intellectual activities; for the elementary teaching, hair washing and prep-taking in my present job could scarcely be called that. In Berlin I had totally neglected my subsidiary subject; it seemed only retributive justice that I should now be compelled to study nothing but theology for two years. I was eagerly looking forward to it.

I told no one but Gertrude about the happy issue of my summer vacation. She was almost as excited about it as I, and suggested I should accompany her to holy communion one morning, as I was soon going to be confirmed in the Church of England. I gladly consented; but when we were discussing the subject in the presence of Miss Goldsworthy, the senior English mistress, whose views were very high church, she objected: I ought not to go to holy communion in the Church of England, as I had not been confirmed in it. Gertrude, whose brother was a clergyman of ordinary Church of England views, insisted that such fussing over formalities was un-Christian, and took me to a not-too-high communion service. It was the second time I went to communion in a Christian church—not now in a militant mood, as thirteen years ago, but accommodating myself to the customs of English Christians whom I loved and esteemed, and to whose Church I sincerely wished to belong.

This last term at S. House went more quickly than the others; for the end of my private purgatory was in sight, and besides I was spending a good deal of my spare time plodding through the Greek grammar, carefully translating all the exercises. What one has learned as a child usually comes back quickly: I soon found myself once more on familiar ground, back in the days when Frau Loeschcke and Herr Schiering had introduced us to the mysteries of aorists and optatives.

From London came good news: I had definitely been accepted for the two-year course of the Archbishop of Canterbury's Diploma. More, Miss Norman had prevailed on the head of Talbot Settlement in Camberwell, a Church of England establishment, to grant me a bursary so that I could give my whole time and energy to studying, without having to worry about either financial or domestic matters. So I could give notice at half term with a quiet mind, to the intense surprise and slight annoyance of Bobs. She prophesied that I should one day greatly regret my decision to leave. She simply could not take it in that "Frolleen," who had hitherto done nothing but teach multiplication tables to the kindergarten and wash girls' heads, should suddenly go to London University to study such a recondite subject as theology. Miss Goldsworthy, too, found it hard to believe, since she tended to consider anything to do with religion her special prerogative.

I took little notice of their reactions, but redoubled my efforts to get through the Greek grammar. This time, I knew,

I should have to take my studies seriously and do a first-class examination, if I wanted to be eligible for a post in the Church of England. Besides, I had an obligation to those who were helping me so generously.

When we broke up for the Christmas holidays this year—on the same day as Eton, naturally—I went to London full of hopes as well as determination to work hard.

11. *Student of Theology*

Miss Norman had invited me to spend the Christmas vacation with her; but for the feast itself I went to Cambridge, where my cousin Werner was now a lecturer; he was married and had two small daughters. When I arrived there, some domestic crisis over the Christmas fowl was in full swing. The hall was littered with parcels of any size and description, which my cousin's wife Hanni asked us to undo before disappearing into the kitchen. After we had unwrapped about eight or ten of them, Hanni reappeared. Looking at what we had done, she broke into a fit of uncontrollable sobbing and moaning. Alas, owing to her defective instructions, we had not only unwrapped parcels that had arrived, but also some she meant still to send, which had all been mixed up together. I could not help recalling the German saying: "Unless on Christmas Eve the mistress of the house lies screaming under the Christmas tree, the feast has not been celebrated properly."

When the tears had stopped and Hanni had regained a measure of equilibrium I staggered the family by announcing my intention to go to King's College to hear the Christmas Carols. Though my cousin had been in Cambridge for about four years by then, it had never occurred to him to attend them. The Carols at King's, in the candlelit chapel with its beautiful windows and woodwork, was an experience I thoroughly enjoyed—aesthetically, not religiously. There had been some discussion whether my relatives should join me, but they eventually decided against it. When I came back, the German Christmas Eve celebrations had just begun; the Christmas tree was lit, the German hymns were sung, the presents given; it was a real Christmas in the emigration.

I was surprised myself when I realized how foreign in these mere eighteen months the German ways had already become to me. But then I had never been an exemplary German. I had even defended the Treaty of Versailles when I was still a student at Berlin; I had been invariably on the side of political compromise against fanaticism. I disliked German sentimentality, and had always been as embarrassed by an unrestrained display of emotion as any English person; therefore people had often thought me cold. I hated bragging and boasting about German superiority, and, perhaps most important of all, I believed in the healing power of a sense of humor that could laugh at oneself.

In my cousin's home I was once more in the atmosphere of typically German earnestness and drama that makes life so complicated; I was longing to get back to low voices and restrained passions, to conversations that were not deep but pleasant. I gave my relatives a further surprise when I insisted on going to church on Christmas Day—I, who had never been known to go to church in my life. I do not think I did it from religious conviction; it was still rather the expression of my determination to belong to a Christian civilization, ready to accept its standards and outer forms.

It was a relief to be back in London. I think it was about this time that Miss Norman gave a party, at which I had a long and animated political conversation with a very interesting gentleman who was most courteous and unassuming.

Afterwards Miss Norman took me aside. "Do you know to whom you have just been talking?" I had no idea. "General Sir Frederic Pile." I gasped. "Not like a Prussian general, is he?" Miss Norman commented. Indeed, no. Not even like a Prussian lieutenant, monocled, arrogant, overweening. It was, to me, a further initiation into the meaning of the untranslatable term gentleman, as well as into the English concept of democracy.

In the middle of January 1938 I moved to Talbot Settlement, then at Addington Square, Camberwell. It was a Church of England foundation for social and charitable work in the slums. The head, Miss Cecilia Goodenough, daughter of Admiral Sir William Goodenough, was a remarkable personality, full of life and sympathy, a good organizer, above all a deeply Christian woman whose religion was part and parcel of her life.

She told me at once that in the Settlement we all called each other by our Christian names, which contributed to the family atmosphere in which I soon felt at home. Most of the young women living there were club leaders or students of social science at the London School of Economics and at Bedford College, full of life and of a variety of interests. I had a large room to myself with bookshelf and writing table; there was a small library with a pleasant atmosphere of peaceful work, where Fra Angelico's picture of St. Peter Martyr holding his finger to his lips seemed to command silence. Adjoining it was the simply furnished chapel. Here we said morning prayers, and once a week there was a Eucharistic celebration. At night we all gathered for Compline, Cecilia leading the singing of the Compline hymn to varying tunes, which at first seemed strange to me, but which I came to love. They expressed so perfectly contentment after the day's work and the peace of evening. I did not then know that what we were singing was the age-old plain chant of the Catholic Church.

I learned also a different kind of song. Among our social activities were parties for the women of the neighborhood, and one of their most popular features was community singing. So my English education, which had begun with "London Bridge is broken down" and "Sing a song of sixpence," was now continued with "Daisy, Daisy," "Two lovely black eyes," and "I'll go the high road." I had been in England for only two years, my passport still showed the German Eagle with the Swastika, I was an alien subject to many restrictions —yet I was already feeling completely at home in this country. Neither my fellow students at the Settlement nor the women and children who came there ever gave me the feeling that I did not belong to them. I worked with them, I sang with them, I shared their life. From the very beginning I had been reading only English books and English newspapers, I not only spoke but thought exclusively in English, and I had never been homesick for a moment.

One morning as I was walking through the Strand, the pavement was lined with people, and I was told that the King and Queen were expected to pass by at any moment. I waited with the others, and after a few minutes there was the open royal car, with the King and the Queen smiling and nodding at the cheering crowds. I remembered in a flash that other scene, which I had watched three years ago, so similar, and yet, how different. Hitler standing on a balcony, and the seething crowd acknowledging the Führer in an outburst of mass hysteria that seemed to reduce them to subhuman beings, at least temporarily deprived of both reason and free will. There was no trace of hysteria in the people round me, waving their arms and shouting Hurrah, delighted to see the monarch they loved and to demonstrate their loyalty. It was all so sane and human, both the King and Queen, in their smiling, friendly simplicity, and the crowds happily cheering the head of the British Commonwealth, or rather the head of their family, for it seemed just like that to me. I joined in the cheering, feeling, not for the first time, that England was a wonderful country to live in—even with an alien's registration certificate.

About this time I formally joined the Church of England, being confirmed in St. Paul's by the Bishop of London. Miss Norman accompanied me to the ceremony, which greatly impressed me. I had never before seen a bishop in cope and mitre, strangely enough these were light blue. There were no red roses for me this time, no feelings of revolt, but no thrills either. It was an act of conforming myself to the established Church of the country of my adoption.

In the Settlement I found again the division between High and Low, and I myself swung like a pendulum between the two. Emotionally I felt attracted to the High Church; on the other hand I did not like the way in which some High Church people seemed to look down on the others, since they all belonged to the same Church. I now went fairly regularly to church on Sunday, sometimes to High Church and sometimes to Low Church, and to the Communion service at the Settlement unless I found it too difficult to get out of bed.

Miss Norman was a friend of Evelyn Underhill, in private life Mrs. Stuart-Moore, who invited me to tea one day. I was very curious to meet her, since she had the reputation of being a mystic and I knew she was a spiritual adviser to a good many clergymen. It was perhaps unfortunate that she was already ailing, and that there was another visitor beside myself, who was evidently venerating her and constantly referred to her sufferings, so that any real conversation was impossible. I came away rather disappointed and, I think, shocked some of her circle by my failure to be impressed.

Miss Norman thought it was time I made a retreat. I had never made one in my life before, knew hardly what it was, and felt no desire for it at all when I was told it was a time of silence and prayer. But as it seemed somehow to belong to my new life, I duly submitted. I arrived one Friday evening

at the Church of England Retreat House which Miss Norman
had selected for me, was supplied with a white veil, which
seemed an essential of feminine religious activities, was shown
my simple blue and white room which looked rather like a
monastic cell, the chapel and the dining room, and was then
left to myself and the few religious books I found on the
shelf. Supper was a strange experience, as I had never had a
meal in silence before except when I had been alone. Then
followed the first conference.

It was given by a well-known religious of the Community of the Resurrection. I remember nothing of the conferences during these three days; they made no impression on
me, they only seemed just as strange as everything else. Miss
Norman had suggested I should talk to the Father, as everybody else appeared to do; so I felt I ought to do the same.
I had heard that some people went to confession in the High
Church—but nobody, not even Miss Norman, would induce
me to take such a preposterous step. Nor had I the slightest
intention to discuss anything with him that was of real importance, for example the strange combination of my theological studies and churchgoing with my almost complete
unbelief. Instead I thought up some totally irrelevant question, simply by way of having some pretext for seeing him in
order to be able to report to Miss Norman that I had done
so. Fortunately in those days, as soon as people heard I had
come from Germany comparatively recently, they at once
asked me about Hitler's intentions and similar subjects on
which they expected me to be an expert. The good Father
was no exception, and to my relief I soon found myself in an
animated political conversation with him, and had the satisfaction to take my leave after about half an hour without
having allowed him the slightest glimpse into my soul, the
existence of which, I at that time, was not at all convinced.

Nevertheless, I did go into the chapel sometimes apart
from the services and conferences to try to sort out my ideas,

and I found myself actually praying that some way might be shown to me to become a Christian, though I had the feeling this might involve sacrifices which I was not prepared to make at the moment.

Miss Norman had told me before that I should probably feel it something of a shock to return from the silence of the retreat into the noise of everyday life. She was judging me by her own standards. If I did feel a shock, it was a pleasant one—I preferred a hat to a veil, and animated talk during meals to monastic silence.

I found work at King's College much easier than at Berlin. The English tutorial system, while rather spoon-feeding the student, saves a good deal of time otherwise spent in trying to find one's way about in a maze of lectures and books. Miss Hippisley provided me with my plan of work; a charming old lady, Miss Blackburn, was in charge of the Lambeth Diploma Library and supplied me with the necessary books; I had nothing to do but to attend the prescribed lectures and study the books. I soon made friends with some of my fellow students; fortunately those studying for Lambeth were about my age or older, which made contact easier than it would have been, had they been the usual undergraduate age.

Though my studies and my keep were paid for me, I needed some pocket money. Miss Norman had thought of that, too, and arranged for me to teach Greek to some young society girls of her acquaintance, who intended to take up theology, one of whom was the Hon. Laura Palmer, the daughter of the then Lord Wolmer.

My days were full, indeed, but I also had some relaxation. Again through Miss Norman, who was a veritable fairy godmother for me during these first years in England, I had got in touch with a very charming old clergyman's widow, Mrs. Beardall, who frequently invited me to spend a weekend with her in her house in Surrey. Very soon she asked me: "What is your Christian name?" When I had to confess to Hiltgunde she decided that this was impossible for English tongues to pronounce. "Why not call yourself Hilda? She was a nice English Saint—I'm going to call you Hilda, anyway." I thought this an excellent idea, so Hilda I have remained ever since, except on my passport and the Election Register.

Miss Norman invited me once more to spend the Easter holidays at her house. Once she took me to a Tenebrae service at an Anglican monastery, I forget which, and on Good Friday she sent me to the Three Hours Service at All Saints, Margaret Street. I obediently sat through the services; but they meant nothing to me, because Christ meant nothing. The biblical criticism with which I was being fed at King's College was more likely to destroy than to arouse faith, and had left my vague, almost agnostic belief in God unchanged. So Good Friday then was to me, as to so many people in this country, no more than a bank holiday with hot cross buns for tea.

In the beginning of August Miss Norman took me to Oxford, for a vacation term of biblical studies at St. Hilda's College. It was my first visit to the City of the Dreaming Spires, which presented itself at its most enchanting in brilliant sunshine. I stayed at an Anglican Convent. I had never before been in contact with nuns, and I found it a slightly alarming experience. As soon as we crossed the threshold of the convent we had to don very long blue veils, which we were never allowed to take off except in our rooms. I had a hard struggle with mine, because it was so long that I invariably sat on it so that it came off. Though we were staying in the guest house, not in the convent itself, no speaking was permitted in the corridors, meals were taken in silence, and the Sisters themselves were very austere and practically never smiled. Fortunately I did not spend much time at the convent, but was busy going to lectures, which I found interesting, and looking at Oxford, which was more interesting still. We also made excursions into the surroundings. I loved the Cotswolds with their mellow stones and shadowed lanes, so different from Surrey, and the old world tea at an inn at Broadway. Naturally I could not escape the inevitable question whether I liked Cambridge or Oxford better. My mind was made up even then. There was nothing that could touch the High, and as to Magdalen, New College, St. John's and their quads and gardens—well, lovely though the Backs were at Cambridge, I did not think they could compete with the charms of Oxford.

Miss Norman had once more invited my mother to stay with me at her house while she was on holiday. This time we were very much less gay than last year. The crisis over Czechoslovakia was just developing, and everyone was talking of war. Like last year, we were looking at London together, we were going for walks in Kensington Gardens or on the Embankment, but at the same time we were anxiously listening to the radio and reading the newspapers. The tension was increasing day by day; and what Mother told me about conditions in Germany was far from reassuring. Hitler was obviously arming, the situation of the Jews was becoming worse. I could see quite well that she was frightened at the things that were to come. She wanted to leave me her gold wrist watch, but I refused. She had already given me a gold bracelet and other valuables she possessed—I did not want to take everything away from her.

When, after about four weeks, I took her to Liverpool Street Station, the crisis was at its height. Two ridiculously tiny anti-aircraft guns were mounted on Westminster Bridge, and three silvery barrage balloons were floating aimlessly in the sky. Heaven help us, if the Luftwaffe attacks London! My friends could not understand why I did not keep my mother here, but it was impossible. She had no permit of residence, she had nowhere to go, I myself had no means of supporting her—what was I to do? All the way to the station I was trying to keep talking as gaily as I could. I saw her into her compartment, then went back to the platform and kept up a desultory conversation through the window. At last the train began to move. I had retained a grip on myself till that moment, but then the thought that this might have been our last meeting was too much for me. I turned my face aside so that she should not notice the tears streaming from my eyes. She had seen them, however, as she told me later, and she herself wept almost continuously all the way back to Berlin.

When Mr. Chamberlain came back from Munich with his message of peace in our time, my anxiety subsided. I knew conditions in Germany too well to imagine that this was a lasting settlement; nevertheless, it was a respite—for England, with the two tiny anti-aircraft guns and the silvery balloons, and for me personally. I might, after all, see my mother again; though I was staggered when she told me in her next letter that her passport had been taken away from her at the frontier.

The next months were filled with strenuous work. Then came the ninth of November in Germany with its outbreak of pogroms. Mother's letters, after that, contained only veiled allusions, but I realized that life was becoming fast unbearable for any one of Jewish origin. I was at a loss what to do. Then a friend said to me one day: "Are you not going to get your mother out?"

"I am constantly thinking of it, but how can I get her here with all those requirements of permits? She is almost sixty—how can I keep her?"

I was told the regulations were now different from those in force when I had come over; all that was required was a guarantee from a British person making himself responsible for her upkeep, if necessary. "Why don't you ask Miss Norman to give this guarantee?"

I felt Miss Norman had already done so much for me that I hardly dared to approach her with this request. However, it was a matter of life and death, and I knew she liked my mother. She agreed at once.

"Of course, you must get your mother out; I will gladly give all the necessary affidavits."

So I wrote to my mother to come to England; the arrangements for a permit would be made from here, all she had to do was to ask for permission to emigrate which would, I devoutly hoped, be given, get her passport back, pack up whatever she was allowed to take with her, and come.

Mother at first raised objections. She had her home and her widow's pension in Germany; was it really right to leave everything, and perhaps be a burden to me ever after? I replied in guarded language that neither her home nor her pension were probably very safe. I did not mind how much or how little she could take with her, but would only urge her to make up her mind at once to come here. To my great relief she wrote in her next letter that she was going to do all she could to get away.

It was just as well I had to work hard all the time, so I had not much time to worry. I heard my doctor uncle and his wife, and my aunt in Vienna were also trying to emigrate. My friends at King's College and at the Settlement were full of sympathy; I realized later how much the burden of those anxious months was eased by their unfailing kindness and understanding. Cecilia Goodenough asked me if I had any plans for Christmas; if not, she would take me home with her for the holidays. I gratefully accepted her invitation. Once more I was living for a few days "in the lap of luxury," but this time, unlike those unhappy weeks at Haarlem, it was in an atmosphere of Christian love and that typically English kindness, which I met in those years wherever I went. Sir William Goodenough, too, promised to write to the Home Office himself if that should be necessary to speed up the permit for my mother, so I was sure that from this side of the channel, at least, there was every reason for hope.

In February 1939 I had once more to go to the German Embassy to have my passport extended. Was I an Aryan? No; my mother was of Jewish descent. Thereupon the official stamped an enormous red J in my passport, and underneath my name: *Vorname Sara hinzugefuegt* (First name Sara added). All non-Aryan women were ordered to adopt Sara as a second name (and men Israel), to be used on all official documents. It was one of the more childish devices of Nazi hatred; but I was glad to show my friends in the Settlement this piece of evidence, since they sometimes suspected me of exaggerating when I told them about conditions in the Third Reich. They stared at it incredulously, unable to comprehend the mentality that relished such inventions, at which I, well away from it all, could only laugh.

My mother, however, could not take things so lightly. There were endless difficulties to overcome; not from the British side, but from the Nazis, until she was at last given back her passport in order to emigrate. Her golden wrist watch, which I had refused to accept from her last summer, was taken away from her, together with all other jewelry and table silver; it was a wonder they left her her wedding ring. In fact she had to queue up to deliver the things herself, and her trunks had to be packed with an SS man standing on either side of her, lest she should smuggle anything out of the country. Eventually, at the end of March, everything had been settled; but I had no peace until I saw her stepping out of the train at Liverpool Street Station, looking haggard and infinitely tired.

I should have liked to give her a good holiday before she took up her work with Miss Hippisley, my tutor, for whom she was to do the housekeeping. But the latter had already waited for her a considerable time, and so she took up her new work at once, after staying one night with me at the Settlement. Fortunately the work was not too strenuous. I myself had been invited by a friend of Miss Norman's, Miss Duff, to spend Easter with her at her cottage on the Isle of Wight.

We travelled there on Maundy Thursday. On Good Friday my hostess surprised me with the announcement that she was going to make the Three Hours devotions privately at the parish church in the village, as there were no Good Friday services anywhere near. I was still as vague in my beliefs as ever, and the prospect of having to spend three hours of lovely sunshine shut up in a deserted church was not exactly my idea of a holiday. However, I realized by this time that religious people do strange things, and being myself a student of theology, I had to keep up appearances. However, Miss Duff was sufficiently human to tell me that she did not expect me to remain in church throughout the three hours; I could go out for a walk from time to time. I was grateful for this concession to my weakness; and after Miss Duff had secured the keys from the vicarage, we settled down in the church at some distance from each other.

I was now thirty-two years of age; I had had the full share of joy and suffering, love and disappointment in my life; I had been teaching religion, I had been, and again was, studying it—yet it never entered my head on this of all days of the year to give one single thought to the event all Christendom was commemorating today. It simply did not occur to me that I might read the Passion narrative on this Good Friday. Instead, after grumbling to myself that I had to sit here in the stuffy church instead of going for a walk by the seaside, I decided that the most useful thing to do would be to pick up the New Testament which Miss Duff had provided and to read through the Apocalypse, because I had so far not done any work on it at all. I interrupted my reading by a walk around the church from time to time, though not too often, so as not to shock Miss Duff. Being a devout Christian herself, she could hardly have understood the boredom of this strange student of theology, who was generally expected to do a brilliant examination and to make religious teaching her career, without believing anything more definite than that there might be a God who had created the world.

The rest of my stay on the island approximated as closely as possible my ideal of a holiday: we were sitting in deck-chairs in the sheltered garden behind the house, reading, solving crossword puzzles, eating chocolates, smoking an occasional cigarette, and from time to time going down to the sea for a swim.

On my return to King's College at the beginning of the summer term my tutor—no longer Miss Hippisley, but her young successor, Miss Mary Grosvenor—suggested I should sit for an examination to gain the Trench Prize of New Testament Greek. I was doubtful about it, as the Prize was open to all students of the College, both men and women; however, it could do no harm to try. I greatly preferred the English way of examination by written papers to the German method, where the professor fires a barrage of questions at the candidate; so I quietly settled down to three hours of translating, annotating and interpreting passages from the Gospels and Epistles. Great was my surprise when, a few days later, I found a foolscap letter from King's College among my post, informing me that I had been awarded the Prize and asking me to select books to the value of six pounds— quite a respectable sum in those days for a poor student like me.

In this last summer before the War I also gained something better than prizes. In the second year of the Lambeth Diploma Course we were introduced to a new subject, Christian doctrine. I had never before studied it; in my school days dogma had been represented to us by our Scripture teachers as something entirely irrational, a hair-splitting exercise for crazy minds, concerned with meaningless iotas in Greek words, a dry as dust subject quite remote from the religion of the heart that Christianity, in their view, necessarily was. Before starting on it we students had been warned that we should find it difficult and perhaps not very inspiring. To me it became a revelation.

For the Diploma examination we were required to be familiar with the development of Christian doctrine down to the Council of Chalcedon in 451. Prominence was naturally given to the great Trinitarian and Christological controversies of the fourth and fifth centuries, especially to Arianism and Nestorianism. So far I had always been told that reason had no say when it was question of religion. Kierkegaard had spoken of the leap-into-the-dark. My Scripture teachers had told me that I must feel and experience things, however absurd they might appear to my mind; that one could, indeed, subscribe to a philosophy that admitted no personal God, and yet know by experience that there was one—and I had never been able to do it. "I cannot leave my reason at home on my writing table when I go to church," I used to say—therefore I had never gone to church in Germany, and in this country, too, I did so by convention rather than by conviction.

Now, for the first time in my life, I was introduced to that highly rational complex of religious truths that is called dogmatics—and at last the scales began to fall from my eyes. If I once accepted a personal God—and I was ready to do that—then it was only reasonable that He should reveal Himself to His creatures. If these creatures had fallen into evil ways—and I could hardly deny that, I need only look at the state of the world around me—then it was to be expected that, by revealing Himself to them, He should also in some way redeem them from their sins. The Church claimed that this was precisely what He had done in Christ. If so, whether true or not, it was at least not unreasonable. And it was in fact extremely important whether this work of revelation and redemption had been carried out by God Himself, or by some subordinate creature; so it was not so ridiculous as I had been led to assume to fight about the first iota in the Greek word *homoiousios*—which, with the iota, meant of similar substance, but without it, of the same substance—for it made all the difference whether Christ was really God or not. Nor was it unreasonable to believe in the dogma of the Trinity, which had hitherto been presented to me as meaning that one equals three, which is absurd, but which, as I now learned, meant that Three Persons were existing in one substance, certainly no mathematical impossibility. So the Christian religion was not, as I had been taught, an irrational experience, "a soft music accompanying existence" as Schleiermacher had expressed it. Luther's hatred of reason had been responsible for my rejection of Christianity; the highly rational speculations of the fathers of the Church became for me the way not only back to the child's faith I had lost more than twenty years ago, but onward to a fullness of Christian life such as I had never thought possible.

Once the intellectual obstacles had been cleared away, the experience, of which my Protestant Scripture teachers had been talking so much, came to me too, when I least expected it. I was sitting in Laura Palmer's room, reading with her the second chapter of St. Mark's Gospel, thinking of nothing but how to explain the moods and tenses of the verbs. I had read the story of the paralytic who is lowered through the roof so many times that I almost knew it by heart, and it is certainly not one of the most inspiring texts of the New Testament. Yet, suddenly, while I was talking about aorists and participles, I saw the scene in my imagination, and, in a flash of insight, realized the infinite love and compassion of Christ: "My child, thy sins are forgiven thee." "And that you may know that the son of man has power on earth to forgive sins, he says to the paralytic: I say unto thee, arise, take thy bed and go home." Thy sins are forgiven thee . . . go home. What power—and what love. And what an infinitely lovable Person He must have been who had spoken these words. This first experience of Christ in a Peer's home in Mayfair cannot have lasted more than a few seconds; for I struggled immediately to regain my grip on myself. I was here to help Laura

Palmer with her Greek, so back to our aorists! But at this moment Christ had entered my life; He had become a living Person for me, for an instant I had been intensely happy in His presence. I was determined to carry on this as yet so strange relationship which He had begun, though I did not yet know how it could be done.

A few weeks later this, too, was made clear to me. Cecilia Goodenough lent me the book of the Anglican theologian, Bede Frost, on mental prayer. I had never heard of mental prayer, and did not know there was such a thing. The author set out all the various methods of meditation: Ignatian, Salesian, Sulpician and many others. The more I read about it the more exciting it seemed to me. So not only doctrine, but prayer, too, was an activity in which one could use one's brains, even one's imagination. It was an altogether new world that opened up before me; but evidently far too absorbing to be embarked on just now, a few months before my examination. I did not finish the book, but firmly resolved to try mental prayer as soon as I had gained my Diploma.

In August Miss Duff once more invited me to go with her to the Isle of Wight, and this time my mother, too, could join us, as Miss Hippisley was away on holiday. The weather was glorious; brilliant sunshine the whole time. We bathed and lay in deckchairs—if only the political horizon had not been covered with the darkest of clouds. Another war . . . what would it mean this time! Every day we devoured the paper, trying to find a glimmer of hope; every day the news was more threatening.

When we returned to London at the end of the month the first thing that struck me was the traffic lights. There was only a tiny slit left to show their colors, everything else was blacked out. The capital was, indeed, preparing for war.

In the morning of September the third I was in the church of St. John the Evangelist in Camberwell. In the middle of the service the clergyman mounted the pulpit to tell us in a grave voice that Britain had declared war on Germany. Almost immediately the sirens began to wail. We were asked to leave the church quietly and go home. As I was coming out, I was addressed by what seemed a primeval monster; while its lower parts were covered by a skirt, its face was almost black, its eyes invisible behind a horrifying mask; in the place of the nose it had a medium-sized trunk, like a baby elephant. Through this trunk it bellowed something I could not understand, but which sounded vaguely like gas-mask. I nodded reassuringly and turned into Camberwell Road to walk back to the Settlement. Nearly all the inhabitants between Camberwell Square and Elephant and Castle were standing in front of their houses, staring into the cloudless September sky all agog to discover a German bomber. But there was nothing to be seen except the familiar few silvery balloons, and before I had reached the Settlement the All Clear had already sounded. The phony war had begun.

Mother, whom I always went to see on Sunday afternoons, rang up to inquire whether I was coming today. Would it not be better for me to stay at home rather than face the dangerous journey from Camberwell to Westminster. After all, there might be an air raid while I was on the way, and perhaps no air raid shelter anywhere near—just imagine! "Nonsense, I'll come, London isn't a battlefield yet."

"But please, bring your gas mask."

"They won't start gas, and anyway I'm sure that little thing won't be much of a protection—but of course I'll take the nuisance."

When I arrived at four o'clock at Miss Hippisley's flat, Mother behaved as if I had made my way through enemy country under constant fire. I had to reassure her that the London streets were no more dangerous today than they had been yesterday, and that it was really quite safe to go for a walk in Hyde Park.

The war soon made itself felt at the Settlement, which became much less lively than it had been; for all our bright young things, the social science students of the London School of Economics and of Bedford College had been evacuated to the country. Instead, rows of gas masks, high rubber boots and tin hats made their appearance in the hall, for some of our girls had exchanged their work as club leaders for that of helpers at First Aid Stations. Cecilia Goodenough had quickly adapted the work to the new conditions. I used to help with a newly opened play center for unevacuated children, which we ran from two to four in the afternoon to relieve their mothers and to keep them off from the streets. One day three of them, aged between three and six, came to me, looking extremely important, and, holding out their dirty little hands showed me proudly thirty dark red fingernails which looked as if they had been dipped into a jampot. They seemed so pleased with themselves that I had not the heart to tell them to take the varnish off.

The mothers, too, were a problem. With their husbands in the army and ration cards and blackout to cope with at home, they needed encouragement and cheering up; so instead of one musical party a month we now had one every week, as well as sewing parties in the evenings. I gave as much help with these as I could, but most of my time was naturally devoted to preparations for my examination, which was to take place next January.

We were evacuated to Bexhill; and there I was busy writing my papers, three hours in the morning and three hours in the afternoon, for three days. A few weeks later the telephone rang. "Congratulations, you have got a First. You will receive your Diploma from His Grace, the Archbishop of Canterbury, in the chapel of Lambeth Palace on the twentieth of April. A formal notice will be sent to you."

The ceremony was impressive. We had all to don white starched veils (veils seemed to be omnipresent in the Church of England) which kept rustling at the slightest provocation; and so we walked demurely into the chapel, sitting down in two rows opposite each other, and reciting parts of Psalm 118 (119). At the words: "I am wiser than all my teachers" a slight tremor on either side of me showed me that my neighbors were as sensitive to the humor of the situation as I. At last I found myself kneeling before the archbishop, Cosmo Lang, who, after laying his hand rather heavily on my starched head in blessing, presented me with a large envelope containing my Diploma, that gave me the right to place the letters S.Th. after my name—Student of Theology.

At the party following in the garden of Lambeth Palace I rejoined my mother, proud of her daughter whom everyone congratulated on her success, and who seemed to be at the beginning of a fine career in the Church of England.

12. *A World Rebuilt*

MY BURSARY at Talbot Settlement had been given me only for the duration of my studies; so after my examination I went to live in the furnished room in Kensington Park Road where I had stayed on several previous occasions. It was at the top of the house and very cheap, since no one liked to be under the roof in London at that time, when we expected air raids to start at any moment. It soon became obvious to me that I should have great difficulties in finding a job despite my good examination, on account of my nationality. Besides, missionary and other colleges which might have provided suitable openings were evacuated, students went into National Service. It was the worst possible moment to embark on a new career. Fortunately Cecilia Goodenough had put me in touch with a charitable organization which helped Germans in this country in cases of need. They made me a weekly grant which, with the help of a few private pupils whom I coached in theology and Greek, was just sufficient to keep me alive. As gas was too expensive, I had a small oilstove on which I did my own cooking. In the morning I would go on shopping expeditions to Portobello Road, where there was a cheap market selling meat, fruit, and vegetables.

I had not forgotten my resolve to try this mysterious activity, mental prayer, and I now had plenty of time for it. I read again the book by Bede Frost, from which it appeared that the most widely used method of meditation was the Ignatian one. So I borrowed an English annotated version of the Ignatian Exercises, and in the early spring I began to "make" them, quite on my own, with such adaptations as I considered necessary, seeing I could not shut myself up completely for four weeks, but had to continue giving lessons, seeing my mother, and providing for my food. By this time my early attraction to Catholicism had reasserted itself, and I found a very high church, All Saints Nottinghill, where I now went to communion not only on Sundays, but three times a week besides.

I had read that, before making the Exercises, one should make a general confession. I had travelled far since that first retreat, when going to confession was utterly unthinkable. I was ready to do so now—if only I could have gone to a Catholic priest! Father Twisaday, the Rector of All Saints, certainly used to hear confessions; still I felt by some unaccountable instinct that a Catholic priest would be different; he would understand, whereas a clergyman of the Church of England. . . . Somehow I could not rid myself of the idea that the "old-school tie" must be lurking beneath his clerical collar. However, there was nobody else to go to, so I made an appointment with him and got it over.

I had never liked getting up very early; between half past seven and eight was my usual time, if work allowed it. Now I rose shortly after five, dressed, and had three quarters of an hour's meditation on strictly Ignatian lines. To my surprise I could meditate without any difficulty. I went through the whole gamut, composition of place, reconstruction of the scene, application of the senses, resolution, without any distractions; but afterwards I felt completely exhausted, and sometimes went to sleep on my knees for a quarter of an hour. I repeated the same in the evening, and during the day I did some spiritual reading and prepared my meditations in writing.

It must have been about the beginning of June, when I had a strange experience which completely changed my life. I was kneeling in the church, at a Benediction service during which the Sacrament was exposed in a monstrance in exactly the same way as in a Catholic church. Suddenly, without ever before having entertained such an idea, I understood that I should make a vow of chastity. I knew, of course, that priests and religious made such vows, but I had never heard that ordinary laymen could make them. I, of all people, had never dreamt of such a thing. I was now thirty-three; I had not given up the idea of marriage, even less was I prepared to forsake those flirtatious relationships in which I had indulged now and again ever since my student days. And yet, in these moments it was made completely clear to me that this vow of chastity which I was asked to make was to be absolute—no kiss, no touch, no glance was to be allowed me—from now on until death.

I stared at the monstrance. This was impossible; it was madness. I could not do it, not now, at any rate. But there was no resisting this incredible demand to which I was asked to consent. With a reeling head, but fully aware of what I was doing, I said at last: "Yes, chastity unto death—but I do not know how I can keep this vow."

When I staggered out of the heavy atmosphere of candles and incense into the fresh air I felt I was coming out of a dream. Surely what had happened a few minutes ago was nothing but a play of my imagination, a wild idea had just entered my head, and which I was now going to brush aside as one does other crazy thoughts. The odd thing was that I could not do it. It seemed that no amount of fresh air and commonsense could make undone what I had done in that church, that I had, indeed, vowed myself to a life of absolute chastity irrevocably for the rest of my days.

As I walked back to my room I began to consider what this must mean to me. A whole lifetime of dull, grey days seemed to stretch out before me in joyless uniformity, a vista of nothing but work and prayer, prayer and work, without happiness, without love. After all, sex is one of the basic elements in the human make-up; and here was I, a woman in the fullness of her strength, condemned by this absurd but apparently unchangeable vow to turn into a repressed spinster. When I had reached this point I thought it best to stop thinking about it. I lit a cigarette and decided to see how it would all work out.

Only very gradually, in the course of years, the real meaning of sex and chastity became clear to me. But what I began to realize almost immediately was that, far from becoming joyless and dreary, my life was now being filled with such intense happiness as I had never known before. Every day the news of the war became more alarming. The French defence was helplessly giving way before the German attacks, the Nazis would soon be firmly entrenched on the other side of the channel. Britain was fast approaching her darkest hour—and my insignificant private life was linked to her fate; for if Hitler, as I had heard, was already preparing to set up residence in Buckingham Palace, then we non-Aryan refugees would soon be driven into the gas chambers. Every morning, as I was reading my paper at breakfast, I became more acutely aware not only of the danger of this island, but also of the danger of the allied armies on the Continent, of the intense sufferings of so many innocent people all over Europe and beyond at this very moment. Yet, against the sombre background of the history of those days, I was living in an intoxication of spiritual joy that gave me almost a feeling of guilt—how could I be so overwhelmingly happy, while there was so much suffering, so much tragedy?

Every morning I made my meditation which brought me ever nearer to Christ; I went to the Anglican "Mass" now almost every day; then, after breakfast, I would fill my briefcase with books and walk to Kensington Gardens, where I sat in a deck chair in the sun, reading. First came St. Thomas. I had started on the *Summa Theologica* to enlarge my theological knowledge by acquainting myself with Scholasticism, which had found no place in the Lambeth Diploma curriculum. After that I read several chapters of St. John of the Cross; and at last, when I could not assimilate any more of this rather heavy intellectual food, I would entertain myself with a novel by Hugh Benson or an essay by Chesterton.

In the afternoon I would go more and more often into a Catholic church to pray. I discovered a small chapel in Chelsea, where the Blessed Sacrament was permanently exposed, and this became one of my favorite haunts. Incidentally this was the reason why I at last conquered my vanity, which had hitherto prevented me from wearing glasses for the distance despite my shortsightedness; instead I wore a lorgnette that dangled from a long silver chain, everlastingly knocking against both people and lamp posts. I could not very well keep looking at the Blessed Sacrament through a lorgnette; so I did eventually what the eye specialist had told me to do for years, and equipped myself with a pair of distance glasses.

I have always looked back on those few weeks of overwhelming spiritual joy as a kind of religious "honeymoon." Gradually it dawned on me that the vow that I had made was nothing negative; not a vow to forsake love, but something like a marriage vow; a vow to give my love to God alone, but not, as in earthly marriage, sadly "until death do us part," but exultantly "until death do us unite."

It is in the nature of honeymoons that they do not last

long. Mine was no exception. Its end was marked by two events, one interior, the other exterior. As I have said, I had been able to meditate extraordinarily well. I wrote out the points for my meditations beforehand, and then reflected on them, visualized the scenes from the Gospels, drew conclusions from the events described there, made resolutions for my own life—it all went off without a hitch. Until, one day, as I was meditating, it suddenly came into my head to ask myself whether the Church of England, to which I now belonged, was the true Church that Christ had founded. I tried to put the question out of my mind and stick to my "points," but it was impossible. Again and again the unwanted thought intruded itself: there was another Church, of which the "high church" to which I had given my allegiance was but an imitation. But if this other Church was the true Church—and even then I had very little doubt that it was—should I not have to join it? And in that case, what of these years of study, on which I was still hoping to build a career, the only one I could envisage in this country? Had it all been in vain? Perhaps, after all, the Church of England was really part of the "Church Catholic." Could it be so? Was it?

How I wished I could go back to my undisturbed meditations, instead of unceasingly rehearsing these questions. There it was, in the New Testament, that Christ spoke with authority, and not as the Scribes. Was there not also a Church that spoke with authority? But it was not the Church of England. "Thou art Peter . . . on this rock I will build my Church." Yes, yes, I knew the Protestant exegesis that it was the faith of Peter, not Peter himself on which the Church was to be built. But what about the keys committed to Peter? Did the Archbishop of Canterbury claim the power to bind and to loose? Which bishop in all Christendom did claim to possess this unique power except the Bishop of Rome?—How I wished my meditations would go according to plan, instead of revolving everlastingly around this subject that seemed to intrude the more inescapably the more anxiously I was seeking to avoid it.

Eventually, it must have been early in August, I could stand it no longer. I went to see Father Twisaday and told him I had "Roman fever." He was evidently well acquainted with this disease, of which he seemed to have suffered himself at one time, and talked about the necessity of keeping alive the Catholic tradition in the Church of England which, after all, was part of the Catholic Church—though he did not attempt to prove this statement. I left him not very convinced, but at least temporarily pacified, and succeeded in making my customary meditations for the next few days without too many distractions, until, after about a week, the disturbance started again and went on increasing.

About that time I woke up one night, because I thought I had heard an odd noise—two bangs, one after the other, sounding rather muffled, as if a good distance away. Could it have been bombs? But I had heard no sirens. Perhaps it had been nothing important, after all; for now everything was once more silent. I went to sleep again. When I opened the paper next morning I read that last night the first bombs had been dropped on London. The honeymoon was over. Doubts and anxiety within, sirens and landmines outside—the next few months must prove whether my newly found love was simply a passing religious emotion, or the foundation of a new life.

Soon the German bombers came night after night, and in the daytime, too, the sirens were constantly wailing. I kept up my daily life as best I could, continuing my disturbed meditations and going to church every morning. Besides, I had begun to write. In the June number of the Anglican magazine *The Church Teacher* there appeared the first of a series of articles headed "Prayer in the Bible," in which I undertook to analyze the prayer life of Abraham and Jacob, of Moses, the Prophets and the Psalmists. They were my first venture in spiritual writing, and showed that my approach to Scripture was no longer the critical one I had learned in Berlin and at King's College. Prayer had become the mainspring of my own life; it was this that I both sought and found in what I had at last come to accept as the revealed Word of God. The editor evidently liked my way of writing and published my simple interpretations month after month.

However, spiritual subjects did not absorb all my interests. In these last years I had come to see Hitler not as a meteor, suddenly arising in the German sky, as he was then so often regarded abroad, but as an authentic expression of the German spirit. To my mind National Socialism had its roots in the non-Christian tradition of German culture. Hegel and Nietzsche, Goethe even and Lessing, however much they might personally have repudiated Hitler had they lived to see his regime, were nevertheless all responsible for his rise. The Viennese paper-hanger could not have gained his hold on the people of "poets and thinkers," as my countrymen chose to call themselves, had not these heroes of German thought, each in his own peculiar way, destroyed belief in God and in objective moral values, and preached their various idolatrous religions of the spirit objectivating itself in the Prussian State, the superman or blonde beast ruthlessly destroying all that is weak after God had been declared to be dead, of the search for truth being preferable to truth itself, of the superiority of the genius to the moral law. If a people subscribed to such philosophies, was it so very surprising that it should succumb to the allurements of Hitler and Goebbels?

Most of the material for these articles I had unconsciously gathered in my school and university days; I now consciously supplemented it in the British Museum. The first result was a short essay entitled "From Hegel to Hitler," written in the early weeks of the "Blitz." It appeared in *The Contemporary Review*. In the concluding paragraph I wrote that, since

National Socialism had struck its roots so deeply in the German soil, and since it drew its strength from such different sources, the Allies would find a real re-education of the German people after their victory very difficult, indeed. I have, since then, visited Germany several times; despite certain superficial impressions to the contrary, I have seen no evidence that would have compelled me to change my mind on this subject.

One morning, early in September, I was just about to leave the house to go to church, when the telephone rang. "Is that Miss Graef? I am an air raid warden. Don't be alarmed, your mother is quite unhurt, but she has been bombed out and is suffering from shock. Can you please come and collect her from the Army and Navy Stores air raid shelter as soon as possible."

I dashed upstairs to put some more money in my purse and then took a bus to Victoria. The scene was terrifying: broken glass cracking under my feet, paneless windows staring under smouldering roofs like the empty sockets of a skull, fire engines and air raid wardens rushing in all directions. I made my way to the Army and Navy Stores and asked a policeman where their shelter was.

"You cannot go there, Miss; it's all cordoned off. There are time bombs about."

"But I have just been rung up by an air raid warden who told me that my mother was there."

"Impossible, there is nobody in that shelter now. They are all having breakfast at the Army and Navy Stores restaurant, you will probably find your mother there."

The restaurant was full of dishevelled looking people drinking their tea, but my mother was not among them.

I went back into the road and asked for the nearest police station. Did they know what could have happened. No, they knew nothing about it, I had better go back and find an air raid warden. I had wasted about three quarters of an hour

by now; another policeman was as adamant as the first one
I had asked, and would not let me go to the shelter. Eventually I met a woman air raid warden. I repeated my story
about the telephone call. "Yes, I know," she said, "there *are*
just three people still in that shelter. I will take you there."
She now talked to the same policeman who had just refused
to let me pass, and finally I was allowed to go to the shelter,
where I found my mother, together with Miss Hippisley and
a friend of hers. Mother was sitting on her suitcase, sobbing
and crying. All the windows in her room had been broken;
it was a marvel that she had escaped unhurt. As Miss Hippisley was going to her brother in the country, there was
nothing for me to do but to take Mother with me to my attic
for the time being, and then try to evacuate her somehow.

As I was sitting with my mother in a taxi I wondered
what my landlady would say to this. She was a Londoner
born and bred, and rose to the occasion with both the kindness and the *sang-froid* characteristic of her race. "But of
course, Graefie (so she had come to call me), your mother
can stay here with you as long as necessary, don't you worry
about it." So we put Mother on my bed, gave her tea and
cornflakes, bacon and eggs, toast and marmalade, and she ate
it all, repeating that she had never in her life enjoyed a
breakfast so much.

The next three weeks were trying, indeed. The sirens were
sounding all day long. While I had been alone, I had never
taken any notice of them in the day time, but had done my
shopping and gone for walks as usual. Now there was a struggle with Mother every time I wanted to go out, in case there
might be a raid; and as soon as the sirens went she would fly
from my attic into the basement, requiring me to do the
same. For the night, my landlady "Chappie" (her real name
was Miss Chaplin) had made a very satisfactory arrangement.
She had let one basement room to a lady who was always on
night duty; so we could sleep there, my mother in the bed

and I on a mattress, if one could call it sleeping. Mother was moaning a good deal.

One morning, about three, when the bombs had been falling on Kensington particularly fast and thick, I tried to comfort her: "Don't worry, there'll soon be an All Clear."

Whereupon Mother, in a sepulchral voice of utter conviction: "There will *never* be an All Clear."

I had made it a habit to say Compline every night according to the rite of the Prayer Book of 1928, as we had done in the Settlement. Mother, whom I sometimes took to High Church services, liked me to say it aloud. The old prayers that had consoled Jews and Christians for well-nigh three thousand years comforted her, too, and gave her new courage. After that, while the guns were firing and the engines roaring in the sky, I would lie on my mattress, reading St. Teresa's *Interior Castle,* letting myself be introduced into a new world, the world of a human soul in close union with God. It is true, I had already read St. John of the Cross, but only his *Ascent of Mount Carmel,* which does not treat of actual mystical experiences. St. Teresa's descriptions of the various forms of mystical prayer, of the prayer of quiet, of union, of ecstasy, spiritual betrothal and marriage, which were really only expressions of an ever-growing love between God and the soul, showed me a form of human life far surpassing anything I had ever known or read about. I realized, of course, that the heights of this way of mystic love were only for the chosen few; but even the lower grades, the prayer of quiet, for example, which St. Teresa seemed to think was given to many sufficiently generous to persevere in prayer, seemed supremely desirable.

At times, when the bombs were dropping very near and the house was shaking, I was gripped by sheer physical fear. Then I would say the first of the Sorrowful Mysteries of the Rosary over and over again: the Agony in the Garden of Gethsemane. It was intensely comforting to realize that

Christ Himself had known such human reactions, that one could turn one's very fear into prayer, as He had done. There was another bomb swishing down—I might be dead at any moment. What use then would be brains, brilliant examinations, intellectual ambitions? God would not ask me whether I had had a First—He would ask whether I had really loved Him above all things and my neighbor as myself. Christianity was not an easy religion, but I was learning a good deal about it, as I was lying on my mattress, listening to the strange symphony of roaring airplanes, hissing bombs, and thundering guns.

I had been writing to several friends trying to find a place in the country for Mother, who became increasingly tense and would have liked to keep me confined to the basement for the duration. So I was greatly relieved when, after about three weeks, we had found two elderly ladies in Ross-on-Wye who required a housekeeper. When I had seen Mother off at Paddington, to the accompaniment of the inevitable wailing of sirens, I had an exultant feeling of freedom. At last I could again go for walks and do my shopping in peace—I should be able to face the bombs much better alone.

While Mother had been staying with me, the Church of All Saints had been bombed, and we had to have services in the small vicarage chapel. As soon as she had left, I went again to pray in that convent chapel in Chelsea, where they had perpetual exposition. But I could not find it. Instead I saw a gap in the row of houses where it had been. It had evidently received a direct hit. But the Carmelite church in Kensington was still standing, and there I now went most evenings to hear the friars sing the Litany of Loretto at Benediction. In the afternoon I often went to the Servite Church in Chelsea, where I used to pray for a long time before the statue of Our Lady of Sorrows. It was a bad statue from the artistic point of view, with seven highly realistic swords stuck into Mary's heart. I intensely dislike this kind of "repository" art and think it disgraceful that so many Catholic churches should be cluttered up with these atrocities —yet I have always been able to pray even before the worst specimens. So I was praying hard before this statue that God and our Lady might find a way for me to become a Catholic. I actually wished a priest would talk to me when I came out of the church—but there was no such help for me.

Instead it happened to my mother. A few weeks after going to Ross-on-Wye she wrote to me that, as she did not like the Anglican church there, she had gone into the small Catholic church to say a prayer. There a lady had addressed her, to whom she confided that, though not a Catholic, she was interested in Catholicism. The lady had immediately taken her to the priest who, in his turn, had sent her to a nun to be instructed. Should I have any objection if she became a Catholic? Might it not damage my career? I was staggered, and almost a little envious that God was making things so easy for her, whereas I was left to my own unaided efforts to decide the issue between my career and the all but irresistible attraction of the Catholic Church. I wrote back I was delighted to hear she wanted to become a Catholic; it would make no difference to my professional prospects, but I said nothing about my own difficulties.

By this time I had become quite used to the air raids and almost shared the feelings of a neighboring shopkeeper, who said to me one morning after a particularly heavy raid: "Shan't we miss the noise, Miss, once the war is over?" I had given up going down to the basement almost as soon as my mother had left. When things became too uncomfortable in my attic, I went just one floor down to a lady whose chief interest in life was greyhound racing. At first she had been very suspicious of me, being firmly convinced that I must be a spy. Once she had told my landlady that I was having conspirators in my room at night; she had heard men coming out of it at three o'clock in the morning. Without telling me anything, Chappie made inquiries, and the matter was cleared up to her complete satisfaction: the girl in the room next to me had gone down to the bathroom at that time! But the witchhunter was not yet satisfied. Soon afterwards she told Chappie I had given light signals from my room in the night. "In that case you had better go and inform the police," said Miss Chaplin very sensibly. The lady went; but even the police did not take kindly to the information: "Yes, yes, we know all about that—a barrage balloon caught fire last night." After that she changed her attitude completely. As she was much more nervous than I, she was only too glad when I came into her room at night to hold her hand when the raids got bad.

Shortly before Christmas Mother wrote that the nun who instructed her had said she was ready to be received into the Church; but she could not possibly do it; it was all too much compulsion, what with having to go to Mass on Sundays, to confession once a year and to eat no meat on Fridays! I could be assured she would remain as she was. She also had an invitation for me to come and visit her at Christmas.

So I spent Christmas with her at Ross-on-Wye. I went to the parish church for Holy Communion on the feast itself; but I also thought it might be a good idea to see the nun who had instructed mother and to tell her about my difficulties. She was very kind; her advice was: "Find yourself a job where you need not teach theology, and then become a Catholic."

It was a sensible answer; yet I was somehow disappointed. It might take years for me to find a proper job, and of what kind I could not imagine, since my only English qualification was the Anglican theology. In the train back to London I stood at the window, thinking. What was I to do? The conviction that the Catholic Church was the only true Church, and the longing to be a Catholic were quite overwhelming. I thought I had better go and talk to a priest. Preferably a

Jesuit. It was the second of January, a Thursday. I would go there on Monday. With my mind thus made up I arrived back in London, only to find that I could not wait till Monday. Some time ago I had bought a map showing the Catholic churches of London; this I now looked up to find where Farm Street was, the famous Jesuit church where so many converts had been received. I went there the next morning.

I wanted first to go into the church to say a prayer, before venturing into the stronghold of the Jesuits, out of whose nets, so I imagined, one could scarcely escape once one had got into them. But the church had been bombed, and workmen were busy mending the roof. I was on the point of abandoning my plan and going home again, when one of them came over to me saying: "You wanted to go into the church? There is a chapel in the house, you can go there. Look, there is the bell you have to ring."

"No, thank you, I won't bother."

"But there is the bell," he persisted. Then he walked with me a few steps until we stood at the entrance to the house. Almost standing over me he repeated: "Ring the bell, lady, ring the bell." I felt I had no choice but to press the button.

When a boy opened the door I could just stammer, the words almost choking me: "Please, could I see a priest. I am an Anglican but would like to become a Catholic."

The boy led me into one of the parlors, which was of a bleaknese and austerity that belied effectively any idea of drawing-room-Jesuits fawning upon the rich, that I might still have harbored from my university days in Germany. A few minutes later the superior appeared. He was a tall man with a calm face, in which austerity blended with fatherly kindness in perfect harmony. To my own surprise he immediately inspired an extraordinary confidence in me. When I told him I came from agnostic Protestantism he drew himself up and almost thundered: "Do you believe that Christ our Lord is God Almighty?"

"Certainly, Father," I replied, much surprised that he should think I should be here unless I firmly believed at least that.

"Oh well, then we can go on."

After some more questions he excused himself: he had just to finish some work; would I wait for a few minutes till he came back. When he had gone I reflected that there was still time—I could go away now, he did not even know my name, and nobody any the wiser. But I could not go. I sat glued to my chair, eagerly waiting for his return.

I then told him of my difficulty. I believed the Catholic Church to be the only true Church, I believed all she taught —but I had done that Anglican examination, it was my only hope ever to build up a career in this country.

Would he say the same as the nun in Ross-on-Wye? The Jesuits have a reputation for being world-wise and diplomatic—would he counsel prudence, material safety first? He reflected for a moment, then said gravely: "You have found the pearl of great price—you must give up everything for it." They were the words of Christ, the words I had been wanting to hear all this time of struggle and uncertainty. I should have liked to be received on the spot, for in my meditations I had worked it all out, from the Divinity of Christ down to Indulgences; there was nothing in the teaching of the Church that I did not believe wholeheartedly.

Father Geddes explained that I should have to be "under instruction" for at least two months.

"I suppose we better turn you over to a nun."

I, meekly, "Yes, Father."

A few more minutes conversation in which I told him in greater detail about my theological studies.

"I suppose you would prefer being instructed by a priest?"

I, with considerably more conviction. "Yes, Father."

Another ten minutes conversation, then: "Well, I think

I'd better take you on myself. Can you come again next Monday at eleven?"

I was too happy to take a bus—I walked back all the way through Hyde Park and Kensington Gardens, very much with a song in my heart. The next day I was feeling rather headachy, and by Sunday I was in the throes of a mild attack of influenza. I stayed in bed, wondering how I should get to my instruction next morning. I would not ring up Father Geddes to tell him I could not come, having a wholly irrational fear he might think it was a pretext, and I had changed my mind. Besides, it would delay my being received into the Church, and I was in a desperate hurry. On Monday morning it was sleeting, not exactly the right weather to go out with a sore throat and an aching head after being in bed for two days. However, I was determined to have my instruction come what may. Father Geddes was explaining to me the first questions of the Catechism, having no idea that I could hardly take in anything he said, as my head was worse than ever, and I was wondering whether I was in for pneumonia. When he had finished, he led me before the Crib, and told me the twelve o'clock Mass was just beginning, and it was the Feast of the Epiphany, a holyday of obligation, on which Catholics were bound to hear Mass. I said, "Yes, Father," and when he had left me, holyday of obligation or not, I made a dash for the bus and back to bed.

My escapade had no bad consequences, and when I went for my next instruction, I had fully recovered. Father Geddes had told me that I need not decide at once whether I actually did want to become a Catholic—but there was nothing to decide any more; it was the one thing in the world I wanted.

There was a Catholic church quite near my home, St. Mary of the Angels, so I started to go to Mass there every morning. But I thought it right to tell Father Twisaday of my decision. When I went to see him, he began by saying that he would not argue with me, but after five minutes he was arguing for all he was worth. His main point was that, if all the Catholics in the Church of England went over to Rome, there would be far less hope of an ultimate reunion, because the Church of England would then be less Catholic than it was now, hence "Catholics" had a duty to remain in it. I did not say much, thinking it all rather confused. Only when I came home I suddenly realized the flaw in his arguments, at least as far as I was concerned, whatever views Anglo-Catholics might hold: I wanted a Church that was Catholic by essence and definition, to whose Catholicity it made no difference whether a few thousand, or even million, people joined or left it. The Church of Rome became neither more nor less Catholic whether I joined it or not, whereas, in Father Twisaday's opinion at least, the Church of England did.

I had decided not to tell anyone of my becoming a Catholic till a few days before the date of my reception. I was absolutely certain, and any discussions with my Anglican friends would have only been upsetting and annoying to them. I did not tell my mother either, because I could foresee her lamentations about ruining my career. As I knew my few theology coachings would soon have to come to an end, I took a job as a copy typist with a firm in Bloomsbury. I had to be there at eight a.m. and work till five, with a break for lunch of about a quarter of an hour, during which we fifteen to twenty girls ate our sandwiches and had a cup of tea before our typewriters, typing addresses for almost nine hours a day at the rate of two pounds a week. I left after a week and determined to learn shorthand, so as to be able to find some less inhuman work. The secretary of the organization who was helping me thought this a good idea and arranged for me a three months' training course at a secretarial college in Kensington.

In February I wrote what I knew would be my last contribution to the *Church Teacher*, an article on the *Magnificat*, for Lady Day. The editor wrote back she liked it very much; there was only one change that would have to be made: her readers might take exception to Mary being called the Mother of God, she had therefore substituted each time "Mother of God the Son." The word *Theotokos,* Mother of God, had been the test of orthodoxy in the controversy between Nestorius and St. Cyril of Alexandria in the fifth century; Anglo-Catholics accepted it without hesitation, but other members of the Church of England evidently did not—I was not sorry I was about to join a less "comprehensive" Church.

At the end of February Father Geddes fixed the date of my reception for the sixth of March—had I witnesses? As a matter of fact, I did not know a single Catholic in the country. However, an Anglican friend of mine had introduced me to the Society of SS. Alban and Sergius, who worked for reunion between the Eastern Churches, Anglicans, and the Catholic Church. At one of their meetings, about ten days before my reception, I met two Catholic young women whom I asked to be my witnesses. A week before I wrote to my mother. Her reply was what I had expected: Did I know what I was doing? Here was I, ruining my career—did I not have a thought for her? How could we ever set up a home in this country if I now threw away the one chance of a livelihood?

Then came the last temptation. Three days before my reception the telephone rang. My Anglican friend, the same who had introduced me to the Society of SS. Alban and Sergius, told me she had heard of a post at lecturer at an Anglican Missionary College; I should write to them at once. I hemmed and hawed, I did not know . . . . She was dumbfounded. "What on earth is the matter with you? This would be just ideal, would it not?"

"Yes, yes, certainly, quite wonderful—but it is so sudden, I must think about it. I'll ring you up again in a day or two."

"All right—but I can't understand you at all."

I replaced the receiver, went back to my room and down on my knees. This was terrible. I would not have minded so much about myself—but here was the great opportunity of making a home for my mother, of finding, at last, my feet in this country. Should I go back now? Could I not remain an Anglican? It was impossible. Rather sweep the roads or type envelopes for the rest of my life as a Catholic than embrace the most brilliant career as an Anglican. It was as clear as that. "He, who loves his father or mother more than me, cannot be my disciple." I got up from my knees. Neither for my own sake, nor even for my mother's could I give up the Church of Christ.

Next day my friend rang up again. She had made a mistake; the post had already been filled. It had ceased to make any difference to me.

After he had received me into the Church Father Geddes congratulated me: "Now you are a child of Holy Mother Church." Once more he had found the right words for me. From without the Church is often regarded as an institution, inflicting a multitude of rules and regulations on its members, limiting their freedom, compelling them to accept in advance any doctrine it may choose to impose. But from within, the Church appears as a Mother, guiding her children wisely and securely, because she herself is guided by the Holy Spirit. And if I could now be called a child of this Mother, this, as I knew then, and was to realize increasingly in the future, did not mean that I was to become childishly dependent in my thought. On the contrary, the more deeply my thought struck roots in the intellectual and spiritual heritage of the Church, the more I appreciated—and used—the freedom that springs from being sure of one's principles. It seemed to me that, by accepting the docrines of the Church, I no more limited my liberty than by accepting the multiplication tables or the rules of syntax. They were as necessary to my spiritual life as the latter are to arithmetic and writing. I was feeling secure and free at the same time, peacefully happy to be where, as I knew with complete certainty, God wanted me to be.

Eleven years later I was sitting before the grille in the parlor of the Carmelite Convent of the Incarnation at Avila, talking to the present successor of its most famous Prioress, St. Teresa. She was thrilled to learn that I was a convert from England, and with naïve inquisitiveness asked me: "And what did you feel at your first Holy Communion?" I tried to smile as enigmatically as Mona Lisa herself, and replied evasively that in England we were rather reticent about these things. The truth was that I had not the heart to disappoint the eager expectancy of the nun, who no doubt hoped to hear from me that it had been the most wonderful moment of my life, accompanied, possibly, by some ecstatic vision.

It had been nothing of the sort. On the contrary, I was thoroughly nervous and distracted, worrying about when to go up to the altar rail—would other people go too? I had heard that Catholics often went to Mass without receiving Holy Communion. Fortunately there were others; but then I had to watch them, because there was a plate one had to hold under one's chin—I devoutly hoped I was not going to drop it with a clang when it was my turn to take it. So my principal feeling was relief that everything had gone without mishap; I knew I had really received our Lord Himself this time, and He, surely, would understand why I had been unable to concentrate. But I was not so sure I could explain the matter satisfactorily to a Spanish Carmelite nun.

Two or three days before my reception I had written to all those friends in the Church of England, who had helped me so generously throughout. It had not been easy. In these difficult years they had shown me the greatest kindness, they had done all they could for me, welcomed me with open arms into their Church—and now I was turning my back on them. I was convinced the Church of England was not the true Church of Christ; I was equally convinced that they were true Christians, living in the spirit of the Gospel, sincerely loving God and their neighbor. Why could they not see the whole truth as clearly as I saw it? In the following months I sometimes tried, with the tactless first fervor of the recent convert, to press upon some of them my own point of view, and naturally thus lost their friendship. Gradually I learned to respect the mysterious workings of God, who Himself respects man's free will. I came also to realize, both in myself and in others, how little use we Catholics so often make of the graces given us, and to admire the more the faithfulness with which those former friends of mine practised their religion despite uncertainties and difficulties. I had no harsh word from anyone of them on my conversion; the theme that recurred in most of their letters was: we are very sorry you are leaving us, but of course we fully understand that you must follow your conscience.

Some letters, however, also made another point, which, in fact, I had been expecting. It was most clearly expressed in a letter from Mrs. Beardall, one of the few who remained a close friend both of my mother and myself until her death. She wrote:

"I am very much interested in your news, and if you are really quite sure yourself, I am glad. I have often felt that no one with abilities and a strong character like yours, can separate themselves from the Motherland (or Vaterland), the only possibility of that is in marrying a native of the land of one's adoption. Personally I just cannot imagine myself ceasing to be British. And, whatever your country and its present rulers have now done, no German can avoid his or her personal share in the matter . . . By joining the Latin communion you have taken your place among a large number of your compatriots, and I am quite sure that it is the duty of all German Christians to go back to Germany after

the war is over, and try to build up afresh the faith and devotion to our Lord and his Church which has been so terribly
destroyed."

So by becoming a Catholic I had rejoined my compatriots.
The Church of Rome was the foreign Church, though such
authentic Englishmen as Thomas More, Challoner, Newman,
Chesterton, had been Catholics. I certainly did not feel one
jot more German for having become a Catholic. I did not
even feel responsible for Hitler, and he himself would certainly have indignantly repudiated such responsibility from
a non-Aryan. There was just one point in this letter on which
I had to make up my mind: was it really my duty to go back
after the war to help restore Christianity in Germany?

I had never been a good German. I had written as quite
a young girl that I wanted the world to be my fatherland.
The re-education of Germany, of this I was certain, would be
a task for generations. This, in itself, would not be a deter-
rent. But was I at all a suitable person to influence the Germans? For you had to feel German for that, above all, to
love Germany. But the strange fact, difficult to understand
especially for English people, was that I had by now ceased
to love my own country. At the beginning of the war I had
said to the Tribunal, before which I had to prove that I was
a genuine refugee, with absolute conviction that I would do
everything to help England, even directly against Germany.
Night after night I had thought of the English airmen as
our boys, who protected us, me, from the enemy. One night
I had been dreaming the Nazis had landed in this country
and I awakened with a start, hearing a bomb exploding in
the neighborhood, and thinking with intense relief: "Thank
God, it's only the bombs, they are not here yet." Churchill's
speeches were an inspiration to me, and his "We will never
give in!" was the one hope for me, too. First to be rejected
by one's own countrymen, and then to live through a World
War with one's heart unreservedly on the other side, must

surely separate a person from his or her country, estrange him perhaps even more than a foreigner. This had happened to me, and the Germans would not be slow to realize that, and reject my missionary efforts even more decisively than they would those of an Englishwoman. Whatever God might have in store for me, I was sure He did not mean me to become a female St. Boniface. Mrs. Beardall would have to resign herself to my firm intention to get naturalized as soon as possible after the war, and to take my place among the three or four million Catholics in England.

When, after my reception, Father Geddes was preparing me for Confirmation, I confided to him that I could not get on with the prayers in *The Garden of the Soul*. I liked so much better saying Prime and Compline, as I had used to do from the 1928 Prayer Book. "So you like the Divine Office?" he said smilingly. "In that case we had better teach you the Breviary. Go and get yourself the *Horae Diurnae*, the Day Hours of the Church, and I will tell you how to recite them."

When I asked for a Diurnal in one of the Catholic bookshops near Westminster Cathedral there were only two copies left; they cost one pound. In those days a pound was a small fortune to me. On becoming a Catholic I had, of course, to give up my few theology lessons, and so I had now to subsist on the twenty-five shillings a week the British German Foundation gave me, my *pièce de résistance* being about six or eight pounds I still had in the Post Office. However, I paid my pound and got the book, wondering how to reduce my expenses still further to make up for this extravagance. Next morning, as I opened a letter from a lady to whom I had given a few Greek lessons, a pound note fell out: she felt she had underpaid me, would I therefore please accept the enclosed.

On the 16th of March I was confirmed in Westminster Cathedral. The two Catholic young women who had come to Farm Street for my reception were prevented from attending; so I had to go alone, having as my godmother an unknown lady who performed this office for those few of us who had arrived by ourselves.

It was the third time I was being confirmed. The first time I had come to it accompanied by my mother and most of my friends, in a mood of rebellion. The second time, only three years ago, Miss Norman had been with me; I had been no longer rebellious but acquiescent, conforming to a Church in which, I hoped, I should be able to make a career. Now, the third time, I was completely alone. As I was kneeling before the bishop who laid his hands on my head and anointed me, I knew by faith that the Holy Spirit was coming upon me to make me a full-grown Christian, to strengthen me with His gifts and to be, to me, too, as He had once been to the Apostles, a Paraclete—a Comforter. Humanly speaking, I was completely alone, and I naturally felt it, but I was not really sorry that it should be so. If my first confirmation had been an act of rebellion and the second an act of conforming, this third confirmation, now at last in the one true Church, was an act of utter conviction. My material future was as uncertain as it could be, but I knew I had truly found the pearl of great price. Nothing else mattered.

13. *Back to the Land?*

SHORTLY after my confirmation the course at the secretarial college came to an end. I had done my best—but I simply could not master the mysteries of Pitman's shorthand. I had learned two different shorthand systems in Germany, one while still at school and another one later on, but I had never achieved anything approaching the speed required for an efficient secretary, and as to reading back my scrawl. . . . Pitman fared no better with me, or rather I with Pitman. Between seventy and eighty words were my maximum, and a hundred and twenty were the minimum needed for a decent job. Nevertheless, I applied conscientiously for any work that seemed possible.

My nationality as well as my insufficient shorthand speed and lack of office experience were drawbacks. A week's copy typing—this time in less trying conditions than before, was all the Labor Exchange could obtain for me. Father Geddes began to get worried. "Have you still not got anything? I had better talk to the editor of our periodical *The Month* about it. It is being published by Longmans, and he could give you an introduction to them. They might have work for you. I will ask him to write to you about it." Next time

I saw Father Geddes he asked if I had heard from the Editor but I had not. He promised to remind him; but the Editor's memory must have been temporarily out of order, for he never wrote to me. At last Father Geddes thought it best for me to chance it and go to Longmans without an introduction.

They were evacuated to Wimbledon at the time; it was quite an expedition to get there. I think I penetrated as far as the staff manager. No, the Editor of *The Month* had never mentioned my name. Indifferent shorthand and typing were not sufficient qualifications for a post with their firm, nor was my nationality exactly a point in my favor. The interview had lasted about five minutes. It was yet another disappointment in an ever lengthening list. When I left, I could hardly foresee that, many years later, I would recall this particular setback with amused satisfaction.

Even now I was luckier with my writing than with my efforts at earning my living as a typist. I had become interested in the German medieval Dominican mystics, and *The Contemporary Review* had just accepted an article on "Meister Eckhart and his Nazi Interpreters," when Barbara Fry, who had been one of the witnesses of my reception into the Church, suggested I should try to write for *Blackfriars,* the organ of the English Dominicans. When I offered the Editor an article on either Henry Suso or John Tauler, he replied to my surprise that he would like to see both. It was a welcome change from dreary visits to the Labor Exchange and abortive interviews with staff managers to ponder over the mystic teaching of the fourteenth century Dominicans, and I produced two articles, which the Editor accepted with flattering comments. I had already written innumerable letters to people who I thought might be able to help me to find work. I now wrote to the Editor of *Blackfriars,* who, till then, had addressed me as Mr. Graef, since I signed my articles only with my initials. Having reluctantly divulged my sex, I gave him an account of my career, qualifications and present predicament.

I had had too many disappointments to expect more than a vague promise to remember my name if he should hear of anything suitable. Instead, I received by return of post a reply not only full of genuine human sympathy, but containing also concrete suggestions. The outcome of the ensuing correspondence was an interview with his father, Mr. Hilary Pepler, well known as a mime producer. He also owned the Ditchling Press, and was willing to employ me as a secretary and proof reader. This seemed a satisfactory solution, at least for the time being—but Ditchling was in the defense zone! Once more my nationality threatened to wreck my chance of employment. Twice Mr. Pepler applied for a permit for me to go to Ditchling, twice it was refused. At last Miss Norman once more solved the problem. She wrote to Lord Wolmer, to whom I was known since I had taught his daughter, and he now guaranteed for my loyalty. Before this testimony the authorities gave way.

In the meantime I had also met my new employer's son, Father Conrad. He had written to me that he was passing through London and would like to see me. I consulted Barbara Fry. How did one meet a Dominican outside his monastery?

"Invite him to come to tea with you."

"But I have only a small bed-sitting room—surely I can't ask a young Father there?"

"Oh," replied Barbara airily, "these young Dominicans will go anywhere. But if you have qualms about it I will ask him to lunch at my house, and you can meet him there."

I had unconsciously pictured the Editor of *Blackfriars* after the pattern of Father Geddes, the only priest I knew: dignified, discreet, inspiring respect, yet distinctly fatherly. It somehow surprised me to find that a priest could be not only lively, full of ideas but even distinctly boyish. It was certainly refreshing, and after lunch was over, we discussed both literary projects and my prospects of eventually coming to Oxford. He told me that a Lexicon of the Greek of the Church Fathers was being brought out there; the Editor, Dr. F. L. Cross, then Custodian of Pusey House Library, needed an assistant; there might be an opening for me later in the year. For the time being, however, I would go to Ditchling, as arranged.

I went there early in August. Mr. Pepler, who was at that time an Editor of *Everybody's*, met me at Victoria on his way home from the office. He was quite different from his son; he spoke very little, and this habit of silence, which was probably due to his Quaker origins, I often found embarrassing. He and his family were living a little outside the town, on Ditchling Common, where he had settled with Eric Gill, and formed a community of craftsmen who rejected the modern industrialized society and sought to return to the simple life, whose prophet was the Dominican, Father Vincent McNabb. When I came to Ditchling, Eric Gill, who had later broken away from the community, was already dead, and the simple life had become not so simple. Though we had to light oil lamps and eat home-made bread, there was a radio (the younger generation had insisted on that) and cornflakes for breakfast.

I was to live with the Pepler family, and go daily to the Press. It was a small family business run on patriarchal lines; a linotype machine was one of the few concessions to modern needs. What exactly I was supposed to be doing apart from occasionally reading a few proof sheets, never became clear to me. I should have liked to be taught my job, if any; but there was no one to teach me. Apparently I was expected to find myself something to do. So I busied myself with tidying up papers and filing away letters, feeling very much an unneeded supernumerary.

I kept up my habit of early morning meditation and went to Mass every day, which involved a twenty minute walk across the common, to a convent of Augustinian nuns which boasted a white "wedding cake" altar of particular magnificence, the exact opposite of the small chapel near our house, which excelled in that strained simplicity characteristic of the Ditchling ideals. These were diametrically opposed to my own. "Back to the land" was a slogan to which I have never been able to subscribe, and why life on the land should be more truly Christian and Catholic than life in the city, as the Ditchling community evidently believed, I failed to see. The LAND, in capitals, occurred continually in their conversations; they talked about it as if it were the object of a cult. They had the typically romantic conception of the city dweller; in fact Ditchling Common smacked more of Bloomsbury and Chelsea than of Sussex. I have never been able to believe in this idea of medieval Catholic England in which all things were good, true, and beautiful, where men were paradisiacally nourished on the fruits of the earth, plentifully yet without gluttony, took wives with whom they lived in perfect harmony ever after, procreated children without concupiscence, and were innocently content with the simple things of life.

If these latter were the object of the Ditchling people, they gaily betrayed their ideals without noticing it. I found it hard to remain serious if Mr. Pepler, after editing a completely industrialized and up-to-the-minute weekly till four P.M., began to chase a recently acquired cow around the common before supper. I could have appreciated it if a Fleet Street editor chased a cow or dug a plot in the evening as a balancing hobby, so as to have some fresh air and exercise. But here such activities were elevated into signs and symbols, more, forged into weapons wherewith truly Christian men and women beat the enemy: paganized and industrialized modern society. Yet, where did the money come from to keep up these pleasant hobbies? Precisely from this wicked, industrialized society against which oil lamps and cows were a horrified protest.

Many years later I read with satisfaction Dom Bede Griffith's account of his own experiment in simple living in his autobiography *The Golden String*. Apart from living that life far more consistently than the Ditchling community did, he saw quite soon that even in his extremely austere version of it, the ideal could not be realized. Whether we like it or not, we cannot jump out of our time. We still depend on this industrial society of ours; the very money needed for setting up such a self-contained community comes from it, we are inescapably enmeshed in the system.

In the Ditchling community this dependence was particularly evident; for few of its members would forego those comforts of the not so simple life that appealed to them. It always amused me to hear them grumble if the bus did not put them down exactly in front of their house: "Could he not go twenty yards further—he might just as well have stopped at the gate." With all their craze for primitivity they disliked walking, and I felt inspired to write an article entitled "We Must Learn to Walk Again." It was published in *Everybody's*, which had already accepted some gruesome stories of mine about the unhappy consort of George I, Sophie Dorothea of Celle, on the famous poisoner Marie de Brinvilliers and other subjects I had read in chronicles in the British Museum. I wonder whether any one at Ditchling realized that they themselves had inspired this plea for going back to the pleasures of a leisurely walk, my own favorite recreation—though I should hesitate to consider it an essential Christian virtue.

Throughout my life I had fully accepted the society into which I had been born; now, as a Catholic, I could not believe that factories should be less subject to divine providence than farms. I agreed that a certain decentralization and a restoration of the balance between town and country were necessary, but there can be no putting the clock back. Christianity had first flourished in the cities, among the up-rooted proletariate of the Roman Empire, whereas the *pagani*, the country people, put up a tough resistance to the new religion and clung to their old fertility rites long after Christianity had been established in the towns. What I saw at Ditchling confirmed me in my view that the Church must adapt her apostolate to the times; it cannot withdraw into a mythical past.

As I was waiting for the bus one morning to take me to the Press, a lady whom I slightly knew addressed me. Did I know there was a German mistress teaching at a convent school at Burgess Hill, which was quite near?

I did not know, nor was I particularly interested. But the lady continued: "Her name is Dr. M."

"What," I said, "Irene M.?"

Yes, her Christian name was Irene.

I had not expected to meet a former pupil of my old school in Berlin in a town in Sussex. Irene had been three classes above me, and, as far as I remembered, had combined a reputation for great intellectual brilliancy with an incomprehensible penchant for pink stockings. Though we had never had more than a nodding acquaintance, I wrote to her, and we arranged to meet on Ditchling Common and go for a walk. She came from the same agnostic background as I, and, strangely enough, had also become a Catholic in this country, a year before me almost to the day. She had just published a book, *The Heresy of National Socialism*, a lucid and convincing exposition of Hitler's system. She had the inestimable advantage of being British by birth, since she had been born in London and spent the first ten years of her life there. Nevertheless, she was far more attached to Germany than I; we sometimes embarrassed each other, she me by her emotionalism, I her by my rational attitude even in religious matters. But for the time being we concentrated on the things we had in common and became very friendly.

I was not very happy at Ditchling. The work was far from congenial, and I felt like an intruder in the house of my hosts. I had by now been living frequently in other people's homes, but it had never caused me any embarrassment. At Ditchling things were different. I may have been mistaken; but as they all indulged that strange worship of the LAND, the Family, too, seemed to have been made into a kind of cult, a self-contained unit that would not admit strangers. Though Mrs. Pepler was indeed most kind and charming, I never felt at ease, and did all I could to efface myself as completely as possible. Perhaps it was only natural that I should have been unable to fit into a circle whose ideals were completely foreign to me; and I was not greatly surprised when, after about six weeks, Mr. Pepler hinted that it would be better if I found myself some other work.

I had written to Dr. Cross soon after my arrival at Ditchling, but had received no answer. I now wrote to him again, asking if there were an opening for me on the staff of the Lexicon of Patristic Greek. This time he replied immediately that he did, indeed, need someone to help him with it, and could I come to Oxford for a fortnight's trial.

I was intensely relieved at this chance of getting away from the LAND and into a more congenial atmosphere. Father Conrad wrote it would be very difficult to find lodgings in Oxford, which was overcrowded with evacuees. No matter; I packed up a small suitcase, went to Farm Street on my way through London to ask Father Geddes' blessing on my new venture, and took a train to Oxford.

14. *City of the Dreaming Spires*

I WENT to Pusey House the same day to see Dr. Cross. Though he seemed very shy, I felt at once I should be able to work with him. He introduced me to the Library, pointing out that it had hitherto been open only to men; I was the first woman allowed to work there. There was Migne's Patrology, above it the Berlin Corpus of early Greek writers, which I would know, of course. I had no idea of either—they had not come into the curriculum of the Lambeth Diploma—but I nodded. No use giving away my abysmal ignorance at this stage; besides, I should probably be able to get the hang of it in a few days.

Then I was led into the vaults of Pusey House, where the precious material for the Lexicon was stored: piles and piles of slips, and mountains of foolscap sheets called "The Draft," as safe as might be from the bombs. It was certainly imposing (incidentally the Lexicon had started its career in the same year as I, 1907)—but should I ever find my way through this maze of references and citations, editions, bibliographies, drafts, critical notes, new slips, old slips, through these masses of different handwritings one more illegible than the other? I gasped.

"And where is the Card Index, please?"

"Card Index? We do not have a Card Index."

"Surely, you cannot make a Lexicon without a Card Index?"

I had scored. It did not take me long to convince Dr. Cross that a Card Index was absolutely essential for producing a Lexicon. I felt confident that the result of my fortnight's trial would be favorable.

After a few days at a hotel Father Conrad advised me to see a young woman graduate who had told him that her landlady had a room free. It was my first experience of the species generally known as Oxford originals. The lady received me attired in somewhat grubby bordeaux-red corduroy trousers and a man's jacket, that contrasted strikingly with her smooth ashen hair gathered into a demure bun at the back of her head. After offering me whisky and cigarettes, she plunged into a highly technical philosophical conversation or rather monologue, for I understood nothing of her no doubt very learned remarks.

When she realized that I could not follow her into these heights, she gradually descended into lower regions, and finally came to earth on the subject of her landlady and the room. The latter was, indeed, available, and the landlady was charming. The only drawback was that there was no bathroom and that I might not find the place very clean. But I had no choice, so I moved in the next day.

I found it somewhat disconcerting that the landlady, making up the bed in my presence, unfolded each sheet, turned it slowly round before my eyes, and said in a deliberately refined voice, sniffing appreciatively at every word: "All quite clean, indeed, perfectly clean." I had never before seen sheets looking such a dusty grey, and they seemed to exude a strange, musty smell; however, I hoped that they had at least not been used for another occupant without being washed. The same performance was repeated when she unfolded the towels. She then spread a torn piece of coarse lace of the same greyish color that distinguished her other linen over the iron washstand. "I will bring you a jug of hot water at night, and a nice little something for your breakfast and your supper." It was perhaps just as well her lodgers were not even allowed a glance into her kitchen, the door of which was always kept firmly closed.

It was the smells of the place that defeated me. I dreaded going to bed, because the sheets seemed to have been wound around decomposing corpses (had she perhaps poisoned mice, whose bodies were putrefying in her linen cupboard?), and I simply had to cease wiping my face with the towels she provided and to make do with some large handkerchiefs. When, after about ten days, Dr. Cross told me he wanted to engage me definitely, I decided to look for another room. Everybody told me it would be impossible to find one.

It was my first experience of this nightmarish business, room-hunting in Oxford. But I had the luck of beginners. I knew all the houses in the neighborhood of St. John Street took in lodgers, so I began simply to ring bells. At the second house the landlord came to the door himself. When he heard I was working at Pusey House, he became very amiable. He had, in fact, a room occupied by a lady who never got up before twelve noon, so that the charwoman had no chance of cleaning it. He was going to turn her out in any case. The place looked a paradise of cleanliness after my purgatory of smells and dirt; the price was reasonable. It almost seemed too good to be true.

Before going back to Ditchling to pack up the rest of my belongings, I visited my mother, who could hardly believe that I had at last secured a definite job, even though the salary was barely enough for me to make ends meet. I promised her to find her some work in Oxford, so that we could be together.

It was a very quiet and pleasantly uneventful life to

which I now settled down. I worked partly in the Library, partly in Dr. Cross' sitting room where I had a typewriter, as I was also doing some secretarial work for him at times. Besides, I continued to write articles, mainly for Blackfriars, and did some typing for its Editor. He asked me one morning would I like to help Mr. Christopher Dawson, who needed somebody to type the manuscript of his new book for him. Dr. Cross agreed that I might take two mornings a week off to go to Boars Hill.

It was yet another secretarial experience for me. I found Mr. Dawson nearly as alarming as Mr. Pepler though in a different way. He was nervous, in bad health; as often as not Mrs. Dawson would ring up early in the morning to say he had been unable to work since I had been there last, and so there was nothing for me to do; in which case I would go to Pusey House. I began to feel that I really was not, and never would be, a competent secretary. I suppose writers rarely are. The perfect secretary should be completely devoted to her boss, readily admire his ideas and make his interests her own. I had my head full of my own views and ideas, and I am constitutionally less ready to admire than to criticize. While typing a manuscript my thoughts go their own ways, and so there is normally a generous sprinkling of errors. After I had finished typing Mr. Dawson's manuscript, he had no more work for me; and this was the end of my secretarial career altogether.

Before Christmas I, or rather our parish priest, had found a job for my mother in Oxford, to do the housekeeping for a Catholic lady who ran a boarding house. She was happy once more to live at least in the same city as I; she would have been less happy had she known what was going on in my mind at this time.

Since my early reading of St. John of the Cross and St. Teresa, the Carmelite way of life had attracted me. To devote oneself completely to silence and prayer, to self-abnegation and communion with God, surely was the highest goal of human existence. Was God calling me to this?

I knew there was a Carmelite convent in Oxford; and while I had been at Ditchling I had the idea that, if I secured the job at the Greek Lexicon, I might later enter the Oxford Carmel. Early in 1942 I mentioned the subject to Father Geddes. He said I could not do it, because I should have to look after my mother. I therefore tried to put the matter out of my head, but found this impossible. I kept on praying that some way might be found for me to follow what I then thought to be my vocation.

Mother and I often discussed religion. She would like to be a Catholic, she said, but there was so much of what she called compulsion. One day I invited Father Conrad to tea to meet her, with the result that she consented to have some further instructions from him.

When I went to see Father Geddes again, about three months after our first conversation on the subject, he asked me whether I was still thinking of the religious life. I said I was.

"Your mother is supporting herself by her work, isn't she?"

"Oh yes, she is. In fact I could not possibly support her at the moment, since I am earning barely enough for myself."

"In this case, I think you may go."

Though I had been praying for this all the time, the sudden reversal came quite unexpected. I realized only later that Father Geddes had been testing me when he turned down my first suggestion. It seemed almost too wonderful to be true that I should really be allowed to become a Carmelite—yet I was afraid at the same time. It is no easy thing for a woman of my age to shut herself up for life behind a double grille. But if God wanted it, I was sure He would give me the strength to do it.

Immediately after my conversation with Father Geddes I went to see the Prioress of the Oxford Carmel; or rather I went to hear her, for she spoke from behind a shuttered grille. She was quite ready to accept me, though I had no dowry and was well over thirty. But I should not be able to enter until I had been in the Church for two years; such were the regulations. This would bring it to the spring of next year.

I was very happy. I now often spent my free Saturday afternoons in the convent chapel, where I said Vespers with the nuns. I cannot say I enjoyed the Carmelite way of mono-toning the Office, especially as I often went to the Dominican church where they sang Compline every night. I had come to love plain chant; however, it would be just one more sacrifice demanded of me in Carmel.

To my great joy my mother was received into the Church in July. This, I hoped, would also make it easier for her when the time came to tell her of my decision.

I could not afford a proper holiday this year; so I went to Begbroke, a small village just outside Oxford, for ten days in August. There is a Servite monastery there; and I once more knelt before the image of Our Lady of Sorrows, as I had done so often in London before my conversion; I went for walks in the woods and prayed a good deal. If I should miss one thing in Carmel more than anything else it would be the freedom to go for walks—I knew that. However, this, too, would have to be left to God. No use worrying about such things beforehand.

The Carmelites have fires normally only in the com-munity room, where they are for two hours every day. All the rest of the convent is without heating, and the extern sisters, who keep up the communications with the outside world, were telling me gruesome stories of having to break the ice on the water of their washing bowls and on the holy water in chapel.

I knew the cold would be the worst physical hardship for me, since I had always had bad circulation. So when autumn was turning into winter this year, I determined to get used to it in good time. Owing to the war there was no adequate central heating in Pusey House, but Dr. Cross had an electric fire in his room. Whenever he came in, he would find me sitting with my coat on, but without the fire. "For goodness' sake turn the fire on, you cannot work in this cold." But I, my blue fingers belying my words, replied bravely that I was quite warm, thank you, and it was really much more healthy to sit in the cold.

At home, too, I was not allowed to practise my austerities without attracting attention. A friendly room-neighbor noticed that I never put on the gas fire, which she thought was due to my lack of shillings for the meter. "You must have a fire, I'll give you a shilling now, come on." It was, indeed, difficult to try to be a Carmelite in the world.

My greatest fear was how my mother would react to my vocation. I knew there would be a most painful struggle; for I was realizing only too well what it must mean to her to be left in a foreign country without the support of her only child. Apart from the consent of my director, my only justification was in the words of our Lord: "He that loveth father or mother more than me is not worthy of me." Father Conrad therefore suggested that I take my mother to see the Dominican nuns at Headington, who were also enclosed behind a grille, though not quite so severe as the Carmelites. She would find them to be very gay and charming, and so she might perhaps gradually grow used to the idea of her daughter joining a similar community.

Shortly after Christmas Mother and I went there. The nuns knew the purpose of our coming, gave us tea in the parlor, and did all they could to show my mother that they were very happy, perfectly normal women, though they were leading such, to her, incomprehensible life.

"Aren't they nice?" I asked, as we were walking back through the park.

"Oh yes, yes. But why did you take me there? You don't want to go to such a place, do you?" The cat was out of the bag. I had better tell her here and now and get it over.

The reaction was even worse than I had anticipated.

"When are you going?"

"Beginning of May."

Then the storm broke. No joy left in life; she would go into the river. How could a child be so cruel to a mother.

I saw that it had been a mistake to tell her so long in advance; for the following months were an agony for both of us. Her only consolation was that her landlady told her hardly anybody ever stayed in that convent, and I certainly would soon be out again.

15. *Carmelite Experiment*[*]

IT HAD been decided that I should enter the convent the Monday after the Octave of Easter, which, in that year, was May the third. I knew it would make things even more difficult if I spent the last days at Oxford with my mother; so I decided to give up my room a fortnight before, be in London for Holy Week and Easter, see Father Geddes once more, and then stay for a few days in Cambridge with my doctor uncle and his wife, who had come to England to join their son soon after my mother.

Naturally they could not understand at all what I was about to do. They were sorry I had been so unhappy that the only end to what they thought must have been a completely frustrated life was an enclosed convent. That I did not look particularly frustrated made the whole thing even more incomprehensible. They looked terribly sad when they saw me off at the station.

I had a last hour with Mother in Oxford; she sounded

[*] The experiences I am about to describe were rather unfortunate and are by no means to be taken as representative of the Carmelite life. I still have the greatest admiration for Carmel and all it stands for, and I consider it a privilege to count several Carmelite nuns among my close friends.

almost unconcerned when she said goodbye to me; but I knew that beneath this seeming indifference there was a bitterness that utterly refused to accept.

"Come and have your last cup of tea before you enter," said one of the extern sisters. "Once you are in, there will be only water."

So I had tea with them in their little whitewashed parlor. Then a bell rang; I was taken to the enclosure door. When it opened, three nuns threw back their veils and embraced me. I could not help noticing that one of them had a number of her teeth out. This would be my fate, too, in a very short time; for I had bad teeth that were preserved only by my Austrian dentist's skill.

Then the key turned in the lock. My God, was I really to be shut up here for life? My throat seemed to be turning into one big lump, my heart beat furiously. What on earth was the matter? Had I not wanted to be locked up in Carmel, to be alone only with God and the Sisters? I could not imagine why I felt as if I had been laid into my coffin alive. Only later it dawned on me that I was in the throes of a violent fit of claustrophobia.

I was first shown my cell. I liked it. It was small, extremely austere: a bed covered with a brown rug, a stool, a sewing basket, a folder for papers, a large cross without the figure of Christ—because the Carmelite herself was to be stretched out on it, symbolically. It was very peaceful, and for a moment my claustrophobia subsided. It reappeared worse than before when I was led into the refectory. I was quite prepared for the skull before the Prioress' place, to remind us of the transitoriness of this earthly life. What disconcerted me was the community, lined up in two rows opposite each other, in their stiff brown habits and black veils, gravely bowing, reciting prayers in a toneless voice—it seemed like a scene from another world, I was overwhelmed by a sense of utter unreality. Was it possible that I should spend my life in this eerie atmosphere—were these really women of flesh and blood like myself?

At least they eat and drank, and the food was less penitential than I had anticipated. For this monastery belonged to what is known as the Nottinghill Carmels, a group of over forty convents that had been founded by a French Carmelite, Mother Mary of Jesus, who had evidently imported French cookery recipes. She had also imported other, to my mind less desirable things, as I was soon to find out.

After the meal there was evening recreation. I was still in my grey costume, feeling more secular than ever; for it is the custom that a newcomer should continue in her worldly clothes the day of her entering. We were sitting in a circle on the floor; I on a hassock, the others had rolled part of their habit into a sort of cushion on which they were half kneeling, half squatting. For Carmelites are never allowed to lean against anything; this, together with the sudden deprivation of all stimulants such as tea or coffee, and the lack of fresh vegetables and fruit, was among the greatest physical hardships for me. After the dumbshow in the refectory recreation was a relief. As the others did not appear to be much inclined to talk I released some of the strain that oppressed me by a flood of chatter which the community seemed to find entertaining.

Recreation was followed by Compline. The Prioress had appointed someone she called the holiest nun in the community to be my "angel." This is an older Sister whose duty it is to introduce the newcomer to the conventual customs, to show her where to go and how to behave. My "angel" was an old nun with a very sweet face, of great kindness and gentleness. She led me into choir and showed me my place; "And from here you can always see our Mother (the Prioress is called 'our Mother' in Carmel), and this will be such a consolation to you."

I was thoroughly shocked. It is one of the deliberate privations of Carmel that the nuns' choir is separated from the altar by a grille, the shutters of which are opened only at Mass and Benediction. It would have been a consolation to me to be able to see the Tabernacle—did the good Sister expect me to put the Prioress in the place of Christ?

At nine I was sent to bed, before the rest of the Community assembled once more to recite Matins and Lauds. The bed, too, is a penitential affair in Carmel; but I succeeded in sleeping on it for a few hours without falling off it—a sure mark of vocation, as I was told later.

The great St. Teresa was a great lover of cleanliness. Therefore she provided for her nuns to wash every morning in about a pint of cold water, which was poured from a brown jug into a small tin bowl standing on a piece of brown paper on the floor. Once a week they were, moreover, allowed a hot foot bath. These were, indeed, satisfactory arrangements for sixteenth-century Spain. They were still the same in twentieth-century England. The convent was a converted private house, and there was a magnificent bathroom. But the bath was boarded up. The Prioress considered baths for Carmelites nothing short of heresy. And in these Nottinghill-founded convents, which were not part of the Carmelite Order, the will of the Prioress reigned supreme.

Yet I liked the Prioress. She was a highly intelligent woman of great understanding; but for her, I should probably have left even earlier than I did. She acted also as novice mistress, so I saw much more of her than of any of the others, to whom I was allowed to talk only during recreation. She was very austere herself; but she fully understood my difficulties; for, so she told me, she herself had found the Carmelite life extremely difficult at first, having, like me, entered late in life; for she was a convert, and a widow. "And look at me now."

Yes, certainly. She was Prioress now. But I could also see that she was incredibly strained; even her laughter—and she laughed quite often—seemed forced. No, I did not want to become like her. I wanted to expand, not to be repressed. However, once the claustrophobia would have worn off I might see things differently. I would not leave under the first impact of shock.

The Prioress herself told me I was suffering from shock. I was always in tears; my eyes were just streaming, I did not know why. Prayer was impossible; during the free period in the afternoon I went into the garden with a book, but I would just stare at the open pages without reading anything. The garden was extremely small, for the convent stood between two main thoroughfares, and the space had been further restricted by an intermediary wall, necessary to protect us from being overlooked from the upper deck of the buses that were constantly passing. As I was sitting listlessly on my backless seat, I could hear the radio from the neighboring houses, the noise of the traffic in Banbury Road, the children playing outside—was I really to be shut up for life in this place? Could God want this of me?

Things were made worse by the lack of reasonableness I met at every turn. As the Subprioress saw me sweeping the stairs on my second day she gave me a sermon on how difficult, but all the more meritorious, this very humiliating occupation was. She had entered the convent at the age of eighteen, well before the first World War; it was quite impossible for me to make it clear to her that I had done quite a lot of sweeping in my life, that it would never have occurred to me to consider this or any other occupation humiliating. It was useless, she simply could not understand. I heard much later that the story had been spread among other Carmelite convents that I had left because I had found sweeping the stairs too much for me!

If I found one occupation there difficult, it was not sweeping, but the very ladylike one of cutting altarbreads. Providing wafers for Holy Communion to the various Catholic churches was one of the main sources of income for the community. The lay sisters did the making; the other nuns cut them out with small cutting machines and counted them into cardboard containers. It was totally mechanical work. I was told it was so wonderful to think, while you were cutting out the wafers, that they would all be turned into the Body of Christ, and to pray for those people who were going to receive them. I was trying my best to fill my recalcitrant imagination with these pious reflections. No good. My mind simply refused to work on these lines. Instead I was wondering how much longer I could stand it all without going crazy.

After four or five days I felt sufficiently composed to write a letter to Father Geddes to tell him about my difficulties. From the first I was trying to do everything exactly like the others; so I had discarded my fountain pen and intended to use the pen and ink provided in my cell. I seized the inkpot—but had failed to realize that the top was far too large for the bottle—and there the former was still in my hand, while the pot had overturned on the floor, spilling the ink in all directions over the white, well scrubbed boards.

I dashed to the washing place—with the boarded-up bath—trying to find a swapcloth. Nothing at all to be seen, except one minute flannel. I tried one or two cupboards—they were all locked. The only thing to do was to call my "angel" to deal with the situation.

This was no longer the older Sister, who had never remembered to tell me the things I did not know, so that I had been constantly missing from where I should have been. After only two days of her activities I had been turned over to the youngest choir sister, who was at the same time the most rigid rule incarnate that can be imagined. I had rarely seen anyone so prim and proper in my life. Though there are no mirrors in Carmel, she was always turned out just so, not a hair showing under her veil, her scapular exactly in the center, her wimple folded with mathematical accuracy. Besides, there was always a large drop of water right in the center of her forehead. At first I could not make out what it was or how it had got there; it greatly intrigued me. It certainly did not belong to the Carmelite habit, since the others did not wear this drop. Then I noticed that she would dip her finger into every single holy water stoup she was passing—and there were holy water stoups in every possible and impossible place in the convent—and sign herself with the sign of the cross. When she came into my cell she dipped her finger into the holy water at its entrance, when she came out after a few seconds she dipped again, passing into the refectory she dipped, back into her cell she dipped—hence the drop was kept everfresh.

This person I had now to find in order to confess my mishap and ask for her assistance. She was shocked. The lovely white floor! But, what was apparently far worse, I had been so independent as to go looking for a cloth, without having asked anyone's permission! She was standing before me, every inch a governess in a religious habit: "You cannot do things without permission in Carmel. I will now go to our Mother and ask her permission to use some Vim and a swapcloth. You wait here till I come back."

Needless to say, the ink had run by this time well over the precious white boards and was seeping in ever more deeply. So a fully professed nun was not even allowed the responsibility to mop up some ink! When she came back at last, armed with all the necessary permissions, at least twenty minutes after the ink bottle had dropped from my hands, I should have liked to take the cloth from her to wipe up the mess I had made myself. Not so. She had been told to do it; and she was now kneeling on the floor, wiping away with all the vigor and precision that were hers. As I was standing behind her I knew—I could almost hear her think it—that she was at this moment rejoicing in the humiliation of having to kneel before the little postulant mopping up the ink I had spilt, offering it up for the salvation of souls, as we were told to offer our humiliations for the salvation of souls in all the approved spiritual books. It was all very right, yes, I knew— but so terribly obvious.

I did not write to Father Geddes that day.

In general, I think, I came fairly near to being a model postulant. I never asked for any relaxation. Not even when I was nearly driven out of my mind by the book that was being read at meals. It was the story of the vocation of a Dominican artist, and when I entered, they had just arrived at the part, which went on day after day, that described his sorrow to have to leave his mother. This was my own greatest difficulty; the Prioress knew I had just got the first heart-breaking letter from my mother; but these readings were continued, presumably as an additional austerity, even after I had once sobbed uncontrollably throughout the meal. The supernatural outlook can be exaggerated; but I was as little inclined to give in and ask for the reading to be stopped as the Prioress evidently was to make the concession without my request.

After the total inability to pray, the unreasonableness of it all continued to be my greatest difficulty. Many of the Sisters seemed to be living by the letter of the law with a vengeance. When working together we were not allowed to speak, except for the most necessary remarks immediately concerning our work. All during May we went at noon before a statue of our Lady and sang a hymn to her. But one morning the whole routine of the monastery was changed, because it was washing day. I did not know whether the hymn would also be left out. So just before twelve, while I was cutting altar breads with one of the nuns, I asked her if we were going to sing this morning. Instead of answering simply Yes or No, she replied gravely: "I cannot tell you this. You must ask your angel." You see, it did not immediately concern the work we were doing! So I had to rush through the house to find my angel, and was late for the hymn in consequence.

We had no electricity in our cells, but the same Spanish oil lamps that had been in use in St. Teresa's monasteries in the sixteenth century. We had electricity in choir, but, to my consternation, there were open gas arms in the passages. When I asked the reason I was told that the electric light there had been removed in order to install gas arms, because "our beloved Mother" (the French foundress, as distinct from "our holy Mother," St. Teresa) had had them in her convent in her youth and had apparently inflicted them on the houses she had founded. What would St. Teresa, this supremely sensible woman, have said to all this? I felt I was constantly walking from one century into the other: oil lamps, gas arms, electric light; minute tin bowls to wash in, but up-to-date sanitation—and boarded-up baths on a Saturday afternoon!

This was the time when we were turning out our cells to give them a good spring cleaning. Not that we were using any water for that; for water, though as plentiful in the tap as anywhere else in twentieth-century England, was used as economically as it presumably was in sixteenth-century Avila, where it had to be laboriously drawn from the convent well. The first thing I was instructed to do was to shut the window of my cell; this, too, probably necessary in Spain —but in England! Then, so the detailed "angelic" instructions ran, all the furniture of the cell (not much, thank Heaven!) except the bed had to be moved outside the door. After which I had to take the broom and sweep in certain, also exactly prescribed directions, the ubiquitous dust into a neat monastic heap, whence it had to be transferred to the tiniest dustpan I had ever seen. It had been explained to me with great pride that these shovels—really only a piece of tin slightly turned up at the sides—were exact replicas of those used by "our holy Mother." I quite believed it; but I simply could not induce the dust to stay on the wretched thing; no sooner had I got any on to it than it fell off the other side. If only the holy Mother had come back to earth—wouldn't she have sent the outsister to Woolworth to buy us some ordinary dustpans!

Instead of on the shovel most of the dust seemed to settle down on me. When I had eventually finished, put the things back in my cell and emptied what fluff I had cajoled into staying on the pan, I felt myself smothered with it. Dust in my hair, throat, lungs, nose, eyes, dust in every single pore. A bath, a bath, a kingdom for a bath—but there was the bath, boarded up, because the Prioress thought bathing a heresy.

Did the Lord want dirty brides? I went into choir to say Vespers, bathed in perspiration.

Then there were Mother Subprioress' chickens. She looked after them, and they were her only topic of conversation, except when she had chats with St. Joseph, with whom she seemed to be on enviably familiar terms. She had given a name to every one of the chickens, which she claimed to be able to distinguish from each other at sight; and whenever she presided at recreation, she would tell us endless stories, mimicking the way in which they raised or bent their darling little heads, making up veritable conversations she pretended to have had with them. If someone dies in Carmel, she is referred to as having "gone to God." The chickens were no exception. "You see, they miss the chicken that went to God." I began to wonder whether Mother Subprioress' heaven was, perhaps, peopled also with haloed chickens.

Mother had been several times to the convent to ask how I was, but steadfastly refused to see me behind the grille. The outsisters told her I was very well and happy. She did not believe it. She was right.

The Prioress, no doubt to comfort me—she was most sympathetic throughout—told me she was sure I was already saving souls, as I had so much to suffer. If I had been able to work myself up into a sufficiently *exalté* state of mind to believe that, I might perhaps have stayed—and left five years later, with a nervous breakdown of the first magnitude. But, for good or ill, I have never been able to kid myself with this kind of pious illusion. The Prioress put my state down to the temptations of the devil—I to the intolerable strain of a life for which I was in no wise fitted.

To give me some relief, my "angel" was once more changed. The place of my governess with the holy water drop was taken by the nun I liked best: a very motherly, gentle, balanced Sister, with a good deal of common sense. Though she, too, would talk to me in the baby language that seemed to be *de rigueur* for postulants even of my mature age. When I had poured water into half a dozen jugs in the refectory I was invariably rewarded with a "You have done that very nicely, little Sister," in tones normally reserved for those under three.

I have a suspicion that this kind of childish talk is due to a misunderstanding of St. Thérèse of Lisieux's "Way of Spiritual Childhood." Much later a nun of Edith Stein's Carmel in Cologne (otherwise a convent of a very different spirit from the one I was in) wrote to me that Carmelites must just be "happy children," and that Edith Stein had become such in Carmel, an assertion belied by her own letters. St. Teresa of Avila spoke a very different language. She wanted her nuns to be "not women, but strong men." It is, indeed, much easier to be childish than to be childlike, and baby talk is no substitute for the authentic way of spiritual childhood, but may well bar the way to spiritual maturity.

"If the Lord does not want you in Carmel," the Prioress said one morning after about three weeks, "He will send you a sign of His will, some illness for example." As I was taking off my stockings that same night I stared incredulously at my ankles. They were swollen to an extraordinary size; the first time this had ever happened. Was this, could it be, a sign of God's will?

When I told the Prioress of it next morning—they had gone down by then—she had apparently forgotten all about the "sign," but said the outsisters would ring up the doctor (there was no telephone in the house) to examine me.

He never came; but my ankles continued to be swollen every night. Mother wrote to me once a week, one letter more desperate than the other. The outsisters still assured her I was extremely happy. Two days after me another postulant had entered, a former Anglican nun. The Prioress had thought her vocation doubtful, but was perfectly convinced of the reality of mine. So was the whole community to the last lay Sister. So had Father Geddes been, who replied by comforting letters to my cries of despair.

On the Thursday of my fourth week in Carmel we had a kind of herring for dinner that seemed to be inordinately full of bones, and besides gave me a feeling of sickness, which I just contrived to keep down. Then, to my surprise, the other postulant left the table. Was she perhaps actually being sick?

As the two of us were sitting in the novitiate room that afternoon waiting for the Prioress to give us an instruction (we were, of course, supposed to be keeping complete silence), I could bear it no longer.

"That herring" I whispered.

"Yes," she replied, "I was actually sick."

"Were you really? I felt like being, but just managed not to."

We exchanged a few more remarks on the difficulty of the life; then the Prioress appeared.

"You have been talking to the other postulant just now."

"Yes, Mother."

I did not make the slightest attempt to kiss the ground

or perform any other act of penitence prescribed in Carmel on such occasions.

"You know this is not allowed, don't you."

I said nothing. If I had opened my mouth I knew I should have screamed. It took my last strength to bite my teeth together. She evidently realized that I had reached the limit of my endurance and spoke of something else.

When I came into choir for meditation at five next morning, something within me suddenly said: "This is the end. Carmel is not for me. I have to go. I have to go now." And with this a peace came over me such as I had never felt in all these troubled weeks. The Prioress had offered to ask Father Geddes to come from London to talk to me. Father Conrad had actually been there one afternoon and quieted me for about half an hour. But I now knew with absolute certainty that nothing anybody could say would make me stay. It was difficult, indeed, to set my own sure knowledge that I was not meant for this against the unanimous opinion of the nuns and my director that I had a Carmelite vocation—but there it was. There was no mistaking the intense joy, calm, and relief that invaded me as soon as I had made up my mind to leave.

After Mass I slipped a note under the door of the Prioress' cell, informing her of my decision. Then I went into the garden to hang out some washing—with a song in my heart, so happy that I thought I might, perhaps, stay after all. But at the very idea all the darkness of the last weeks seemed to return.

The Prioress came to see me. She was coolly polite. "Of course you must know what you are doing." She sounded as if I were going straight to hell. Nevertheless, she was very concerned that I might have nowhere to sleep, Oxford being still as crowded as ever.

"Never mind, I shall find something."

"But have at least something to eat before you leave."

"No, thank you. I can't eat. I must go at once."

Once more the three nuns came to the door; the keys were rattling. The heavy door opened. I was free. There was the road, the buses, the people, in short: "the wicked world." And I loved it!

16. *Austerity Time —*
National and Individual

NATURALLY my first visit was to my mother. After we had been sobbing a while in each other's arms, she said. "You know, I have an idea your room it still vacant. I have never seen the window open or the curtains drawn back when I passed there."

It seemed incredible that a room in the center of over-crowded Oxford should have remained untenanted for six weeks. Nevertheless, I went there. Yes, the room was free; the landlord had stored some furniture in it.

"Can I have it back, do you think?"

"When do you want to come?"

"This evening."

"All right. It will be ready for you."

A minor miracle, surely. Now to get my job back, something I was pretty sure would not be difficult. Dr. Cross seemed only too pleased to see me again. It did indeed look as if my place "in the world" had been kept open for me. At night I plunged into the most wonderful—and necessary—bath I had ever had.

I was determined not to go to hell as the only alternative to Carmel. What surprised me was the unsettling effect these

barely four weeks had on me. The difference between life in
a completely enclosed convent and the modern world is so
great, that even a short spell as a postulant is bound to throw
one off balance. With some this takes the form of drowning
themselves in a whirl of amusements. I went to the opposite
extreme. I was trying at first to live like a nun in the world.
I had my long black postulant's dress made into an ill-fitting
costume; instead of hats I wore headscarves, to the horror of
my mother, to whom this was still a symbol of nunnery, and
I would firmly avert my eyes from any shopwindow displaying fashions, quite an effort for someone who had once
wanted to be a fashion journalist and never lost her interest
in clothes. It was a help that austerity was the order of the
day in those years of rationing; my own deliberate dowdiness
passed unnoticed in the general lack of elegance.

It was inevitable that, now and again, I should hold a
private *post mortem* on my abortive Carmelite vocation.
One thing was certain: I had none, though I knew the whole
convent was of opinion that I had wickedly turned my back
on it. Even if I had been in a model Carmel, I did not think
I could have stayed. I was simply incapable of living shut up
with fifteen to twenty other women. Later I have often sat
in the parlors of other Carmelite convents, chatting with
charming, highly intelligent, lively Prioresses and their nuns.
But if I asked myself: Would I like to be here, behind this
grille? a cold shiver would run down my spine.

While I had been a postulant I was in too abnormal a
state of nerves to reflect much on what I observed. This came
now. I could see more and more clearly the wisdom of the
Church which insists on preached retreats, conferences, and
complete freedom for enclosed nuns to consult priests other
than the regular confessors of the community. "Our beloved
Mother" had been riding roughshod over the provisions of
Canon Law; in her convents the Prioress was an absolute

queen in her small realm, and unlimited power is perhaps more dangerous even to women than to men.

Moreover, women are far more conservative than men; to make even the most necessary adaptations required by changed conditions of place or time is regarded as a betrayal of the ideals of the holy foundress, even though she herself would have been the first to demand them.

In later years I have heard much discussion about the crisis in the religious vocations especially of women. Often this is attributed to the instability of the modern girl, her lack of enthusiasm and materialistic outlook. I do not think there ever has been a time when the older generation has not accused the younger of exactly these failings. My own experience, and what I have seen of contemporary young women, seem to point to a different cause. Between the foundation of nearly all the women's orders—dating from the Middle Ages to the nineteenth century—and our own days, there has occurred the emancipation of women. We no longer emerge from the shelter of our parents' home only to be received into the protection of a husband or, alternatively, a convent. We are now trained for a profession; we know independence and responsibility; we have shown our mettle—surely not our lack of stability—in two major wars. We are used to being taken seriously and expect to be trusted just like men.

Yet, on entering a convent, women immediately become minors, and in all too many cases, in contrast with the male religious, remain minors throughout their lives unless they are made superiors. Or else how is it possible that a fully professed nun should have to ask the formal permission of her superior to mop up some ink spilt on the floor?

It is true, this was an extreme case. But I have rarely been with a woman superior in the parlor for more than twenty minutes without a knock on the door, and an ensuing whispered consultation on some immediate problem incapable of being resolved by anyone except Reverend Mother. I have also frequently had conversations with superiors of men's communities—yet never have there been any such interruptions. Evidently the men are expected to get on with their jobs on their own responsibility, whereas the women are not.

This failure to develop an adult outlook often shows itself also in an unwholesomely sentimental devotional life. Once I was visiting a nun friend of mine. As soon as she came into the parlor, she threw herself into my arms, sobbing disconsolately.

"What has happened?" I asked, afraid that some major disaster had occurred.

"Oh, it is quite terrible—I am no longer sacristan!"

I stared at her incredulously. "Is that all? What on earth does it matter?"

"But just think, I am no longer allowed to prepare the altar linen for our Lord. . . ."

It was typical. Being sacristan is a much coveted job in women's convents, because it provides ample food for pious imaginings of helping our Lady laying the Infant Jesus in the crib and so forth.

This attitude, which is very unhealthy and, as in the present case, leads rather to pious egoism than to true charity, seems to be actually encouraged in some quarters. For about the same time I had a similar experience with an intelligent, lively young Scots girl, who entered a teaching order. From the first letter she wrote to me from the convent I was unable to find the girl whom I had known "in the world." Everything was pious commonplaces, the lovely flowers on the altar at Benediction, the beautiful vestments, the helpful retreat of Father So-and-So, the heavenly peace . . . It was really distressing to see how a fresh, open girl was being cast into a spiritual mould that did not suit her character at all besides being sentimental rather than spiritual. I have never seen this happening with men; the Jesuits are popularly thought to be mercilessly conditioned till they are all the same; but I have known a good many of them of the most amazing variety of character, ideas, outlook, and behavior. It seems that at least in some orders new methods are needed to fit the new situation of women's social status in order to attract modern girls to the religious life and prevent the latter from using methods of devotional automation.

As far as I myself was concerned, however, it did not seem that God meant me to work out my salvation in a convent. It was to be the Lexicon of Patristic Greek for me—and a very purgatorial kind of work it was, looking up references all day long, without even the consolation of pious motivation! Yet this I now did for another twelve years, proving at least to my own satisfaction, if to no one else's, that my failure to stay in Carmel had not been entirely due to "the modern woman's lack of stability."

This monotonous work was suddenly interrupted on my mother's next birthday, the first of April. We had not yet been able to find a home together, as in 1944 Oxford was as crowded with evacuees as ever. My last memory of the day is that I went to see her in the morning and asked her to come to my room at four in the afternoon to have a birthday tea. A fortnight later I found myself lying immovable in a hospital bed, with a sensation in my head as if a sword had been driven right through it.

When my mother had come into my room on her birthday she had found me lying on my bed, just sufficiently conscious to ask for a doctor, before falling into a coma. The doctor whom the landlord finally ran to earth—it was a Saturday—diagnosed cerebral haemorrhage. So my mother, whose last birthday had been overshadowed by my decision to enter Carmel, had this time to take me in an ambulance to the Radcliffe Infirmary, where she was told it was uncertain whether I should regain consciousness. On the next day, Palm Sunday, I received Extreme Unction while still unconscious.

I have never quite understood what actually happened during the next fortnight. I came out of my coma that same afternoon, asking where I was and evidently immediately remembering that the day before had been my mother's birthday, for I told her, as she was sitting by my bed, that I was sorry I had made it such a bad day for her. During the next two weeks I was told that I slept a good deal, but when I was awake I spoke perfectly normally, knew that I had bought chocolates for some friends for Easter, and asked Mother to send them on, had letters read to me and commented on them, thanked people who were bringing me flowers.

Yet, when I finally came to, I remembered nothing of all this. I told Mother I was so sorry that those friends of mine had not got their Easter presents.

"Why are you worrying about that? They have got them."

"But how could they?"

"You asked me to send them on and I have done so."

"I? Asked you? Impossible."

I asked had there been no letters. No, none. Only three weeks later, when I was once more able to move my arms, I pulled out the drawer of the table beside my bed and found several letters which had been slit open. I read them—I was quite certain I knew nothing whatever about them. Next time my mother came I asked her why she had never told me about these letters, and why they had been opened.

"But you know all about them! They came at the beginning of your illness; you asked me to read them to you, and I did."

I gave it up. In the intervals of consciousness during these weeks my memory had obviously been working perfectly, yet when I finally regained my normal state of mind everything that had happened during the first fortnight of my illness was completely blotted out. It was quite difficult to make my mother realize this; for she would refer to what I had then said, and could not understand that I knew nothing about it.

Many years later, when I had to investigate a case of stigmatization which, among other strange happenings, involved a similar loss of memory, I remembered this illness and was less inclined than other writers on the subject to attribute it to supernatural intervention.

After seven weeks in the hospital, it took me many months to regain my strength. Fortunately the doctors told me my illness, whatever its cause which they had been unable to ascertain, was not due to nervous strain but had been completely organic. As soon as I should be restored to my normal state of health, I could work as much as I liked; there was no question of a relapse.

It was a wonderful summer that year, and Dr. Cross allowed me to take my books out into a secluded part of the garden of Pusey House and work there. I had been given something new to do for him. Besides the Patristic Lexicon he was also editing a popular reference work, *The Oxford Dictionary of the Christian Religion,* and I had been temporarily assigned to writing articles for that, a much more congenial task than looking up references for the Greek Lexicon, and through which I learned, incidentally, a good deal of theology which stood me in good stead later on. Pusey House garden, then not yet partially converted into garages, was a most peaceful place to convalesce in, while doing as much work as I could stand without fatigue. Its red wall was lined with fig trees which even bore fruit; from time to time the old gardener would come to cut the lawn and tend the flowers and we would have a chat; and every morning, as soon as I was settling down on my bench, a cat would appear, jump on to the seat beside me and demand to be stroked.

She did not like it if I became too absorbed in my reading. Then she would gently get up and try to establish herself on the *Dictionnaire de Théologie Catholique* or another learned tome I was just consulting, and be most indignant if I tipped the book so that she landed on the path in front of me.

In August I went to a convent of German missionary nuns near Stoke-on-Trent. They took in guests, as their ordinary work of training missionaries had been interrupted by the war. Here I was given a most romantic abode. For the community was housed in a medieval castle, and one of its old towers had been made inhabitable. There I was lodged, quite by myself, in an octagonal room with thick stone walls pierced by small windows that looked out over the magnificent garden. I felt like a heroine out of a novel of Walter Scott.

I was the only nonpermanent guest; the others were mostly old ladies, evacuated there for the duration. One of them was a retired Irish schoolmistress. She would go into the convent chapel or the adjoining small parish church twice a day to say her prayers, which took exactly forty-five minutes. She really said, or rather sibilated them, nonstop, and what greatly intrigued me was that in the course of her uninterrupted and, apparently, rather one-sided conversation with the Lord she would suddenly hiss about a dozen times: "Sweetheart . . . Sweetheart . . . Sweetheart. . . ." I wondered what this incongruous-sounding expression could possibly mean. Next time she came into the chapel when I was there, I frankly abandoned all pretence to be praying but listened. After a time there it was again: "Sweetheart . . . Sweetheart . . ." But then the whispering became a little louder and at last I understood: "Sweet Heart of Mary, pray for us."

When the Reverend Mother learned that I had lately been trying my Carmelite vocation, she told me that their Congregation, too, had a contemplative branch. I seem to have a certain attraction for Reverend Mothers which, however, is invariably doomed to disappointment. I listened with no more than Platonic interest, though I had a vague feeling that once the war was over I might find out what God really wanted me to do.

My holiday restored me sufficiently to be able gradually to get back to a full day's work. As the end of the war seemed now in sight, editors and publishers began to think of new ventures. Father Conrad was adding a supplement to his periodical *Blackfriars*, called *The Life of the Spirit,* and asked me to write for it a series of articles on Catholic mystics. So, in addition to my Dictionary work at Pusey House, I began now to occupy myself more methodically than I had done before with the great figures of the interior life, Catherine of Siena, Gertrude, Francis de Sales, as well as with the more theoretical problems of infused contemplation and its relation to faith and the gifts of the Holy Ghost.

My friendship with Irene M., which had been very close at the beginning of my Catholic life, had become considerably strained after I had left Carmel. I had written to her rather flippantly in the first flush of my regained freedom, and she had reprimanded me for my levity. It was bad enough that I should have left the convent; but that I should even rejoice in it was more than she could understand. Early in 1945 our friendship broke down completely—over politics. In the February number of *Blackfriars* I read an article entitled "Reflections of a Refugee." The anonymous author (it was signed X.Y.Z.) therein told her English hosts: "I am not sure whether I have learned to love your country. . . . I have learnt many things in your country, my friend . . . your people have taught me to appreciate the value of friendship, though I should never have learnt from them the lesson of love . . . You will always hold a second place in my heart."

It was enough to make me see red. I was a constant contributor to *Blackfriars,* many of its readers knew me, and of course knew that I was German. They would immediately jump to the conclusion that I was the author of this uncalled-for confession—in the middle of the war—of being unable to love England and the English, which, in my case at any rate, was as far from the truth as it could well be. It was typically Teutonic tactlessness—bull-in-the-china-shop, as usual.

I soon enough found out the author. It was my friend Irene. Irene, whose father had been a Bulgarian, herself British by birth, who had spent the first ten years of her life in this country, who, with her British passport, had never known any of the difficulties of us other refugees, our struggle for labor permits, our years of dependence on charitable organizations, on *au pair* domestic jobs—telling the English without even being asked she could not love them. If she must broadcast this to the world, why accept all the advantages of her British nationality? If she had at least had the courage to sign her name to these sentiments! My fury exploded in a letter to her in which I mentioned all these points. She replied with some irrelevant excuses, and after that our correspondence ceased altogether. I was sorry, as she had been a congenial friend in many ways; and a later *rapprochement* from my side was rejected.

While peace was coming to Europe this spring, my private life became a mess of upheavals. My landlord had sold his house, which was to be turned into a licensed boarding house for undergraduates expected soon to be once more filling the University. For the first time I experienced to the full the worries of room hunting in Oxford. As I had to leave within a fortnight I had not much chance to find something suitable. At last a friend offered me a minute attic as a temporary abode. When I came back to it the third evening after moving in, I found most of its ceiling on the floor. . . .

Next morning I descended into the basement kitchen of

our Jesuit presbytery, where Mother had been acting as housekeeper for the last three years, to inform her of this latest catastrophe. Luckily she remembered that she knew somebody who might give me at least a bedroom for a few weeks. In fact I stayed there for about three months, leading an unpleasantly ambulatory existence, since I could not work there, and so had to do my writing as best I could in Pusey House.

I had had the idea that my vocation would somehow be decided when the war was ended. In May a friend was talking to me about a new contemplative foundation of Dominican Third Order nuns in France. There was no strict enclosure as in Carmel, intellectual work was encouraged, and there would be many opportunities for apostolic activities. It did, indeed, seem most suitable. Just about this time I was going up to London for one of my periodic talks with Father Geddes. Without my even having mentioned the subject he suddenly asked: "Are you again thinking of the religious life?" It seemed providential. I told him of my idea, and he once more approved. So I plucked up courage and wrote to the superior of the community. She wrote back enthusiastically; they were very keen on making a foundation in England, so I should be most welcome, and she hoped I knew some *jeunes filles* ready to join me. As the war was as yet over only in Europe and there would be no possibility for me of going to France in the near future in any case, I gave myself time to consider the matter. The strange coincidence of Father Geddes bringing up the subject just as I was thinking about it seemed to indicate that there was really something in it—yet I had misgivings.

At the end of June I went to the Isle of Wight for a holiday. I was staying at Carisbrooke, near a convent of Dominican contemplative nuns, in whose chapel I prayed a good deal for light to see my way. The Prioress and Subprioress whom I met quite often in the parlor were delightful—yet again I had not the slightest desire to retire behind the grille with them. The French community which I was thinking I might join had no grilles!

After a few days the Prioress asked me to accompany one of the nuns to Guildford, where she had to enter a hospital for an operation. We arrived there in pouring rain. At the station there was no taxi to be seen anywhere. I rushed into a telephone booth trying to ring up a garage—but there was no directory, and no one able to give me any information. After about ten minutes I came back, very flustered, to the nun whom I had left sitting on a bench. She received me with an angelic smile.

"We are going to get a car."

"But how? There is no taxi anywhere in this wretched place."

"Oh, I just said a prayer to the Little Flower (St. Thérèse of Lisieux), and immediately a lady came to offer her car, as she is going the same way. She is outside the station waiting for us."

It was one of those situations that might well have given me an inferiority complex, if I were liable to this psychological disease. Here was I, never thinking of enlisting supernatural assistance, but using all the natural methods of procedure to no effect, getting hot and bothered in the process—and there was this nun with her childlike faith producing a car by simply saying a prayer.

This was not the end of the day, however. On my way back I was sitting alone in a self-contained compartment when, just as the train was beginning to move, a man got in and sat opposite me. I did not like the look of him, and presently he started a conversation, in the course of which he moved over and sat beside me. I instinctively gripped my umbrella more firmly. He suggested he would put it in the rack.

"No, thank you, it's no trouble to me." After all, it was my only weapon should the situation become really unpleasant.

He then informed me he would like to marry me. After about five minutes acquaintance this seemed pretty fast going. "But," he said pensively, "there is the question of religion. You are a Roman Catholic, aren't you."

I stared at him. I was displaying neither a crucifix nor a rosary nor any other outward sign of my religion on my person. "Yes, I am a Catholic—but how do you know that?" He muttered something about its being unmistakable; the only explanation I could think of was that he might have seen me with the nun, or going into the convent, though I had never set eyes on him before.

The rest of the journey was taken up with glowing descriptions of his car in which he would take me around the country both before and after the wedding. "How would *that* be?" he asked after each further addition to the delights to which I was expected to look forward in the course of the courtship.

It was greatly relieved when he eventually got out just before Carisbrooke. There can rarely have been such an uproarious session in the parlor of the Dominican nuns as when I went there in the evening to report on my trip.

"I think the man must have been mad," said Mother Prioress.

"But, Mother, this is very impolite to Miss Graef, isn't it?" quoth Mother Subprioress.

If I had still any doubt whether contemplative nuns could have hysterics as much as other women on such highly irreligious topics, I was quickly disabused.

My holiday helped me little to settle my difficulties about trying once more my vocation. Early in September I had another letter from the French nuns, inviting me to come and stay with them. This definite offer brought me down to earth with a jolt. So far I had been playing with the idea, influenced no doubt by the fact that a good many people still seemed to think I ought to be a nun, despite my failure to stay in Carmel. But now, as I had really to make up my mind whether to go or not to go, everything in me revolted. The very idea of becoming a religious made me miserable. No, it simply could not be done. I could not live together with a crowd of other women—I must be free. I wrote the nuns an apologetic letter that I had been mistaken.

This, now, was final. I was as convinced as ever that I had to realize my desire for prayer in some form—but it had to be done in the world. Besides, I had by then received a very definite hint about what I was really meant to do—only I did not realize that this, too, could be a vocation till much later.

At the end of July I had a letter from an Irish publisher, hitherto unknown to me. "We have been informed by the Editor of Blackfriars," so it ran, "that you are a good writer on mystical matters. Perhaps you might have some manuscript on these subjects suitable for publication in book form. If so we would be glad of an opportunity of considering it."

I stared at the document incredulously. I knew that unknown authors used to send around manuscripts to refractory publishers—and here was I, an author without a manuscript asked by a publisher to submit one. As he mentioned the editor of *Blackfriars*, I went round to see Father Conrad. I greeted him almost indignantly: "What have you done now? Look at this letter. I haven't a manuscript and not the faintest idea what kind of a book I could possibly write."

He grinned at this novel kind of author's predicament. "Why not take the articles you have already written for *Blackfriars* and other reviews, enlarge them a bit, write a few more and an introduction? That should make quite an acceptable book." It did, indeed, seem feasible. I went back to the attic I was occupying at the moment, outlined a plan for grouping together the mystics on whom I had already written and adding a few more, and sent it off to Eire.

I had not yet found a satisfactory abode, and much of my time during these last months had been taken up with answering advertisements and interviewing landladies. One morning early in August I was sitting in the garden of Pusey House reading, when my friend Vera arrived. She was the only German in Oxford I knew, a Jewess who had been converted to High Church Anglicanism, and one of the most kindhearted, and, despite her own poverty, most generous people I have known. "I have just heard of a very nice room being free here round the corner in St. John Street—go there at once."

I had had too many disappointments to be unduly keen. Vera insisted. "Don't be silly—it's only two minutes from here." I put my books back into the library and went. A charming old lady answered my ring. Yes, indeed, she had a room free. She took me up to the first floor and showed me the most comfortable room I had been in since coming to this country—armchairs, settee, bookshelves, two large windows . . . it was clear that the price would be far beyond my means. To my amazement she named a sum just a little more than I had to pay for my present minute attic. It was as perfect a place as Oxford could provide. I could really settle down now to write a book.

The war ended on August 15th, the feast of the Assumption of Our Lady. It seemed almost incredible that there should really be peace. I remember shocking my mother when she rejoiced in what our gallant Russian allies had done, by sombrely prophesying: "Yes. But if there is to be another war, it will be fought with Germany against Russia."

"How can you say such a thing—the Russians are our allies!"

"At the moment—but they won't remain so."

"You are mad to say this."

"I wish I were."

After our sober, really half-hearted rejoicings—after all, there was no question as yet of easing the national austerity regime, and the future was too uncertain—life did, indeed, become different. Dr. Cross had left Pusey House some time ago to become Lady Margaret Professor of Divinity and Canon of Christ Church; he now had the Lexicon material removed to a room in the New Bodleian Library and was going to reorganize the work. It had been carried on in a desultory fashion for almost forty years; the Committee responsible for financing it was gradually losing patience, and Dr. Cross asked me could I suggest other people willing to give their time to it. The rate of pay was now fixed at five shillings an hour; holidays would have to be made up by working overtime!

I did not think it would be easy to find collaborators on such terms, which no trade union would have countenanced; besides, the work demanded many qualifications. Apart from having a good working knowledge of Greek, the Lexicon staff were expected to be conversant with the theological controversies of the first eight centuries of Church history, and the part played in these by the various authors; moreover, they must be clear-headed, concise, conscientious. It simply would not do just to guess the meaning of a word from its context; if it could not be found in any of the existing dictionaries, it had to be carefully investigated, even if this should take many hours and involve ordering a shelf full of books from the stacks of the Bodleian. There was next to no scope for creative work: the word in any given context simply did mean one particular thing; preconceived ideas or interesting theories were poisoned baits to be avoided under pain of making fatal mistakes. Many an internationally famed patristic scholar's reputation crumbled to bits, at least in our estimation, as we found time and again that his references were unverifiable, his translations wrong, his interpretation a figment of his fancy, far removed from the thought of the father he pretended to elucidate for his readers. We ourselves trembled before future critics of our work—for in the thousands upon thousands of tricky passages how was it possible *not* to misinterpret from time to time? Especially as we were none of us (except of course, Dr. Cross, the Editor), trained patristic scholars. These were in the chairs of the Universities—here, on the Continent, in the U.S.A., hardly to be expected to slave away looking up references at the rate of five shillings an hour, or in monastic libraries all over the world. They would pull us to pieces once the work was published; but by that time the staff would long have been dispersed—*après nous le déluge!*

However, so far there was no staff except myself. When Dr. Cross asked me for suggestions, it occurred to me that Miss Grosvenor, for a few months my tutor at King's College in the last stages of my studies for the Lambeth Diploma, would be the right person to approach. She had become a Catholic some time after I had, and was now working in a government office in Edinburgh, but was soon to be "demobilized." She had all the qualifications—if she could only be persuaded to consent to the very unsatisfactory financial arrangements. On the other hand, there was the advantage which I pointed out when writing to her, that our staff would be quite free to suit their working hours to their personal convenience. As long as we kept to the number of weekly hours we had arranged with the Editor, it did not matter how we fitted them in. We could come and go exactly as we liked, take off a long weekend or suddenly disappear for a fortnight, if only the weekly hours were made up somehow or other during the year. As a matter of fact there was no control at all; we were simply trusted to work as many hours as we were paid for. On the whole this system worked very well, apart from one notable exception. This was an attractive young woman, who suddenly did not turn up for months, though she received her check as usual. When the Editor at last made enquiries, she gave as an excuse that time seemed to have stood still for her! A few weeks later she became engaged.

To my relief Miss Grosvenor decided to join us, and after her came the newly appointed chaplain of St. John's College, Mr. Lampe, who had recently returned from the war. While Dr. Cross was often kept away by his duties at Christ Church, the three of us began to evolve a method of coping with the enormous and as yet almost totally disorganized material which we were supposed to put into shape within a few years. I may as well confess that, though I conscientiously worked off my hours at the Lexicon, my heart was nevertheless far more in my writing than in the everlasting looking up of references. Nothing infuriated me more than when people, on hearing what I was doing, exclaimed admiringly: "What a wonderful work! How very interesting it must be!" If I could only have set them to work on it for four weeks! First look up the passage in the old edition, for which we had the reference in our slips; then try to find it in the modern one—if it was there, it might have been a spurious passage left out, in which case we ought to ascertain where it came from, if possible. And when actually all seemed to be well, you looked at the wretched word again, only to find that the man who had put it down on the slip as a new word had mistaken the form, and it was really quite an ordinary word which need not go in at all. Well, some people actually throve on this kind of thing, but I did not. I was always only too glad when I could go back to my mystics in the evening.

About this time my mother's sister in Cambridge fell seriously ill. Unlike her three sisters, she had never become a Christian; her husband, too, was a Jew, though neither of them was practising their religion. A few days before Christ-

mas we received a telegram that she had died, informing us
that the Requiem would be on such and such a day.

"Requiem?" I said to my mother, "Requiem? What on
earth do they mean by that?"

"She can't have become a Catholic?"

"Impossible. She never showed the slightest interest in any
religion, let alone Catholicism."

"Can't imagine what they are calling Requiem there."

Mother and I were both baffled, but quite certain that,
whatever the word Requiem stood for in the telegram, it
could not be a Catholic Requiem Mass.

Mother went to the funeral alone, because I was unable
at the time to leave Oxford, owing to an accumulation of
work. When I met her at the station on her return her first
words were: "Aunt Hermine died a Catholic." I was speechless. She was about the last person whom I should have
credited with a death bed conversion; yet there it was. About
three weeks before her death she had asked the hospital nurse
to call a Catholic priest, she was sure only a priest could help
her. He came, talked to her, and from that time continued
to see her every day. She then asked her husband if he had
any objection to her being baptized a Catholic. He had none,
and himself told my mother he was amazed to see how peaceful my aunt had been afterwards. When I sent a Mass offering to the priest who had both baptized and buried her
within a few days, he wrote me a letter fully confirming
what my uncle had said. From that time the latter, whose
medical studies had estranged him from his ancestral religion,
began to read the Bible, including the New Testament,
though he never took the final step to follow his wife.

I finished the manuscript of my book in May, 1946, but
the publishers suggested I should include another chapter, on
the Franciscan mystics. So I set to work again, immersing
myself in St. Bonaventure, Angela de Foligno and a stigmatized Tertiary of the nineteenth century, Louise Lateau.

I had read only a small book on her of the devotional kind, but it seemed to provide enough material for a short account of her. It was my first acquaintance with a case of stigmatization—soon this strange phenomenon was to dog my steps for years.

This year and the next went by in a rather monotonous routine of work and prayer, from which only two events stand out in my memory. The one was my first acquaintance with a Benedictine convent, St. Mary's Priory of Princethorpe, near Rugby, where I went for a private retreat just before Whitsun, 1947, and where, since then, I have returned each year at least once, if I could not arrange a second visit. It was a place after my own heart, where I could pray, read, sit in the garden, go for walks, or simply relax. The Benedictines have PAX as their motto, and this happy spot seemed indeed replete with peace. When I wanted a break from the silence, the Retreat Mistress would come and talk to me, and already during this first visit we became friends, as our tastes and views were very similar.

The other happening was of a different kind. A German Jewish refugee had recently moved into a top floor room of the house where I was staying. She was in poor health—ulcer of the stomach, as she told the landlady and myself. Just before Christmas I had taken her to the Radcliffe Infirmary, when she had been feeling very seedy, but she had come back after a few days, and, after that, spent most of her time in her room. I often went upstairs to sit with her, and soon realized that her illness was something worse than ulcers. She was interested in religion. A German woman who had herself been converted from Judaism to some form of Protestantism had caught hold of her and was trying hard to make a convert of her as well. She plied her with a vast amount of tract literature and upset her by implying that, unless she were baptized, she would without any doubt go to everlasting torment. I quieted her, explaining that this was not the teaching of the Church, that she would never be punished for following her conscience; that faith in Christ was a gift, and if she had not received it, no one could force her into it. This impressed her, and she told me repeatedly: "If I ever become a Christian, I want to be a Catholic."

Shortly before Easter her condition became worse and she had to go to the hospital again, not to the Radcliffe this time, but to one where they took in only old people and incurables. It was the first time I saw someone slowly dying of cancer. I could almost watch the flesh disappearing from her face, which became frighteningly skull-like, and from her arms and fingers. "Nurse can hardly find a place where to put the needle in to give me my injections," she said with a wan smile.

Her pains were evidently atrocious, and she rapidly reached a stage when the drugs lost their effect. Still she would keep calling out in peremptory tones whenever the nurse did not come at once: "My injection, nurse, immediately! Immediately!!"

The two Irish nurses in the ward humored her in every way. She had told them she was interested in Catholicism, and they had great hopes that she might yet want to be baptized on her deathbed. One of them, whom she liked particularly, gave her a medal of St. John Bosco, which she wore around her neck. Despite her weakness she insisted on discussing religion with me as well as with them.

As I came in one Saturday morning the two nurses were very excited. "She has said she wants to be baptized. We have asked the priest to come this afternoon. We have given her a sleeping tablet now, that she will be a bit more rested for the ceremony."

It seemed almost too good to be true; but, after all, my aunt had been baptized on her deathbed, and she had appeared to be much farther from the Church than our poor patient.

When I came again next day I saw at once from the face

of the nurse that something had gone wrong. "A very strange thing has happened. Just before the priest came yesterday she woke up. She said she had had a terrible dream. She had seen a dreadful place, where people were being tormented, but she could not remember the name of it. I suggested it might have been purgatory, and she said Yes, that was the name. When the priest arrived she told him she could not possibly be baptized because of that dream and that awful place. He told her that, if it really was purgatory she had seen, she need never go there, because if one died immediately after baptism one went straight to heaven. It was no use. She would not be baptized because of that dream, whatever it was. So he told us if she should yet express a wish to be baptized after all, we had his permission to do it ourselves. So we keep a bottle with holy water near her bed, just in case."

When I came to her bed—I noticed at once an outsize bottle with holy water on the table—she seemed quite changed. She had always been very friendly with me; but now she was almost hostile. As she did not seem inclined to talk much and looked more than ever like a living skeleton, I walked a little away from her bed, where she could not see me, and began to say the Rosary. Almost at once she grew strangely restive. She kept sighing and moving about in her bed, and at last asked: "What are you doing? Stop whatever it is." I did not want to upset her; she evidently sensed that I was praying for her; so I left her. When I came back next day I knew the end could not be far off. But she insisted on yet another theological discussion. I had to make an effort to answer her questions. Only her eyes were still alive in the fleshless face; I felt like arguing with a voice from a corpse.

Early next morning my landlady came in to tell me that the hospital had just called up to say she had died that night. Though I had known when I left her it could hardly be more than a matter of hours, I was badly shaken. The disease had been so painful to watch, her struggle for life had been so fierce. I went around in the afternoon to ask the nurses about her last hours. She had requested to be buried in a Jewish cemetery in London with the full ritual of her faith.

The thought of her pursued me for a long time. There had been my aunt, whom no one had ever dreamt of converting, asking for a priest; and here this other woman, herself seemingly so near to the Church, surrounded by Catholics praying for her, talking to her, with the priest all ready to baptize her . . . God's ways were inscrutable. I had to leave it at that.

17. *The New Look*

I APPLIED for naturalization as soon as this was once more possible after the war. I waited for a year to hear from the Home Office, not daring to enquire because I was afraid of upsetting the authorities by undue importunity. When I heard that other people had only to wait a few months, I at last wrote again and received a very apologetic answer. There had been a typically English muddle: the Home Office had moved to other quarters and my application had been mislaid. Within three months, in the beginning of January 1948, it was granted, and on the thirteenth I went to a commissioner of oaths to swear "allegiance to His Majesty, King George VI, His Heirs and Successors, according to law." For me it was much more than a mere formality; it was an act by which I now in fact became a member of the nation to which I had belonged in heart for many years. It was with a feeling of intense relief that, a few days later, I went to the police station with my grey Alien's Certificate for my name to be removed from the register of aliens. I was British at last—and immediately proved it by the desire to go abroad!

Oxford had got on my nerves. Rationing had got on my

nerves. The Greek Lexicon had got on my nerves. My feelings exploded in a poem I called:

Holiday Song

I feel I want a holiday in some place far away
From publishers and editors,
From dentists and from creditors—
It's May, my friend, it's May.

I want to go to the Continent in a light blue
    fairy train,
Where they have a spring
And the milkmaids sing—
Please, give me an aeroplane.

I've had enough of the Lexicon, and the Fathers
    bore me stiff.
I want a pink frock
And a glass of hock,
And of Alpine air a whiff.

I am a woman, I want a break from all this
    austerity,
I want a new hat
And a self-contained flat—
I suppose that's temerity?

I am fed up with life as it is, and just about
    ready to crack.
I must arrange
To have a change—
And perhaps I'll never come back.

Let editors and publishers, all the gentlemen of
    the Press
Talk lots of hot air,
I won't turn a hair,
I'm off, goodbye, God bless.

I'm off in a frock as pink as can be and a light-
   blue aeroplane
From the Oxford mists
And publicists
To the happy land of Cockayne.

What was the Englishman's favorite holiday country?
Switzerland. So Switzerland it had to be for me.

I seemed to be in a new mood altogether. For years I had
been wearing that same old black costume or, on hot days,
some unmistakably "austerity" cotton frock. I had religiously
refrained from looking at a fashion journal. I had proved to
myself that I could resist the attraction.

Then M. Dior invented the "new look." Everybody was
talking about it, there were to be "new looks" in policy and
even in religion. Besides, St. Francis de Sales who, indeed, was
a Doctor of the Church, had said that he wanted his "devout
women" to be well-dressed. After all, it was not much of an
advertisement for religion to go about looking like a scare-
crow.

One Saturday I was going to London for a study week-
end on mysticism at a convent in Hampstead. But before
going there, I went to a shop in Oxford Street and bought
a "new look" dress with a flaring skirt. I could not refrain
from spreading it out on the conventual bed that afternoon,
a sign, as it were, that the two sides in me were about to be
merged, and I would now live my religion without sacrificing
my interest in the world around me.

While I was planning my Swiss holiday I had a letter from
my Irish publisher: "I am anxiously looking around for someone to write a good biography of Therese Neumann, and it
has occurred to me that you would be the ideal person to
undertake this task. . . . If you agree to undertake this work
we can supply you with most of the modern biographies of
her."

Therese Neumann. I remembered that a long time ago, in the late twenties, I had read about her in the Berlin papers, when the case of this stigmatized Bavarian peasant woman who was supposed to live entirely without food and drink had set Germany buzzing with rumors and legends. She seemed lately to have been in the news again, for I had also read an article about her in *The Life of the Spirit*, and had actually been wondering whether I could not combine my projected Swiss holiday with a visit to her native village of Konnersreuth. And here was this publisher asking me to write a book on her! It seemed a strange coincidence. I considered that the straightforward account of a holy woman who bore the wounds of Christ in her body would not be difficult to write. Indeed, the book might perhaps even turn out to be a "pot-boiler," with which I could really do very well. I wrote back I would gladly undertake the work.

In due course three volumes on Therese arrived; two of them were simply pious stories, the third was a large tome, written by an Archbishop, Teodorowicz by name, entitled *Mystical Phenomena in the Life of Therese Neumann*. In this I now immersed myself.

When I was half through its five-hundred odd pages of glowing descriptions of her ecstasies and other marvels I said to myself: "All this sounds fishy to me. I have never yet heard of a mystic who, while having a vision of Christ on His way to Golgotha, wants to save Him and points out a secret way of escape, sending messages to His mother: 'Tell her, the Resl (Bavarian abbreviation for Therese) says He won't die!'" The archbishop had commented: "She (i.e., Therese) is no despairing, helpless witness of the terrible tragedy on Calvary, like the Mother of God. . . . She is personally active, a Joan of Arc in the presence of her Saviour. . . . She does not despair for a moment as to the success of her attempt to rescue Him." If the archbishop was so carried away by his enthusiasm for the stigmatic of Konnersreuth to place her above the Mother of God and, indeed, above Christ Himself to whom she was to play a Joan of Arc—well, let him square this with his theology as best he could. I certainly could not accept his version of the happenings at Konnersreuth, and was not prepared to write a book on them—potboiler or otherwise—without very careful investigation.

I wrote therefore to the publishers, if they wanted a panegyric on Therese I was afraid it would have to be written by someone else. The affair seemed very strange to me; it would need a good deal of further examination.

I fully thought this would be the end of it. Instead, the publishers wrote back: "We are quite in agreement with the principle of your approach to Therese Neumann. It would be senseless for you to produce just a pious document in which you did not believe, and it seems to us that only something reflecting your own impressions, conclusions etc., after a careful examination of all available data, would be worthwhile doing."

So I was given a free hand! Little did I know then what a hornets' nest I was going to bring about my ears.

At that time we were allowed only thirty pounds foreign currency, so I told the publishers I should like to combine my proposed Swiss holiday with a visit to Konnersreuth, but needed more money for that. They promised to approach the Eire government for a further thirty pounds worth of Swiss francs.

Next I had to obtain a permit from the American occupation authorities to go to Bavaria. Before going to London for this purpose, I went to an early Mass. As I was just entering the church I met one of our "devout ladies," evidently in a great state of excitement.

"Oh, Miss Graef, I know you are interested in mysticism. I must tell you, something wonderful has happened. You know about Mary, don't you." Mary was a girl who had wanted to enter a convent but had been refused.

"Yes. What about her?"

"Something quite marvellous. She came to see me last night and told me that the pope has had a vision about her. She is going to enter, after all—but the Holy Father himself will clothe her in the Sistine Chapel. And she is going to receive the Stigmata on the feast of St. Dominic, the fourth of August."

At this point I was digging my nails into my palms to make sure I was really awake and standing before the church, and not still in bed dreaming. After all, all this stigmatic business in which I was involved might have affected me, so that I could no longer distinguish between waking and sleeping. However, I really was awake, and there was the good lady carrying on her tale: "You will see, it is quite true, for it will all be given out at Blackfriars before the half-past seven Mass this morning."

"My dear Mrs. X," I said, "the poor girl is evidently suffering from religious mania."

"What, religious mania?" the lady cried indignantly. "I thought you were so interested in mysticism, that's why I told you. Nothing to do with religious mania."

"I am very sorry; I am afraid I have to leave immediately after the early Mass because I have to go up to London. I can only advise you to inform this young woman's confessor and her doctor; she is evidently suffering from hallucinations."

Mrs. X. gave me a withering look. "And I thought you knew something about mysticism!"

It was incredible what "pious people" not otherwise certifiable were capable of believing. It should have given me an inkling of what to expect if I dared to cast doubts on a popularly accepted "mystic" like Therese Neumann.

When I was back in Oxford that night after filling in all the various forms for being admitted into the American military occupation zone of Germany, I met Mrs. X. again, now in a less exuberant mood than in the morning. "I am so sorry—you were right; please don't tell anybody. The girl's mother has already arrived to take her home."

I had thought a permit to enter the American zone of Germany would be all that was needed; but a German Dominican who was staying at Blackfriars at the time told me I should also have to obtain the permission of Therese's bishop to see her. This would not be easy, for visits to her were discouraged by the ecclesiastical authorities, and he suggested in what terms to apply. To my relief the permission,—given "exceptionally" (*ausnahmsweise*)—arrived by return of post. Now I was only waiting for the American permit.

A fortnight before I was due to leave for my Swiss holiday I came home from Mass as usual about eight o'clock, to find among my post a letter from the American authorities—refusing a military permit to enter Bavaria! I gulped down half a cup of cold milk and a couple of biscuits, by a sudden inspiration seized the episcopal permit, and dashed off to catch the 8.40 to London.

The American office dealing with military permits was full of Germans and Austrians trying to go to the Continent to see their relatives. My British passport secured me preferential treatment, and I explained my case to one of the secretaries. "We should have given you the permit," she said, "but you will not be able to see Therese Neumann, because the Church authorities won't allow visitors." Triumphantly I waved the bishop's permit at her. "I see, this is a different matter, of course. If you will leave it with us, we will send it to Berlin, and you will then get the Permit from there."

"How long will that take?"

"Three weeks at least." Heavens, and I had arranged to go away for my holiday in just a fortnight. Eventually she suggested that the permit should be sent to their office at Berne, which could then issue a visa. It certainly was going to be complicated—but it seemed the only possible solution.

I had hardly sat down in the train to Paris after landing

at Calais, when a youngish woman beside me dropped a leaflet in my lap. I picked it up; it was a tract stating in the first sentence that its author wanted to convert people from the various Christian denominations, including Roman Catholicism—to what was not quite clear. I stopped reading any further and looked at the person thus anxious to convert me. She was a girl in her thirties; her face would have been attractive but for its almost inhumanly tense expression. "So you convert people *from* Roman Catholicism? This is interesting. Do you know at all what Catholics believe?"

She sputtered forth the popular misconceptions about worshipping the Virgin Mary instead of our Lord and the pope being always right whatever he might say. I tried to explain the real position of the Virgin and the infallibility of the pope, but she would not believe me. She then held forth about the general immorality of people, expressing the hope that I should agree with her on the wickedness of dancing, theaters, and cinemas, interspersing her remarks with frequent allusions to covering oneself with the Precious Blood. She was evidently a member of the Plymouth Brethren. Her seriousness and obvious devotion to an austere life impressed me, if only her religion had not made her so fiercely censorious of any innocent human enjoyments, which I had to defend against her bitter denunciations. She was sitting bolt upright all the time, as she proclaimed her gospel of unremitting austerity for all. Then I made a fatal mistake. I offered her a chocolate biscuit. Whether she thought it might contain "Popish poison," or whether eating chocolate biscuits was as sure a sign of immorality as drinking alcohol and dancing I did not know; anyway, she refused it indignantly and, as I was evidently inconvertible, took a religious paper from her handbag and read it furiously, without ever looking at me again all the way to Paris.

This was the first of a series of three attempts to convert me within quite a short time. The second was made by a

Jehovah's Witness when I was sitting in the garden of a private house near Stanbrook Abbey. Having spread out a vast amount of literature before me the lady assured me that Catholics were most welcome in their communion which was, indeed, the oldest religion in the world.

"The oldest?" I asked incredulously.

"Certainly," she replied, "far older than the Church of Rome, for we were founded by Abel, who was the first witness."

"Nonsense—you are simply a modern American sect, don't kid yourselves."

Madam, outraged and purple in the face, snatched up her papers and beat a hasty retreat.

The third, and funniest attempt to convert me, once more took place in a train. While it was standing in Bletchley, dreariest, draughtiest, most desolate of junctions, a gentleman in black, with a muffler round his neck, sat down opposite me, placing a black leather-bound volume beside him. I was reading a book *Philosophical Understanding and Religious Truth,* which my one-time fiancé, Erich Frank, then professor at an American University, had written. After a few minutes the person opposite me began a philosophical conversation. When, after about ten minutes, he had guided it to the existence of God and the creation of the world, he suddenly drew himself up and announced dramatically: "You see, I am a Catholic priest."

I grinned. "I thought so, Father. I am a Catholic." I do not think I have ever seen such an expression of acute disappointment on anybody's face.

"Oh," he said at last (I had fully expected an unpriestly "damn"), "and I had intended to lead up so cleverly to the subject of the Church."

"Too late, Father, too late—I am sorry you have wasted your time on me instead of reading your Breviary."

*   *   *

When I arrived at Estavayer-le-Lac, looking apprehensively at the skies exhibiting the same "clerical grey" as in Oxford, my hostess said: *"Il ne pleut jamais à Estavayer."* It was obvious I was indeed away from England, where such a flagrant case of overstatement was altogether unthinkable. In fact it rained nearly every day, and to add insult to injury I was blamed for having imported *la pluie d'Angleterre*. But there was worse to come than merely rain.

The proprietress of the Catholic guest house where I was staying suggested that I should talk to a German Swiss Dominican Father who was interested in Therese Neumann. When he heard that I was taking a critical view of the case he threw up his hands in horror. "But don't you know that the Holy Father himself called her to Rome this Easter, to consult her?" I stared at him incredulously. "After this," he continued, "it is of course quite impossible for any Catholic to take a negative view of her."

"But Father," I objected, "are you quite sure that this is really a fact, not just a rumor? It does seem unlikely that the Holy Father should have consulted her."

"Not at all. It is absolutely true. She was indeed in Rome last Easter to advise the Holy Father."

I went back to the guest house somewhat dazed. If it were really true that the Holy Father had consulted her (on what? I could not help wondering), who was I to doubt the supernatural origin of the phenomena attributed to her? It seemed more important than ever for me to go to Konnersreuth, and I waited with growing impatience for the American permit, that ought to have arrived by now.

I was really perturbed. So far I had not come across a single Catholic authority to share my sceptical views—if the worst came to the worst I should have to abandon writing the book altogether. Then my hostess suggested I should go to Fribourg, which was quite near, and discuss the matter with Monsignor Journet. The famous theologian, a thin, elderly man in a well-worn soutane, received me with the unassuming courtesy of the true scholar. I explained my difficulties in hesitating French. His first words made it clear that he, at least, held no brief for Therese. But the most important result of this visit was that he suggested I should read a book on the case, written by a Polish doctor a few years ago, and highly approved by the Roman authorities, which attributed all the phenomena to natural causes.

This was news, indeed. I at once went into a bookshop to buy this work of Dr. Poray-Madeyski, but they did not have it. Instead, when I mentioned to the girl who served me that I was hoping to go to Konnersreuth in a few days to see Therese, she said, her eyes wide with wonder and admiration: "She is sure to know already that you are coming."

She was, indeed, sure to know that; though not by supernatural revelation, as the girl only too readily assumed, but because I had written several times to her parish priest, Father Naber, informing him of the bishop's permission and asking him to arrange an interview for me with the stigmatic. Though I had enclosed international reply coupons each time, he had never answered my letters. Only my last, despairing note from Switzerland received a curt reply, written in a curiously uneducated hand and style, saying he regretted being unable to make any arrangements for me, as he could never say beforehand whether Therese was going to be at home or not. The bishop's permission, which, as I had been informed, had been communicated to him, had evidently not made much impression.

My hostess suggested I should go to Einsiedeln, the famous place of pilgrimages, which Therese Neumann had often visited, and where I might glean some more information on her, besides its being interesting in itself.

When the local train from Lucerne wound its way to the medieval shrine, up the wooded mountains with the Rigi in the distance, my first impression was incongruity. The rich, overladen baroque of the Abbey contrasted all too painfully with the magnificent simplicity of the Alpine scenery. I was frankly disappointed. Having found a room in one of the large hotels opposite I wandered into the church, which was filled with a strange, high-pitched, monotonous noise for which I could not account until it occurred to me that they must be tuning the organ. I walked around among the many statues in the agitated postures characteristic of the baroque, until my eyes came to rest on the small black face of the Virgin of Einsiedeln, dressed in a richly embroidered scarlet mantle, and surrounded by gilded clouds and gold and silver votive offerings. I went to Mass early next morning, having been awakened at a quarter past four by the tremendous noise of the bells of Einsiedeln calling all the neighborhood to church.

I do not always find it easy to follow Mass with full attention; the innumerable preoccupations of daily life intrude themselves so often into one's consciousness. But before the Black Virgin of Einsiedeln it appeared scarcely possible not to be completely recollected. The prayers that had been offered there without interruption for eleven centuries seemed almost to materialize, invading the soul on their own account.

At night I went to the Rosary. It was a poignant experience, poles apart from the impression of distracted gabbling I had so often had in English churches. Here a handful of old women and peasants had gathered, as they did every night, after the day's work was over, to pay homage to the Mother of God. Kneeling before the black statue as their forefathers had done down the centuries, these simple people said the prayers slowly, deliberately, in a loud voice vibrating with a love and conviction that were overwhelming. Here, I felt, was a faith that had been transmitted from one generation to the other these last thousand years; that had never known a doubt, not even a wavering, something as robust as it was simple, and with which the very air seemed to be imbued. These people were children gathered around their Mother with absolute trust. It seemed as if a strong current went out from this Mother to her children, and from them back to her. I felt myself drawn into this current, in which all problems and complications fell away, and there remained but simple faith uniting the soul to its God.

I needed this spiritual refreshment, for the day had been full of random interviews with people regaling me with un-verifiable marvels that added nothing to what I already knew about Therese Neumann.

I had hoped to be in Konnersreuth on Friday, July 9, to witness the so-called "passion ecstasies." But the American permit did not arrive, and I had already made up my mind to go back home without having seen her, when I at last received a communication from Berne telling me to go to the American military office there to have a visa for Germany made out. It would be impossible to see her on the ninth, since it was now the sixth. The Friday after, July 16, would be the Feast of Our Lady of Mount Carmel, on which day she was sure to have no ecstasies, since they never occurred if one of the greater feasts fell on a Friday. However, it could do no harm to see her in her ordinary state; perhaps I might even find out more about her in that way; for books containing minute descriptions of her trance states abounded. For the purpose of discovering whether these were caused by divine intervention or were merely the effects of strange psychological faculties that might, for example, be found also in spiritualist media, it would even be more useful to speak with her while she was not in trance.

In Berne it took some persuasion to make the American authorities realize that I had neither unlimited time nor money at my disposal; but once they had grasped this they sped up the visa and even opened their office for me on Sunday, so that I could collect my passport with the visa on that day and take the one and only train to Regensburg the same afternoon.

It was my first visit to my native country after almost exactly twelve years. I had left it, a refugee, a non-Aryan without rights, whom the Gestapo might arrest at any moment for an ill-considered remark, or even on the grounds of a completely unfounded denunciation.

At the Swiss-German frontier at Lindau the dreams of a refugee became reality. The exile without human rights came back as a citizen of one of the occupying powers. When I heard the customs officials in the adjoining compartment question some Swiss travellers with German thoroughness, making them open all their cases and reveal their foreign currency, I put my British passport on the table in front of me and waited what would happen. I had cigarettes, coffee, tea, Swiss butter and so forth in my luggage for my relatives with whom I was going to stay in Regensburg, to which diocese Konnersreuth belonged.

The passport had an almost miraculous effect. The customs official practically apologized for his existence. When I told him the contents of my luggage he nodded: "Certainly, certainly, Madam. So sorry to trouble you." There was no question of opening anything. "Do you want me to enter your foreign currency in your passport? Of course I have no right to do so, but you may find it useful on coming back." He next complimented me on my excellent German ("Yes, I had been staying in Germany for some years before the war!"), and then entered on a respectful conversation about the recent German currency reform and asked about conditions in England.

When the frontier formalities were finished the train at last moved into war-wrecked Germany. It did give me a shock. After the superbly clean and prosperous Switzerland, the contrast between the two countries which now became

visible was particularly striking. The very landscape seemed
to be dreary and dirty; but what, in the growing twilight,
gave it a strangely unreal look of utter hopelessness was the
lines upon lines of burnt-out rail carriages. Now I was passing two charred goods-trains standing within fifty yards of
each other, now a windowless express whose center carriages
had evidently been hit by an H.E. bomb, again what must
once have been a local train, as could be seen from one fairly
intact coach—all the others were unrecognizable skeletons.
And this went on for miles. Then there were the piles upon
piles of felled trees. Whole forests seemed to have been cut
down. Now and again a village came into sight, many of its
houses still in ruins. And over it all the same atmosphere of
dull despair—though it was a fine, warm summer evening.

Sitting alone in the compartment I tried to sort out my
feelings. It had been my country. Whatever my nationality
now, should not my heart be bleeding for this unhappy,
humiliated land, this Germany, *Deutschland,* should I not
feel its sorrow in my own soul? Had not an English friend
once written to me one could never really give up the country of one's birth?

This homecoming surely must be the test. I looked again
out of the window. I was, indeed, shocked to see the burnt-
out trains and the cut-down forests. But I was shocked in the
same way as if I had seen the destruction in France or Italy.
I well remembered the immediate, shooting pain in my heart
when I looked out one morning in London to see the whole
sky over the city an orgy of pink and red. There was nothing
of this now. My heart remained cool, untouched. It was *an*
unhappy country to which I was coming back, it was no
longer mine.

It was well after midnight, and I was pleasantly dozing
in the empty compartment, when the train stopped at a small
station behind Munich, the door opened, and a crowd of
American soldiers in various stages of intoxication, beer

bottles in their pockets and under their arms, burst in upon my sleepy solitude. Before I knew how they had got there, two of them were already in the luggage rack over my head, the others sat packed like sardines beside and opposite me.

"Mom, are you Amurrican?" one of them asked.

"No, I'm British," I replied, in what I hoped resembled the accents of a dowager duchess.

This announcement was followed by a respectful silence. I wondered what to do next. I did not relish the prospect of spending hours in this somewhat alarming company, though they were really very considerate; for I heard one of them admonishing his buddy, who had evidently made an unsuitable remark (I did not understand most of their slang conversation anyway): "Mind, there's a woman in the compartment." I was probably embarrassing them as much as they were me.

After a quarter of an hour or so a woman attendant of the train appeared. I quickly said to her in German: "Please, can you find me a compartment where there are *no* drunk American soldiers?"

"I am afraid the whole train is full of them; but I think I may be able to find you something." She went out, came back almost immediately and took me to a compartment where there were several strange-looking women and a child on their way to Czechoslovakia.

It was just as well I had left the Americans, for soon after I had installed myself again, the train came to a standstill. There was no sign of a station anywhere, but we did not move any further. We were to be in Regensburg about one-thirty, it was almost one o'clock now. I knew my uncle would be waiting for me at the station. I did not know Regensburg; of course there would be no taxis, and all the hotels, so I had been told, were requisitioned by the occupation troops.

I tried to go to sleep. After what seemed an eternity I

looked at my watch. 1:25. The train was as immovable as ever. I went out into the corridor which was full of G.I.'s, most of them drinking, of course. I went back into my compartment. At last a ticket collector turned up, who had an argument with one of the women who appeared to be in the wrong train. He explained the situation: the cable of the electric train had been torn by a falling tree, and they had just telephoned to Regensburg for some engineers to mend it. How long would that take? I asked apprehensively. At least two hours. Surely my uncle would not wait for me all that time! I was dead tired, and the prospect of arriving at a roofless station (as they all still were after the bombings) quite alone in the middle of the night, was not very cheering.

I eventually got there at half-past-four—and there was my uncle, having waited for me almost three hours. "I could not possibly have let you arrive here alone," he said; and as we were walking home, he entertained me with a selection of gruesome tales of rape, though by now, he assured me, things had become considerably better, and there were far fewer cases of it than during the first year of occupation.

Regensburg was overcrowded with refugees. What struck me most was the dirt, the smells, the drabness—and the absence of rags. I did not see a single unmended hole in the clothes of these people who had survived bombings, exile, occupation—every tear had been meticulously darned. I thought of English workmen—fifteen pounds a week or so—in their torn shirts and trousers, and of the Oxford landladies who did not mind washing their steps down every morning in atrociously laddered stockings. I raised my hat, metaphorically, to the German housewife.

Before going to Konnersreuth I went to a bank with my aunt to find out how I could change some Swiss francs into German money. I had hardly voiced my innocent question, when the bank manager drew himself up to his full height, the veins swelling on his forehead, and bellowed in a voice like the last trumpet: "Change Swiss francs? Don't you know that according to paragraph so-and-so of the currency law of such and such a date (he rattled off the figures with preternatural speed) you are not allowed to possess any foreign currency?"

While I was trying to control my mirth, my aunt said quickly: "But the lady is a foreigner."

The man remained quite literally speechless. His colleague came to the rescue, stammering abject apologies: such strict regulations, had to be so careful, so sorry this should have happened, would I perhaps try the American Express.

I was reminded of this scene when I landed at Newhaven about a week later. Soon after the war, when watches were still very rare, I had bought an airforce watch, which had already bitterly disappointed the hopes I had pinned on it. Its masculine shape now attracted the lynx-eyed customs official.

"Where did you buy this watch?"

"In Oxford."

"Surely not."

I became very angry. "It's an airforce watch, I bought it soon after the war for a wicked price, had already to have it repaired, and am certainly not going to pay any duty on it!"

"Please show me your passport." I did. His manner changed at once to smiling politeness.

"Thank you, Ma'am." And he put his cross on my luggage without any further question. Could there be a better illustration of the different attitude of English and German authorities to foreigners?

I went to Konnersreuth on the Wednesday following the interview at the bank. It took me seven hours to reach Waldsassen, the nearest railway station to the stigmatic's village. In the train I met a nun from the neighborhood. When I mentioned Therese Neumann, she shut up like an oyster. This seemed strange, seeing that in Switzerland everybody had been ready to tell me exciting tales of the marvels with which her life was believed to abound. So I ventured the remark that I was none too sure about the supernatural origin of the phenomena. The Sister's face brightened up at once. "We don't think much of her ourselves," she confided. "She is so terribly rude and conceited. But we may not say anything. People here think she is a saint. But we don't believe it."

I walked the three quarters of an hour to Konnersreuth, as there was no bus at that time. The scenery was not very exciting, meadows interspersed with woods (it was quite near the Czechoslovak border), now and again I met a wayside crucifix, a *marterl* as they call it in Bavaria. Konnersreuth itself seemed no more interesting than its surroundings: a collection of poor, white-washed houses, many of which still bore the marks of the shelling, to which the village had been subjected in the final stages of the war. The crooked streets, populated by geese, were rather dirty, and presented a striking contrast to the clean, fairly large baroque church in the center. I walked straight to the presbytery and rang the bell. When I received no answer, I went to a neighboring inn to book a room. There they told me that the priest's housekeeper had gone into the fields accompanied by her sister, the famous "Resl."

When I returned to the presbytery about an hour later, I had to ring and knock for a long time, before a rather bad-tempered woman opened the door. She immediately scolded me for making so much noise. As I knew she was Therese's sister, I thought it better to swallow my annoyance and try to make friends with her if I could. When she heard I had come from England, she became a little more amiable, and we were soon deep in a very feminine conversation about the difficulties of rationing, the unpredictable character of cats, and similar subjects far removed from the real purpose of my visit. At last, however, she led me into the sitting room, where I should wait for Father Naber, though she kept grumbling that people always went to him when they wanted to see Resl, whereas that was a matter for her family rather than for the priest.

When I had been waiting for about five minutes the door opened and a stout peasant woman dressed in black bustled in and told me to wait outside, because someone else wanted to see the Father. Instinctively I glanced at her hands. There, without anything to cover them, were the famous stigmata. I thought them rather disappointing: they were square bright red marks of the size of a postage stamp. They did not look like real wounds at all and seemed, moreover, quite incongruous on the hands of this somewhat fussy middle-aged woman whose personality failed to impress me.

She apologized for keeping me waiting. I said it did not matter because, being on holiday, I had plenty of time. She replied tartly that for her there was never a holiday. Then Father Naber came in with a man and a woman, relatives of Resl, as he later told me. Resl joined them, after showing me back into the hall, where I was left standing, there being no chair, for the next three-quarters of an hour.

When her relatives had eventually left, Resl once more showed me into the sitting room, instructing me not to keep Father too long. The priest then gave me what was evidently his usual lecture, on how she lived without any other food except Holy Communion, a living proof that the Eucharist was Food, indeed. When I expressed my regret at having been unable to be there last Friday, he told me that I had not missed anything, because her ecstasies had not occurred on that day; by way of explanation Resl had shown him "in an old prayer book" that there had been a feast of our Lady unknown to him. I later made thorough investigations, but failed to discover any Marian feast on July 9. He further told me, rather naively I thought, that Resl's temper could be very violent and had shown itself only the other day, when a Swedish newspaper had alleged that she accepted money from the American occupation troops who visited her frequently. She did, indeed, sometimes accept presents from them; for the following day he himself pointed out to me a cart with a horse and a coach boy they had given her, all of which were housed in the stable belonging to the presbytery. Before taking leave I asked him to make an appointment for me so that I could talk to her, pointing out that I had the bishop's permission to see her. He told me to come back the next day at noon, as that was her time for receiving visitors.

I had supper at the inn, where a garrulous old man entertained me with an endless tale of Therese's "expiatory sufferings," pains she is supposed to endure almost every day for the sins of others. The whole atmosphere of Konnersreuth seemed to be saturated with religious sensationalism. As soon as I could do so without unduly hurting Resl's devotee, I went up to my very primitive room and noted down my impressions.

As I had nothing to do next morning, I went into the parish church where, so I had read, Resl had a special electrically heated chair to herself behind the high altar. As there was no one in the church I quickly climbed over the altar rails to investigate. There was the chair, which looked exactly like the priest's part of a confessional. I pulled the curtains back, and sure enough the whole contraption was fitted with electrical cushions, on the seat, behind the back, on the arm supports—an American millionairess could not have been seated in church more comfortably. But a stigmatic, with a special vocation of suffering for others? I had seen quite a few rheumatic old women in church early at Mass that morning, who did not claim to have any such vocation, and had yet to put up with the drafty church as they found it. . . .

When I came out again I saw several American cars parked in front of the church and opposite Resl's house. I wondered what was going to happen, as we were all evidently intent on seeing her, and Father Naber had told me that she liked the Americans particularly. I went to him once more to ask had he made an appointment for me. Though he had promised it the day before, he had not done so. And what with the Americans there, he did not know whether she would see anybody. The official permission of the bishop seemed to count for nothing; indeed I had the impression that it was rather the reverse of an asset.

"What am I going to do then?" I asked.

"That I cannot tell you. You will just have to take your chance."

So I joined the G.I.'s who were standing before her house waiting. They were not asked in either, probably because of the unpleasantness with the Swedish newspaper about which Father Naber had told me.

I had almost abandoned all hope of seeing her again when I suddenly noticed a black figure hurrying towards the gate of the back garden behind the house. It was now or never. Fortunately the Americans, who kept staring at the front door like hypnotized haddock, did not realize what I was doing, when I was dashing off in a different direction. I arrived at the back door just in time to catch her.

"What d'you want again now?" she asked rudely. "Why, we had already a chat yesterday." She evidently considered a few insignificant words with her an outstanding favor. I told her I had some letters for her, inwardly blessing the friends who had been so eager to commend themselves to her prayers. "Give me the letters then." I handed them to her, and she was just going to slam the gate behind her, when I told her in a very humble and diffident voice that I had a personal question.

I had prepared two questions, not, I may say, for my own information, but to test her alleged "supernatural" knowledge. In the books I had read about her it had been stated that she knew such intentions of the questioner. She certainly did not in my case, since, she answered me with the readiness of the professional oracle. The first question concerned the proposed activities of some religious order, to which she replied in a very common sense way, without any claim to extraordinary enlightment. The second was a poser. I said that people who were trying to lead a contemplative life in the world were often exposed to criticism. What should these do, give themselves to prayer, or sacrifice their inclination for the sake of activities? She replied quickly: "Work by day and pray by night," looking meaningly at the stigmata of her hands, as if to say: "Anyway, that is what I do."

There was no object in prolonging the conversation. I had found out what I wanted: outside her trance state she had evidently no abnormal knowledge of her visitors' intentions, and her rudeness could be overcome by deliberate flattery. If I had seen her bleeding out of every pore it would have made no difference to me, because I had come to Konnersreuth determined not to let myself be impressed by any external phenomena. Instead I had tested her humility in the most obvious way, and she had promptly fallen into the trap. So I said goodbye, asking her to pray for me, and she made me promise in return that I would not give her away to the Americans, who were still waiting in front of the house to see her.

When I continued to make notes of my impressions in the afternoon, I suddenly realized that I had never found out whether Therese had been in Rome that Easter, as the Dominican Father in Switzerland had asserted. This had simply slipped my memory. Luckily I happened to meet Father Naber before the church in the evening and fired my question. He assured me that she had never been in Rome except "in spirit," for the canonization of St. Nicholas of Flue.

"So she has never been in Rome at all, I mean bodily?"

"No, never."

So this was how legends came into existence! Somebody thought it appropriate that the Holy Father should consult Therese Neumann, so appropriate, indeed, that it must have happened. He told it as a fact to someone else, this other person was at once ready to swear to it—shades of the Holy House of Loretto flying through the air from Nazareth to Italy!

While I was still talking to Father Naber, Therese came into sight, standing on the horse-drawn American cart, shouting to him to come and look at something. She was evidently displeased that he should be talking to me. He hastily took leave of me and hurried after her.

Before boarding the bus next morning, I could convince myself that she did not have her Friday trances that day; for she was bustling around the church, loudly talking to the workmen who were mending the roof. If the stigmata in her feet were so painful that she could hardly walk, as I had read in the various pious books about her, she must be extremely clever at concealing her discomfort, for she was rushing hither and thither as nimbly as a squirrel. I remembered the scene three years later, when the ailing old bishop of Regensburg said to me in the course of an audience: "I wish I were in such good health as she is."

Back in Regensburg my relatives pressed me to stay at least till the following Monday, though I could not eat anything and was feeling permanently sick, owing to the water which had been so heavily chlorinized that even a cup of tea would make me ill. Nevertheless I decided to make the best of being there and went to the bishop's residence. A nun opened the door; when I told her I wanted to discuss Therese Neumann with one of the bishop's theologians she raised her eyebrows, but lowered them immediately on hearing that I had been given the episcopal permission to visit her.

I then had half an hour's conversation with the Vicar General, who was very affable, and in reply to my question assured me there was no objection to my writing a book on her taking a critical view of the case. "But if this is your opinion, you had better go and see Professor Waldmann, who is also sceptical. You will probably find him quite ready to give you all the help he can."

I found Professor Waldmann, a tall, scholarly priest of over seventy, well wrapped up in rugs on account of his rheumatism, in his flat in a street called *Am Oelberg* (By the Mount of Olives). When I told him about the purpose of my visit, he was frankly delighted. He would have liked to have written a book on Konnersreuth himself, but his bishop was opposed to it. He would be only too pleased to give me any information he could. He drew my attention to a series of articles the late Father Thurston had published in the Jesuit periodical *The Month,* in which he explained phenomena kindred to those of Konnersreuth on parapsychological lines, and he gave me his own views on some of the happenings that had so far mystified me. When I came away I was more convinced than ever that I had followed the right track; it was time to get back to Oxford and work.

Soon I was beginning to wonder whether the redoubtable Therese was exercising her strange powers to revenge herself on me. When I arrived at Berne I found every hotel was full to capacity. I was already considering the prospect of having to camp out in the park, when the manager of the last hotel I resolved to try said he had still a bathroom available. I was by now prepared to sleep even in a bath, but fortunately there had been enough room to put a bed in. It was a very warm night, the hot water pipes close to my head were near boiling point, the tiny window made no difference at all to the stifling atmosphere inside. I fell into a very heavy sleep from which I awoke next morning feeling like a fly in December. My right eye was aching and part of my nose was swollen, besides, I seemed to be getting deaf, my ears were feeling quite blocked up. I had meant to break my journey home in Paris, but I was so miserable that I thought it best to go straight back to England.

In Oxford I first presented myself at the casualty ward

of the Radcliffe Infirmary, where they mercilessly syringed my eye for twenty minutes, and then sent me to my own doctor to have my ears treated—evidently all the dirt of post-war Regensburg had collected in my sense organs. I was as yet only half restored when the next blow fell: my landlady had made over her house to her son, who was going to turn it into an undergraduates' lodging house—so I had to room-hunt once more.

It was still the long vacation, yet every decent room in Oxford seemed to be already booked. I interviewed land-ladies without number, wanting two guineas for a room without even a table let alone a bookshelf, expecting me to be out all day and come in only to sleep and, of course, to pay the rent. The publishers wrote would I please come to Cork in September to discuss Therese Neumann with them. The Lexicon had not grown any more interesting in my absence.

I at last found a room in a none-too-clean house with an oddly unpleasant atmosphere. It was run by an old man, a refugee from Central Europe, quite kind but a bit queer. There was a newly installed bath near the coal cellar, and one's towels invariably bore the marks of this vicinity. How-ever, the room had running cold water, a large table and a book shelf, and the old man, though himself a Jew, had touchingly hung a small crucifix over my bed since I had told him I was a Catholic.

In the middle of September I went to Eire. It was my first visit to the green island; the woods and meadows on either side of Cork Harbor looked their most emerald in the bright morning sun, as the boat was slowly steaming past them. The publisher had arranged for me to have dinner at a hotel with him and a theologian. The latter was a learned Canon of Cork Cathedral, very favorable to Therese Neumann, and we were to fight a verbal duel over the lady with the pub-lisher and his secretary as seconds, so to speak.

As we were ordering the meal there was an incident that could have happened nowhere except in Ireland. When asked what kind of soup we wanted, clear or thick, all four of us opted for clear. There ensued a whispered conversation between the publisher and the waitress, after which he turned round to us and said: "Not allowed to have clear—it's Ember Wednesday today, and the clear soup is made with meat." Its being a day of fasting and abstinence, the latter was on the menu only for the apostate English!

Then the Canon and I began our theological disputation. It was blow and parry, blow and parry all through the soup (thick), the fish and the pudding. I left none of his arguments unanswered. As he said goodbye to me after the coffee, he admitted: "You have shaken me." Next morning he sent a note to the publisher to say he had had no idea that there were so many possibilities of a natural interpretation of the phenomena.

In the afternoon I had to undergo another ordeal. I was taken to the Dominican house of studies and confronted with one of the Fathers there. There the issue was whether, the situation being what it was, it was desirable that such a critical account as I was going to produce should be written by a Catholic. The verdict of the Dominican was that, since the case was doubtful, it was better that this should be pointed out by a Catholic rather than be left to unbelievers. It would, indeed, be a service to the Church to raise a critical voice in this dubious matter.

At last the publisher was satisfied that he could risk it. Next day I relaxed, going to look at the shops. As I was buying a pair of stockings I had a conversation with the assistant. The world was in a bad state, wasn't it. In the end it all came to the question of religion—people no longer believed in God.

"We have our religion," she said, "and you have yours. . . ."

"But I am a Catholic, too."

She beamed. How wonderful that I should come from

England (neither Irish nor Americans usually notice my slight foreign accent) and yet be a Catholic. Did I know Blessed Martin Porres? Yes, certainly, as he was a Dominican lay-brother, I being a Dominican Tertiary. When she heard that, she then and there produced a small picture of him with a relic from her handbag and gave it to me over the counter. I have kept it in my prayer book ever since, a reminder that religion can be part of human life even in a modern department store.

The next months were filled up with work on the book. It was no pleasant task. Wherever I probed there were samples of pious fraud, if fraud could ever be pious! Alleged miracles that had never happened, approvals by authoritative ecclesiastics that had long been withdrawn and were yet repeated over and over again as proof of the authenticity of the phenomena, flagrant evidence of conceit hushed up or twisted till it appeared as a virtue . . . I admit I sometimes found it difficult to keep my temper. Not that I blamed Therese herself; she was but the victim of circumstances. But there was St. John of the Cross, made a doctor of the Church for his unique contribution to mystical theology, the most sceptical of men where strange phenomena were concerned, forever deprecating visions, trance states and the rest—yet hundreds of priests and even a goodly number of bishops were prostrating themselves at least metaphorically before the stigmatic of Konnersreuth as if they had never read a line of his works. No wonder that the multitude of the faithful, to say nothing of the Catholic popular press, followed suit and made Konnersreuth a place of pilgrimage, regardless of the caution of the diocesan bishop, and in flagrant contradiction to the practice of the Church which forbids pilgrimages to living people. No, my book would not be popular, but it would at least reflect the teaching of the Church.

Early in 1949 I could at last move to a less unpleasant

room. I had been there only a few weeks when one morning, as I was just sitting down for breakfast, a child arrived with a message that my mother had been taken seriously ill quite suddenly, would I go around to the kitchen of the presbytery at once. She had been suffering for some time from high blood pressure; when the doctor arrived he looked serious and told me she would have to give up work for good—after all, she was nearly seventy, and needed a complete rest immediately. I took her to her room in a taxi wondering what to do. If we had had a home together, the problem would not have been too difficult, but with each of us in a furnished room in different parts of Oxford, things were not easy. I myself was struggling with an influenza and drugging myself with aspirins to keep on my feet. At this juncture I had a telegram from the publisher that he was in London and would I please come and see him. During our conversation he mentioned the possibility of my moving to Cork to join his staff; there would be little difficulty of finding a flat there for Mother and myself, since housing conditions in Eire were better than in this country. It seemed a ray of hope, for by this time I was sufficiently desperate to take any job anywhere as long as there was a chance of making a home for the two of us.

While Mother was making a slow, but sure recovery, I finished my book on Therese Neumann and sent the manuscript to Cork. After that I felt ready for a holiday. Mrs. Beardall had invited Mother to stay with her while I was away; so in the middle of May I went to Rome.

I had given myself three weeks in the Eternal City, for I wanted to enjoy it at leisure. I hate "doing" places, guidebook in hand. If I miss some three-asterisked sights—well, I simply don't mind. I like to get the feel of a place, to relax in its atmosphere, look at the people (at the shops, too, I must admit); I unblushingly confess to having been in the rue de la Paix in Paris before going to the Louvre, and I like to return to spots which, for some reason or other, hold a special attraction for me.

So perhaps it is not so surprising that I should have spent my first afternoon in Rome in a somewhat unorthodox manner, having tea with three bearded Capuchins in an American club opposite St. Peter's—there being no other place in Rome where a religious could sit down to have a meal, as one of them, whom I knew from Oxford, ruefully informed me. We did, however, look at St. Peter's afterwards.

Next morning I went to Santa Sabina, the Dominican House on the Aventine Hill to see one of the Fathers who had once been Prior at Oxford and was now a *Socius* of the General. I squeezed myself into the Circolare, that useful and permanently overcrowded tramline which takes you almost anywhere in Rome, and was soon elbowed right into the center of the roaring, jostling, smelly mass of humanity seething in its belly. Here I learned to divide Italians into people who kick their elbows into you while apologetically shouting *Permesso* and those who do the same without such formalities. Though the good nuns at the convent where I was staying had given me minute directions where to get out, I was too preoccupied trying to avoid elbows to notice where we were going. Then, at one stop, almost everybody was surging forward, so I thought it just as well to let myself be disgorged with the rest, especially as the smells had become quite overpowering.

As I was standing in the road wondering what direction to take I suddenly saw a Dominican habit on the other side. I dashed across and, not knowing Italian, said inquiringly: "Santa Sabina, Padre?"

To my utter relief he asked back in unmistakably trans-atlantic accents: "You speak English?"

I was in luck this morning, for Father Tindal-Atkinson was at home and ready to take me in hand. Of course an audience with the Holy Father must be arranged; he would see to it that I got a special one, with only a few other people. But first of all he must show me around the church and the house, with the cells of St. Dominic himself, and of St. Pius V, the Dominican Pope. Oh yes, I was allowed to go in, for there was no enclosure, as the buildings were under government protection.

I at once lost my heart to the church of Santa Sabina, a marvel of restoration, coming as near as possible to the original sixth century basilica. As I walked in, the dazzling rays of the Italian sun were falling through the windows above the high altar and the nave, caressing the two rows of exquisite marble columns into a delicate pink, filling the sanctuary, playing about the choir stalls, and, reflected from the inlaid marble floor, transforming the whole church into a harmony of light, space, beauty that expressed to perfection the purity and freedom of the Christian faith. It was utterly different from the great abbey church of Einsiedeln where I had been the year before; it was almost incredible that the same faith had inspired both the stucco angels and the marble columns; indeed only a faith that was Catholic in its very essence could have shown itself in such totally different forms.

This was borne in on me even more forcibly when I went to see the other great churches of Rome, Santa Maria Maggiore, Santa Maria in Domnica, St. John Lateran. It was May, the month of Mary, and the first sight that struck me in almost every church was a large picture of our Lady, surrounded by an outsize halo. The picture was invariably a trashy oleograph, the halo gilded sheet metal. Men, women and children were kneeling before it, praying with great devotion. Then my eyes would wander to the apse. Yes, there it was—a ninth century mosaic of our Lady with the Child surrounded by angels. The light was playing on the tesserae, the colors, dark blue and shining gold, emerald green and a

deep, warm brown vied with each other to express the realities of another world, the majestic gentleness of the Mother
of God, the omnipotent smallness of the divine Child, the
rapt angelic adoration. It almost forced one into prayer, with
its silent symbolism, its contemplative grandeur. Was nobody
looking at it? No; they were all gazing at the gaudy Madonna
and her sham halo. I could hardly blame them; it was the
only beauty they knew in their daily life, the peroxide
glamor of Hollywood translated into religious terms.

For religion was, indeed, part of their daily life. It did
not shock me, as it had once shocked Luther, that they behaved in church with a familiarity which, in Northern countries, would have been stark irreverence. They regarded the
church as their home, and it is our Father's house, after all.
Though their nonchalance could take embarrassing forms
sometimes.

I was in the Lady Chapel of Santa Maria Maggiore; in
front of me a woman deep in her devotions, with her small
daughter kneeling beside her. Suddenly the child began to
cough, with the unmistakable noise of whooping cough.
Once, twice—then she was violently sick, all over the marble
floor. Mama just gave her one irritated glance, then continued her prayers. The same thing happened at least three
times during the next ten minutes, by which time the mother
had become either so used to it or so abstracted in her pious
exercises that she did not even look around any more. Quite
unperturbed she finished her program to the last Amen, then
took her daughter and walked out, carefully avoiding the
prodigious mess on the floor. A few minutes later a uni-
formed attendant appeared, gave the mess one glance and,
without so much as raising an eyebrow, walked off to fetch
a cloth to mop it up, as naturally as a maid would clean a
nursery, while the famous old icon of our Lady looked down
on the scene with a faint, motherly smile.

Father Tindal-Atkinson had kept his promise to ask for

an audience for me. When I came home one evening early in June, the nuns told me excitedly that a messenger from the Vatican had left a *billetto* for me. I was to present myself at 11 o'clock on June eighth. Fortunately Pius XII had considerably relaxed the rules for women's clothes: only in private audiences the long black dress was still *de rigueur,* but mine was a special one, long sleeves and a high neck was all that would be required. So I put on my grey travelling costume, black shoes and stockings and a black mantilla, and took a bus to St. Peter's.

When I presented my card I was entrusted to two Swiss Guards who led the way to the audience room. Walking between these giants I began to feel considerably reduced in size, and this feeling continued to increase as I had to walk through room after room, all gold and white and crimson and, so it seemed to me at least, one larger and higher than the other. By the time I had arrived at my destination I had shrunk to Lilliputian dimensions, while my surroundings, including the black and purple Monsignori, seemed to have come straight from Brobdingnag. The only people that appeared to be of normal size were the two American nuns already there, who were evidently to be received together with me. But even they had an uncanny touch about them: for their arms, from their elbows to their wrists, were covered with rosaries. For one crazy moment I wondered whether everybody had to arrive with loads of rosaries for the Holy Father to bless and whether it was a horrible *faux pas* that I should have come without any. . . . But then I realized, with an inaudible sigh of relief, that they must be carrying the rosaries of their whole community. It was hardly to be expected that a private individual like me should take the pious objects of all her friends and acquaintances with her to Rome!

The two nuns and I exchanged a few whispered words. After about a quarter of an hour the pope entered, the tall, slender figure in white familiar from innumerable pictures. For a moment it looked to me as if the nun whose turn it was first was about to shake hands with him; I once heard the story of an American bishop who exclaimed, when an English priest had kissed his ring: "Gee, Father, that's a new one on me." So perhaps the Sister was not quite sure at first, but on a sign from one of the Monsignori she went down on her knee, after all.

When the two had left it was my turn. It was one of the rare moments in my life that found me all but tongue-tied. I was acutely conscious of standing beside the Vicar of Christ, the "Christ upon earth," in the words of St. Catherine of Siena. He first spoke to me about the Patristic Lexicon, such a great and much needed work, as indeed it was (if only I had not to look up all these references day by day —but I did not tell him that) and gave his blessing to it. When I told him, that I was a native of Germany, he immediately changed into German, asked about my family, and finally, at my request, sent a blessing to my mother adding: "And for all those dear to you." Then he motioned one of the Monsignori who handed him a medal which he gave to me, as I knelt for his blessing.

Though I had really been somewhat overawed, the chief impression I took away with me, as I walked back through the endless flight of rooms, was of the extraordinary simplicity and fatherliness of Pius XII. As he was speaking to me I felt he was actually concerned at that moment with my work and well-being, as the earthly Father of the Church with one of his children. There was around him all the pomp and circumstance of the Vatican: the Monsignori, the Swiss Guards, the imposing rooms with their precious tapestries, the whole apparatus of the Church as an earthly institution and source of power, whose chief representative he certainly was. But there was another side, the side which I had realized far more deeply during these few minutes the audience had lasted. For the Church is not only an organization, it is the Body of Christ, whose head He is Himself, the High Priest. What impressed me most was the priestly quality of Pius XII, this mystery of the Catholic priesthood which can make the celibate a father far more strikingly than natural fatherhood. I had often felt that with other priests; but in this brief encounter with the man whom Catholics all over the world call "the Holy Father" it was brought home to me more vividly than ever before, as a reflection of what the divine Fatherhood must mean.

I saw the pope once more before I left. On my arrival the Reverend Mother of the convent where I was staying had told me that there was going to be a canonization on the fourteenth of June; and though I had planned to leave earlier, it was too wonderful an opportunity to miss, especially as Father Tindal-Atkinson had promised to get me a good ticket.

About a hundred people had arrived at the convent for the canonization; so we all had Holy Communion at 5:30 next morning, then a snack of breakfast, and after that set out for St. Peter's; for though the ceremony started only at eight, one had to be there about an hour and a half before, even if one had a ticket for a good seat.

The Dominicans had indeed done me proud. My place was on a tribune just opposite that of the Diplomats, between the papal throne and the high altar, so I missed nothing. St. Peter's lit up by thousands of electric lights and candles, filled with purpled bishops and scarlet-robed cardinals, was a wonderful spectacle in itself. The entry of the pope on the *sedes gestatoria*, to the sound of the famous silver trumpets and the excited *Viva il Papa!* of the enthusiastic crowds was all the more a thrill for that it had happened for centuries in exactly the same way. Here, in St. Peter's, at one of the most impressive ceremonies of the Church, a Catholic could not help feeling at the center of a Christendom of all places and all ages. This universality was borne in on me with particular force when the Gospel and the Alleluia verse of the Mass were chanted in Greek as well as in Latin. However much I might often writhe under my constant occupation with Greek patristics, I could not help being carried away by the magnificent Greek chant now filling St. Peter's, as if it had been a particular greeting for me and my work.

I was interrupted in my musings by a slight movement on my right: the Italian nun sitting next to me suddenly dropped forward as if she were about to faint. Her Sisters on the other side gave her one glance but evidently decided it was not sufficiently serious to interrupt their attention to the service, rather in the way of the mother of the child with the whooping cough. I remembered that I had put some very strong peppermint lozenges in my handbag in case of emergency. I passed one to the drooping Sister; after a moment's hesitation she took it, put it in her mouth and under its influence gradually revived. I had the satisfaction that next time she was feeling faint she trustingly turned to me to provide some more.

The papal blessing on the Lexicon which I brought back with me from Rome caused great excitement in our room in the New Bodleian. Our Editor was no longer Dr. Cross but Mr., now Professor, Lampe; under him the staff, Catholics, Anglicans and Free Church, whom an orthodox monk from Mount Athos was to join later, were working together as harmoniously as we had done under his predecessor, and he was as thrilled as his Catholic collaborators that the pope had blessed our work.

I personally felt I needed every possible blessing to enable me to cope with my double job, Lexicon and writing. I was now anxiously waiting what the publisher would say to the book I was soon to call my *enfant terrible*. A few days after my return from Rome I had a letter from 'him telling me that his most trusted ecclesiastical advisers had warned him not to publish it. He himself gave a vivid account of the extraordinary affair in an American periodical, *The Vincentian*. "These men," he wrote, "warned me that we were playing with fire and begged us to have nothing to do with the whole affair," and he admitted to handling the parcel with the manuscript on its arrival "as if it contained an atom bomb about to explode."

Despite the fears of his advisers he decided to publish the book, but first the manuscript underwent a thorough examination, as a result of which some of my more vigorous statements were toned down. Unfortunately this process resulted in a manipulation of various passages which I felt had to be left as they stood, so I suggested I should come again to Ireland in September and go point by point through all the alterations.

So it was Cork once more, a city I shall always remember as the scene of theological discussions. We spent two days re-revising the manuscript, until it had at last reached the state we agreed should be final. Then I went for a fortnight to Blarney, just outside Cork, to recover from my exertions.

My visit to Eire had also another purpose: I wanted to ascertain whether there really might be a chance of securing a job—and a home—there. But it all looked very uncertain. So I resolved to make a decisive assault on divine providence, a Novena to our Lady involving the recitation of the fifteen mysteries of the Rosary each day. But as I belong to the school of thought that believes in combining supernatural with natural means, I also wrote a letter to a person in Oxford who, I knew, sometimes had information on houses or flats available. His reply came by return of post. My letter had come at a very opportune moment—there was a small house just about to be vacant; he enclosed the notice.

I could hardly believe it possible. I sent my mother the notice asking her to look at the house, while I was finishing my Novena and went to kiss the Blarney stone to receive "the gift of the gab," so necessary for the forthcoming controversy on my book.

When I returned to Oxford my mother was waiting for me in my miserable attic room. With studied politenes she asked: "How was your holiday? Did you have fine weather?"

"I don't care two hoots, darling—what about the house?"

She smiled. "Go and sign the contract first thing tomorrow morning."

"But I must see it first."

"No need for you to see it—it's just what we want, make sure of it at once."

If Mother was as enthusiastic as all that, I felt I could safely sign the contract without having seen the house.

I think one must have lived in rooms for years, as I had, in order fully to appreciate what it means to have a home of one's own. It seemed unbelievable at first, and I was quite sure that it was true only after we had actually moved in, and I had slept the first night blissfully conscious that there were no other people above, below and beside me, playing the radio, stampeding over my head, using the bathroom just when I wanted it. Living in "digs" can be an excellent training in unselfishness; but I felt I had had just about enough of it. I was deeply grateful to have at last a stable background, my own four walls where I could live and work and see people, without having to worry whether my nextdoor neighbor would let his phonograph blare till I was driven crazy, or whether the lady in the room below was going to complain that I disturbed her morning's rest when I was going out to Mass.

The Lexicon, too, had temporarily acquired a new look. A young Scotsman had joined the staff, John B.; he was an excellent classical scholar, but almost entirely devoid of theological knowledge and understanding, slightly neurotic, interested in spiritualism and Indian religions, and apparently given to experimenting with the emotions of some of the younger feminine members of the staff. I have never quite understood why he got into the habit of giving me toy animals of every description. One morning I would remove a large tome from my table, which suddenly released a tortoise creeping noisily towards me; another time there would be a hen which, when you pressed her back, began to lay eggs. There were bears, geese running along the floor, monkeys, long-tailed mice as well as children's trumpets which he would have liked me to blow, and at least half a dozen rubber thimbles to help me turn the pages of the hundred and sixty-one volumes of Abbé Migne's *Greek Patrology*.

Besides, he was very clever at making things out of pipe cleaners, and soon a whole collection of white devils in various postures were displaying their wicked charms on the top of our filing cabinet.

The craze had begun before Christmas, and it was carried on into carnival time. My place was by one of the windows, and the dozens of toys with which John had presented me were by this time all assembled on the windowsill. Then one morning he came in with a wonderful red balloon on which a white face was outlined. I could not resist the temptation, I simply had to blow it up. But where was I going to put it? I selected a chair opposite the Editor's seat, to which I attached it. Mr. Lampe had a great sense of fun and was sure to laugh at it when he came in.

About 11 o'clock the door opened, enter Mr. Lampe. But he was not alone. Horror of horrors, on this of all the days of the year someone who had never visited us before came with him: the Curator of the Bodleian. Mr. Lampe gazed at the balloon floating gaily in the air, making a face at the Curator who stared at it, speechless. Had the Bodleian, most venerable of libraries, Duke Humphrey and all that, been turned into a dancing-hall? With truly admirable presence of mind the Editor rose to the occasion and remarked nonchalantly: "I suppose it must be somebody's birthday." And with this he took the Curator to the Card Index, where the pipe-cleaner devils, alas, gave further evidence of the most frivolous of Patristic lexicographers. But by that time I had at least brushed my entire collection of toys from the window-sill and hidden them beneath piles of quarto sheets soberly covered with Greek characters.

The only uncanny experience I have so far had in my life occurred while John was with us. Among the quantity of rubber thimbles he had given me there was one black one, which I used a good deal. When I came in one morning I looked for it in the drawer where I normally kept it, but it was not there. I hunted for it all over the place, no sign of it. I began to work without it. About 11 o'clock I was looking out of the window for a moment, when I sensed—whether I heard or rather felt it I could not say—something like a swish. I turned my head: there, on my blotting paper, right in front of me, was the thimble. There was nobody sitting near me. I had been using that blotting paper all the morning, there was absolutely no chance that I might have overlooked it. About five minutes later John came in. I asked him what he had done with the thimble; he grinned, but denied all knowledge of it. I had had to read a good deal about poltergeists and other strange phenomena for my Therese Neumann book, and I have no doubt that this was an, admittedly very minor, case of telekinesis, and that John, who dabbled in spiritualism, had been responsible for it.

18. *"Masonry, Rationalism and Miss Graef . . "*

1950 WAS one of those years which one likes to remember in retrospect, but which are nightmares to be lived through. My *enfant terrible* was looming large on my horizon. Even before *The Case of Therese Neumann* was actually published, it had lost me several friends. That I, a laywoman, hence doubly inferior by definition, should dare to contradict an archbishop, that I should take it upon myself to cast doubts on the authenticity of phenomena which had been accepted as supernatural by a large number of priests to say nothing of the devout laity, was more than some of them could stomach. I was not a safe person to consort with. That the book had received the *Imprimatur* in my own archdiocese did not seem to make any difference.

I remember one evening, after a study week-end at a convent in London, when I was asked to explain my views. In the course of the discussion I was confronted with several "miracles" which the good ladies who had attended the week-end had heard about and considered authentic. They were totally unsubstantiated stories which no diocesan commission, let alone a Roman one, would ever have accepted as miracles in their dreams. I pointed out the weak spots in these tales, but succeeded only in convincing my audience of my own intolerable scepticism and conceit. It was a foretaste of what to expect at the hands of a devout, uncritical Catholic public, as ready to believe in signs and wonders as their Protestant counterparts in walled-up nuns, and priests seducing young girls in the confessional, as I had read myself in a contemporary novel not so long ago.

However, the book was not published yet. If I was to be taught one particular virtue that year, it was patience. In May the publishers wrote resignedly that they had urged the printers to do their best to speed up production but had received no answer to their repeated enquiries. In July I was told the printers were on holiday. In September they were on strike. And all my "friends" were asking me every time they saw me: "When is IT coming out?" not, I was almost sure, entirely without a touch of malice. The final straw was an Irish railway strike just before Christmas. However, when I came back from Mass on Christmas Day, I found a large parcel on the dining room table. I could not refrain from putting one copy of the *enfant terrible* among my Christmas Cards.

When I had a friend coming to tea next day I drew her attention to the book on the mantelpiece. She gave it one uninterested glance and then talked about something else. I awaited the reviews with some trepidation.

I breathed a sigh of relief when two prominent Jesuits, Archbishop Roberts and Father Martindale, and one well-known Catholic doctor, Letitia Fairfield, wrote very favorably about it in the leading Catholic weeklies. Nearly all the other English Catholic publications followed suit; but, to my great grief, Father Conrad, for whom I had been writing ever since my reception into the Church, flatly refused to review the book in his periodical *Life of the Spirit*, and soon afterwards returned, without an explanation, several articles

of mine which he had already accepted. It was the end of a
long literary as well as personal relationship.

In Eire, where the reception had been mixed, the then
President of Cork University, Professor Alfred O'Rahilly,
attacked me so violently over Radio Eireann that the publishers asked that I should be given the opportunity of a
reply. It was the first of a series of attacks not only on the
book, but also on my personal character and faith. The professor accused me, *inter alia,* of "systematic denigration of an
inoffensive living person," of "a lot of intimate prying, slick
insinuations and some really cattish remarks." He then advanced an argument which I was to hear more often, namely
that any investigation of the supernatural origin of the phenomena was of interest only to experts: "As against Miss
Graef I hold that a description—still more a sight—of what
is happening is of far greater importance than an inconclu-
sive investigation." It was unfortunate for my critic that he
held this not only against me, but against the authorities of
the Church, who are most meticulous in ascertaining the origin of strange phenomena. Just a few months before Professor O'Rahilly's radio attack the official attitude of the Church
had once more been stated in no uncertain terms by Monsignor, now Cardinal, Ottaviani in an authoritative article in
the *Osservatore Romano.* Secure in the knowledge that the
official doctrine of the Church on my side, I wrote a meas-
ured reply for Radio Eireann. It was read for me by someone
else, for by this time I was taking a holiday from controversy
at Florence.

As I have said before, I have no conscience at all about
missing world-famous sights in which I am not interested.
I "did" the Uffizien from a sense of duty, but I do not think
I spent more than an hour in this celebrated museum; for
most museums give me backache. Instead I had three mornings in San Marco, the former Dominican monastery now

turned into a museum of Fra Angelico. Fra Angelico ranges
for me immediately after icons and mosaics, together with El
Greco and before Rembrandt. It is probably a defect that my
taste should be so very selective; indeed, I have a Platonic
appreciation also of other great artists, say Michelangelo or
Frans Hals or Renoir. I respect their art, their genius—but
I do not love them. I cannot gaze at their pictures spell-
bound, tearing myself away from them only with an effort.

San Marco is unique in that the pictures are still where
they were originally intended to be, on the walls of the
monastery cells on which many of them were painted directly. The prayers of the Dominican friars that went up to
the bleeding Crucifix, to the tenderly smiling Madonna, seem
still to hover around the images painted by one whose art was
itself the overflow of prayer. To me the criterion of religious
art is the presentation of angels. The hieratic, dark-winged
figures of the mosaics embody all the majesty of the spiritual
beings, as it is described in the "Celestial Hierarchies" of the
Pseudo-Dionysius and in St. Thomas Aquinas' treatise "De
Angelis." Fra Angelico's angels, though less hieratic, yet have
an unearthly charm; musicians, they, before the throne of the
Almighty. But the fat-cheeked babies of the Renaissance—
no. Perhaps it is partly due to these modern representations
that our contemporaries find it so difficult to believe in
angels. The babies as well as the anemic young females of
modern repository art can scarcely claim to be symbols of
invisible powers; there is no suggestion of another world
about them, as there so patently is in the paintings of the
medieval Dominican.

San Marco, the black and white cathedral with its exquisite campanile, and, yes, the fireworks one night and the fair
along the river with its stalls of fruit and sausages and con-
fectionery—this is my memory of Florence, the city, too, of
Savonarola, his preaching, his burning at the stake—but I

was on holiday, on holiday especially from controversy, I did not fancy being reminded of burning!

After another ten days complete rest at the Chiemsee in Bavaria, with orgies of sunshine, whipped cream, and bathing, I once more went to Regensburg, where Professor Waldmann was ready to take me in hand and make me work. For the book on Therese Neumann was indeed finished, but he wanted to supply me with additional material so that I could refute attacks more effectively. Besides, it was essential that I should see Therese's diocesan, Archbishop Buchberger, so he arranged an audience for me, during which I presented my book. The archbishop was very amiable, indeed. He greatly regretted the sensation mongering of Konnersreuth and authorized me to state in public, if necessary, that his attitude to the case had remained unchanged since 1937. In that year Therese had refused a request from the entire German episcopate backed by the Holy Office in Rome to have herself examined in a hospital in order to prove her alleged complete fast from all food and drink for the last ten years. Consequently the archbishop had declined to give any more permits to visit her except in special cases, and to take any responsibility for the authenticity of the phenomena. This cautious attitude of the responsible ecclesiastical authority, however, had never prevented either faithful or priests from flocking to Konnersreuth in their thousands and make it a veritable center of pilgrimage.

In the course of the conversation the archbishop asked me: "Did my permission help you at Konnersreuth?"

"I am afraid not, Your Grace."

He smiled. "I thought so."

On my return to Oxford I found a letter from an editor of one of the Catholic weeklies asking me to write an article on Therese. This brought Professor O'Rahilly on the plane again, who once more attacked me with all the violence of his

Irish temperament. I was beginning to learn that reasoned judgement and objectivity have little place where religious fanaticism is concerned, and contented myself with pointing out that two opinions on the case were possible, reiterating the arguments for mine. In the course of this correspondence a letter appeared from a gentleman who had recently visited Therese. His description of her greatly amused me. "I expected to see a gaunt, haggard and ascetic-looking person because of her suffering and of her total lack of material food or drink for 30 years—except daily Communion. I was delighted to discover a lovely woman, warm soft skinned, round faced and plump. . . . My heart glowed." Perhaps it is just as well that the Church never canonizes a living person, else the judgement of the experts on a beatification commission might also be in danger of being swayed by a soft skin and a round face. Naturally I was less susceptible to these physical charms of hers.

About the same time the controversy started with even greater fury in the United States. I had been quite ignorant of the fact that Therese Neumann was not only an article of faith for many devout American Catholics, but also a vested interest of certain popular Catholic papers, which regaled their avid readers with an inexhaustible flow of miracles of the "Saint." One gentleman wrote me a five page letter informing me that I must be "a willing or unwilling instrument of the devil." The non plus ultra was a chapter in a book on quite a different subject by a well-known priest headed: "Hilda Graef and Theresa Neumann." After calling me an "ignorant trickster," "hoodwinking our Catholic book reviewers" with "charges of sinful fraud" on the part of Therese Neumann which were "an insult to the Catholic priesthood," he finally broke out into the *cri de coeur*: "Masonry, Rationalism and Miss Graef are . . . destroying the influence of Therese Neumann." As, in the course of his peroration, he had also called a good Catholic doctor (J.

Deutsch) now dead, "a fanatical rationalist and fallen-away Catholic" whose disciple he alleged me to be, though I had never either known him or read his publications, I wrote him a very polite letter pointing out all his errors which were, indeed, many. As he had devoted eight pages to a discussion of, or rather assault on, my book, I was somewhat staggered when he admitted in his reply that he had never even read it! He had derived his information from the pamphlet by another priest, which he enclosed. Though he had not the grace to apologize for his offensive and quite unfounded remarks, he informed me at least that he would "step out of the controversy," and the chapter was actually left out in the later editions and translations of his book.

Despite this outburst of popular fury, however, the book received favorable reviews in many quarters, also in America; the Jesuits particularly took up the cudgels on my behalf, but also a good many other priests and lay reviewers felt that the book had done a service to the Church by investigating the phenomena impartially. For it was simply not true that I had attacked Therese Neumann, as so many of my opponents wrote, unless the word be used in the hitherto unknown sense of "examine." To examine the facts of a strange case of stigmatization, including the behavior of the stigmatized person herself, surely is not "attacking" her. I did, indeed, attack something in my book, and I shall continue doing the same unrepentingly. But this object of my attacks is neither Therese Neumann nor stigmatization in general, but credulity, superstition, and false mysticism, which have always been a danger to the true faith and are especially so in the present age.

The controversy eventually died down in America, only to flare up again, this time with unprecedented violence, in Switzerland and Germany, especially Bavaria, when the German translation of my book was published in Einsiedeln. It began even before the book was out with an avalanche of abusive letters to the publishers. One of them stated that the book was "a real work of the devil." I personally like best the terms in which it was described on an open postcard as "the vile book of the vile witch of Albion" (*das gemeine Buch der gemeinen Hexe Albions*), but greatly regret they left out the "perfidious" before Albion. Next, a highly colored account appeared in a small Swiss newspaper in which I was alternately described as an "English Miss" and "the German-English-American" (no less!) Hilda Graef, and in which the author expressed the pious hope that my book would appear without an *Imprimatur*. The gentleman's expectations were doomed to disappointment. The Swiss edition appeared not only with one, but with two *Imprimaturs,* the original Birmingham one and another from the Swiss diocese of Chur. Consequently the bishop of Chur, too, received abusive letters from Therese's friends. In fact, the ecclesiastical authorities were soon reviled as vigorously as I myself, for Chur refused the *Imprimatur* to a wild pamphlet entitled *Justice for Konnersreuth*. This refusal produced a pink leaflet which ended with the extraordinary statement: "We do not think that He (Christ) would stroke the contemporary scribes and rationalists with velvet paws (*Sammetpfoetchen*). Not even the prelates!" It was soon followed by another, in which the author (who gave his name and address) ventured the following prophecy: "After the Marian Year (1954) there will come a catastrophe such as the world has never yet known. Then the Church will be purged from the rationalists."

I had by now a powerful ally. Father Siwek, a Jesuit expert on psychology, had written a book on Konnersreuth in which he approached the case from a different angle, but came to the same conclusion as I. Naturally he, too, was a "rationalist." This was rather confusing; for in one of the abusive letters to the Swiss publishers it had just been stated that people like myself were responsible for keeping Switzer-

land closed to the Jesuits! Besides, his book was prefaced by
a very laudatory letter from no less a personage than the
Secretary of the Sacred Congregation of Rites. Nevertheless
from now on Father Siwek and I were usually condemned
together; but at least it could not be said of him, as it was of
me, that his book was "the revenge of an offended female"
(*die Rache eines gekraenkten Weibes*), because my reception
at Konnersreuth had not been as favorable as I had expected.

Nevertheless the campaign against the book effectively
prevented its wider distribution, and the German reviewers
hardly dared express a favorable opinion, after one of Therese's personal friends in the Bavarian clergy had written a
whole series of outsize articles on my book, reproaching me,
inter alia, for such faults as having been born in Berlin and
living now in Oxford! Yet Professor Waldmann, who had
not these disadvantages of nationality, but was a Bavarian
born and bred, had been of the same opinion as I. Evidently
any broomstick was good enough to beat the witch!

My former countryman Friedrich Schiller has written:
"Even the gods fight in vain against stupidity." Credulity is
even more difficult to conquer, and, linked with superstition,
is indeed all but invincible, enclosing the mind with an iron
curtain that cannot be penetrated by reason. It is faith that
seeks understanding, credulity and superstition that abhor it.
The controversy in which I had been involved during these
years had taught me a good deal about the difference between
them, but also about the need for patience and charity in
dealing with those unable to grasp this difference. Anger and
personal abuse are bad weapons with which to fight for the
cause of truth; the tone in which the controversy was conducted on the side of Therese Neumann's adherents failed
to commend belief in the supernatural origin of the phenomena she exhibited.

19. *New Friends and Trends*

THOUGH I was still groaning under the boredom of my Lexicon work, nevertheless, at this time the Greek fathers provided a salutary relief from the tantrums of the Konnersreuth fans. Throughout 1951 all my spare time was taken up with translating two treatises of Gregory of Nyssa for the *Ancient Christian Writers* series.

It was difficult work. The complicated language of this great Cappadocian was none too easy to puzzle out, but it was even more difficult to render it into smoothly reading English. Fourth century Byzantine Greek is florid and diffusive, its writers indulge in luxurious strings of epithets, synonymous nouns heaped one upon the other, exotic compounds, far-fetched metaphors, all flung recklessly into one enormous hodgepodge of a sentence, which the ill-fated translator has to break up, smooth out, pare, turn inside out and upside down, yet all without in the least changing the meaning of the original, in order to make it not only accessible, but pleasing to English readers.

Yet it was in many ways a labor of love, both for the Greek fathers and for the two languages, whose genius is so different. For if Greek may be called the tongue of metaphysicians, English is perhaps that of politicians, of men of action, with its wealth of verbs, its aversion to compounds, its richness of nuances and its unlimited possibilities of insinuation and implication. It is difficult to *sound* profound in English. Try, for example, to translate some German profundity into English, and out comes more often than not either nonsense or a commonplace. In a similar way the metaphysical finesses as well as the emotional exaggerations of Byzantine Greek are difficult to reproduce in modern English, to which speculation for its own sake is foreign, and which conveys emotion only by hint or understatement.

But these difficulties of the translator are also his exciting opportunities. Sometimes, after brooding for twenty minutes over a particularly obstinate passage, the inspiration will come in a flash: "Yes, that's it—I am sure this is how Gregory would have expressed it had he been writing in English." I hope I shall not be considered reactionary if I venture to suggest that no electronic brain, however many words may be fed into it, will ever be able to do the work of a human translator, except for scientific textbooks.

In September the Greek Lexicon staff was in a state of excitement, for in connection with the celebrations of the fifteen-hundredth anniversary of the Council of Chalcedon, the First International Conference for Patristic Studies was taking place at Oxford under the auspices of Professor Cross. Professor Lampe was giving an account of our work, I myself was reading a communication on the concept of ecstasy in the Greek fathers, besides reporting the Congress for *The Tablet*. The program of lectures was extremely heavy, and in the lunch hour Professor Lampe and I had to be in our room in the New Bodleian to show visitors a carefully pruned collection of our materials. We had, like all such scholarly undertakings, a whole assembly of skeletons rattling in our cupboards, or rather filing cabinets, which we did not want to frighten our visitors. We were all very much on our best behavior, no balloons floating above the editorial chair this time, and I arrayed myself in a black costume to look as clerical as possible in this clerical assembly, in which women were in a devastatingly small minority. It was a sign of changed times and tempers that the festal lecture on the Council was delivered by a German Jesuit standing beneath the portrait of Henry VIII in the hall of Christ Church.

If my *enfant terrible* had lost me some old friends, it also gained me new ones. A few months after its publication I received a most extraordinary letter. It came from Madrid. The writer, after stating that she knew Konnersreuth and Therese Neumann very well, indeed, went on to tell me that she had just received two registered letters emanating from the circle around the stigmatic, accusing her, whom I will call Miss X., of the authorship of my book and urging an explanation. One of the letters was actually addressed to "Miss X., alias Miss Hilda C. Graef."

My first reaction was: a hoax, heaven knows what these Konnersreuthers are up to. But my correspondent had anticipated this and, to prove her good faith, affixed a snapshot of herself. Her next letter contained the copy of a Munich publisher's letter, in which she was once more accused of having, if not written, at least inspired my book: "You deny," so this gentleman wrote, "having in any way contributed to the book by Hilda C. Graef, *The Case of Therese Neumann*. This plain affirmation of yours absolutely contradicts a statement coming from a quarter where Hilda Graef and the whole situation are well known. Since the injuries done to Therese Neumann in this book cannot remain uncontradicted . . . sooner or later this discrepancy will have to be discussed in public. I only wanted to tell you this, in order to give you an opportunity to explain your position."

This was strange, indeed. Anyone who knew me "and the whole situation" was aware, of course, that I had never so much as heard the name of the lady in Madrid. I had only two explanations: either the publisher was trying to bluff Miss X. into an admission of her "guilt," or Therese herself had suggested this connection in one of her "mystic" states, when she was wont to give all kinds of supposedly inspired information. Why Miss X. was thought in Konnersreuth to be connected with my book, I am not at liberty to divulge, but there was some reason for it. It was certainly an odd way for a friendship to start; but our correspondence soon became so intimate that I decided next year to go to Madrid for my holiday and collect, if possible, also some more material on this peculiar case.

After I had finished my translation of Gregory's treatises, I had originally intended to write a book on the spirituality of the Greek fathers, and had already started on it, when my attention was diverted to another subject.

Through some article I had written, correspondence had developed between a German Dominican nun at Speyer and myself. At the end of the year (1951), she asked me in a letter whether I had ever heard of Edith Stein. She had been teaching at her convent school and she, the Dominican, owed her much. I had read some extracts from Edith Stein's biography some time ago, but my immediate reaction had been: too intellectual for me, too feminist, and somewhat cold. I communicated this view to the Sister, who wrote back that it was quite wrong; Edith Stein had been a most warmhearted, kind, and saintly woman. I was not convinced. I had always had a certain aversion against modern philosophers, and now a woman philosopher! God forbid. The nun insisted. "She had a fine sense of humor," she wrote, "though she was never heard to burst out into loud laughter." This was quite enough to confirm me in my prejudice. I love laughter and have always privately disagreed with St. Thomas Aquinas who asserted that our Lord never laughed but, at the most, smiled.

Then, about two months later, I had a letter from an

American Capuchin Father in Italy with whom I was carrying on a correspondence about Therese Neumann. He wrote that he had just read a book on Edith Stein (the first biography by her own former novice mistress and prioress, Mother Theresia Renata) and had been very much impressed. I wrote back: "I have always had a certain unreasonable dislike of her, because she seemed so frightfully serious, ascetic, and philosophic, which I think is somehow opposed to my light-hearted and very un-German temperament. I far prefer people like the great St. Teresa and heartily concur with her saying: 'The Lord preserve us from frowning saints.' But of course Edith Stein may be really quite different from what I imagine her to be."

By way of answer the Capuchin sent me the biography. When I read there that, as a Carmelite, she could laugh at recreation till the tears rolled down her cheeks, I was already half reconciled, and what I learned about her end did the rest. My next reaction was that, after finishing my proposed book on the Greek fathers, I wanted to write a book about her myself, for this first biography was not much more than a collection of materials, and made no attempt at an interpretation. When I communicated my idea to the publishers, they suggested I should write this book first and postpone the Greek fathers. As I myself was very keen to write a book on a truly Christian woman whose life was yet entirely devoid of stigmata and other marvels, I scrapped all other literary plans and started work on Edith Stein.

The German nun who had been such a great friend of hers wrote that she was going to take the sixth form of her school to Paris in July for a vacation course. I made up my mind quickly. Paris was only an hour from London by air. There might not be another opportunity to see her so soon, and it was essential for me to meet somebody who had actually known Edith Stein well. So I flew to Paris on a very hot summer day. It was my first flight, and I thoroughly enjoyed it. To be high up above the clouds, with the channel, on which I was so easily seasick, far beneath me, relaxing in a comfortable armchair while smart air hostesses were serving tasty meals, was surely the ideal way of travelling. I had scarcely finished my coffee, when we were descending on Paris.

The nun had secured a room for me at the same convent in the center of Paris where she herself was staying with her twelve girls. The mid-July heat of Paris nearly finished me. Fortunately the Sister had a lecture in the afternoon; so after I had spent a couple of hours lying on my bed, moaning, for a change, about the Continental instead of the English climate, I went out to have a cup of atrocious tea and buy a flask of cognac. The cognac restored me almost miraculously, and by the time the Sister had returned I was ready to fire my barrage of questions at her, which she answered patiently, if sometimes a trifle hagiographically.

Next afternoon we went for a long walk through the sunbaked Bois de Boulogne and along the boulevards. I was consumed with the irrepressible desire for an ice cream on the pavement, watching the traffic and the Parisiennes in their chic and not quite so chic dresses. There were cafés all around us, the heat was overpowering, and I was feeling like the driest of sponges.

"What about an ice cream, Sister?"

"Oh, but not here."

"Why not? Such nice cafés."

"But I can't sit out here on the pavement in my habit!"

"Come, come, Sister, you are on holiday—and I am so dreadfully thirsty; it will be a positive act of charity if you sit down here with me and have an ice cream."

Thus argued the temptress in an up-to-date garden of Eden with a reluctant Eve in religious dress. What could Eve do, as the appeal was slyly made in the name of charity? She sat down with the serpent—and with a very bad conscience

—and had an ice cream on the boulevard, in open defiance of all the rules and regulations that govern the lives of European nuns. They are quite different in the States, I believe, where they rush about in cars and think nothing of staying in a hotel, as the men do, if there is no religious house to give them accommodation.

In return for all the information she had given me, the nun asked me to talk to her girls about England, and about the austerity which was still governing our life, since these German young women were so very materialistic and, at an age when they ought to be full of high ideals, seemed to think of nothing but good food, plenty of clothes, and a life of comfort. So she brought them down into the convent garden in the evening, and I began to describe our life in England, how we were still putting up with a good grace with rationing and all the discomforts inflicted on us in the interests of an equitable distribution, and the unselfish kindness that I had always found to be one of the most striking characteristics, especially during the air raids. I told them how, when I had come back to Germany last year, I had found a very disturbing one-sidedly materialistic outlook on life among a good many people I met. Even in Catholic Bavaria I had been unable to get fish one Friday in a restaurant on the border of the Chiemsee, a large lake teaming with fish; and when I had complained to the waitress she looked at me as if I were ripe for a lunatic asylum.

Then the girls answered with one accord: "But you see, we have suffered so terribly—all these years of starvation! You cannot imagine what we have gone through—it is only natural that we should now enjoy ourselves a little."

There they were, sturdy and pink-cheeked, whining about the privations they might, perhaps (they all came from the country, where starvation was not nearly so bad as in the cities) have experienced for not quite twelve months six years ago. I deliberately lost my temper. I shouted at them, because that was the only way of talking that might conceivably impress them a little: "Yes, that's typical. In English one calls it self-pity, the outstanding German fault. Who started the war? If you had won it, you would not have cared two pence about other nations starving. Goering or somebody of the Nazis said so in so many words: Whoever is going to starve in Europe, it will not be we. Now you had to go hungry yourselves, and the world never hears the end of it. You also complain that people are not very friendly to you if you go about speaking German in Paris. Do you realize that the Germans have invaded France three times within seventy years? What do you expect? That they will welcome you with open arms and ask you to do it a fourth time? You have no reason whatever to pity yourselves. You should rather be sorry for all the wrong Germany has done in the past."

They stared at me open-mouthed. But they had to be told the truth at least once, and in accentless German, though I had little hope that they would accept even part of it. I was the more angry because I had had a few extraordinary experiences with my former countrymen after the war. When one could once more correspond with Germany I had written to a cousin, a daughter of Sabine Lepsius, who had died during the war. I sent her one or two parcels, which were then allowed to contain only rationed foodstuffs, so that meant we had to deprive ourselves of our own meager allowance in order to help them. I did it gladly, but I had not expected that this would result in her demanding many other things, including a dozen electric bulbs. I pointed out to her that English bulbs did not have Continental fittings; besides, I doubted that they would arrive unbroken—after all I had no electrical shop. Her husband then wrote me a twelve-page letter, almost every sentence beginning: "Do you know that . . ." followed by an enumeration of all the unprecedented sufferings Germany had to endure, about which I should inform the English public. I pointed out that I was neither Prime Minister nor Foreign Secretary, and that, moreover, Germany had only herself to thank for the results of Nazism. With this the correspondence ceased.

Another acquaintance of mine, who had been a prisoner of war in Russia, thanked me for a food parcel I had sent him, but wrote he would prefer two pounds of tea. I replied our ration was a quarter of a pound per week, how could I send two pounds? He wrote back sneeringly, surely I could get enough in the black market? When I pointed out to him that the black market in this country was practically non-existent, besides that I was the last person to have any such connections, he demanded either several pounds of various spices or a thousand cigarettes. This was soon followed by a letter asking for ten meters of the best tulle for his small step-daughter who was training to be a ballet dancer. Fortunately I also had other experiences, but these certainly made me less inclined to take kindly to the orgies of self-pity in which these young women indulged in a Paris convent garden.

In September I carried out my plan to see Miss X. and flew to Madrid. I was surprised to find it a very modern city, where the cinemas are larger than the churches, and which boasted even a few skyscrapers. The women promenading on the Avenida José Antonio or emerging from taxis and private cars in the Puerta del Sol were all well dressed, with superbly groomed hair which it would, indeed, have been a pity to hide under a hat. I could see no evidence of a dictatorship holding the country in its iron grip, as had been only too obvious in the Berlin of the Third Reich. Though there was, of course, far more evidence of poverty than in England, and I soon learned to distinguish the noise the many unattended blind people made with their sticks on the pavement, life seemed gay and carefree under the cloudless gentian sky, and I fell headlong for my favorite pastime of loitering about in the streets of foreign cities, wandering into dark churches with their dressed up statues of the Madonna, or gazing at the beautifully decorated windows of the fashion shops.

I was staying at a very luxurious convent, waited on hand and foot by lay sisters and maids. They even had a shower in the bathroom which had been installed at the request of some American students. At the moment the only guests besides myself were a charming old lady, who was very much the *grande dame* and connected with high diplomatic circles, and an Italian school teacher. The latter informed me immediately that she also spoke English (generally the conversation at table was in French, as I do not speak Spanish), besides, of course, French, Spanish and German, in all of which she asserted to be equally fluent. After every two words in French she asked me condescendingly: "Do you understand that," in an English which, though not actually broken, was pronounced in such a way as to be almost unintelligible. As I understand French quite well, I was determined to get my own back; and every now and again, after she had said something which was really almost impossible to make out (she talked incessantly—Spanish, French, English), I looked at her with the blankest of blank expressions and asked back: "What do you mean?" When she repeated it louder, though no more correctly, I would administer the final blow and say, to the great amusement of the Spanish old lady: "Please repeat it in French, I really do not know what you mean."

She had the extraordinary custom of coming in for breakfast in her dressing gown, and made herself further unpopular by treating the serving nuns like her personal maids and holding forth nonstop on every subject under the sun. The climax came when I announced my intention to go to the Escorial with an excursion of Cooks. "But this will be much dearer than if you went by train! How much is it?" I told her. She threw up her hands. "But this is dreadful. This will be much dearer than if you went by yourself," I was trying to point out that I did not fancy going by train not knowing any Spanish, that I should have the advantage of English-speaking guides, and would not have to bother about arrangements for meals and so on. Then she rolled up her sleeves, metaphorically, and gave me a lecture, in which the most frequently occurring word was *pésètes*, the flow of French being only now and again interrupted by the inevitable "Do you understand?"

I did, indeed, understand; but took advantage of a second's pause while she was trying to think up yet another argument, to point out that it was, after all, my own affair, and if I wanted to waste my pesetas in this way it had nothing to do with her. This, however, completely failed to impress her, and before I had finished my sentence she was at it again. Only twenty pesetas for this, thirty for that, fifteen for something else—how could I be so foolish, if I went to the station at such a time, and from the station, and the guide, and so many pesetas, pesetas, pesetas. . . .

At last the old lady had had enough and interrupted the niagara. "But if the English lady wants to go with that excursion. . . ."

"Be quiet, I must still explain. . . ." This was too much for the Señora, who was about twice the age of the Italian. With an inimitable gesture she rose and left the table. The serving nun, in a great flutter, rushed after her. The Italian stopped the pesetas abruptly. The two of us sat in silence, wondering what would happen next. The nun came back. The Señora would return to the table if the Signorina would apologize. Re-enter the Señora, whereupon the Italian made an abject apology. She had not meant it, in the heat of the argument. . . . Would the Señora please forgive her.

So I was allowed to go to the Escorial in the way I wanted, without any further interference. A few days later the Italian left, very early in the morning. When I came into the break-

fast room the Señora smiled at me: *"L'italienne est partie."*
The serving nun chirped: *"L'italienne est partie!"* The por-
tress who opened the door when I was going out afterwards
sang: *"L'italienne est partie!!"* The whole convent breathed
with relief—the Italian had gone!

Naturally I went to the Prado to revel in El Greco. A
French girl offered to show me the way to the famous museum. The walk there was a nightmare, for at every traffic
light she would make a dash to cross just before the orange
lights came on, to save twenty seconds. She simply had to be
there the moment the museum opened and, so she told me,
would stay till it closed, about four hours later. She had
assigned one morning to each room which she "did" without
missing a single picture. It was her idea of a holiday. I arrived there, breathless. She suggested we should meet again
at the entrance hall at closing time, but despite all my devotion to El Greco this was more than I had bargained for.
I intimated that, being of a less studious frame of mind than
she, I should probably be tired after an hour and a half, and
walked off to the Grecos.

El Greco has been called the mystic among the painters,
and if the spiritual experience of St. Teresa and St. John of
the Cross can be reflected in art at all, it is surely reproduced
in his paintings. As Rubens is the painter of the flesh, El
Greco is the painter of the spirit. The eyes of his long-faced
saints, large and wide open, or almost closed, gaze into another world, into that "interior castle" of which St. Teresa
writes, that is dominated by his Christ, a figure of light and
strength even on the Cross. His worldly grandees, too, are
men and women of spiritual stature, ascetic-faced, often
violent, but of that violence that is needed to conquer the
kingdom of heaven.

I gazed at them enchantedly, as I had gazed at the mosaics
in Rome and the Fra Angelicos at Florence. For all their difference in style and conception, they had a deep affinity that

sprang from the contemplation they strove to express. The reality they were designed to convey was a spiritual reality which invested shapes and colors with a meaning far beyond the material representations that delighted the eyes.

One day I went to Toledo, where El Greco had lived the greater part of his life, and where most of his paintings were assembled. The fierce city, with its narrow, winding streets, was intense, vibrating under its outward calm, hard, unyielding, yet supple like its steel. I stood in the ruins of the Alcazar; I walked through its cool, dark vaults, where, twenty years ago, the women and children of Toledo had sheltered from the Communist fury, where General Moscardó had made his supreme stand for Christian Spain against a foreign creed of atheist materialism. Here, where I was now standing with a crowd of English and American sightseers, had come the fatal telephone call, when he was promised the life of his young son, a hostage in the hands of the enemy, if he would surrender the fortress. And here, through the telephone, he heard the shot that killed the boy when he had refused to barter away the city for the life of his son.

The mood did not change, whether I walked into the church of Santo Tomé, to look at Greco's masterpiece, the Burial of Count Orgaz, or into the Greco museum, his house, the famous medieval synagogue close by, or to a workshop where they were making the famous Toledo blades by the same methods as their ancestors had used in the time when St. Teresa founded one of her convents in the city, and when St. John of the Cross was imprisoned, scourged and fed on a diet of salt fish by his Carmelite brethren who resented his reforms. Here, in Toledo, I felt I was in Spain far more than in modern, americanized Madrid. Here I was near to the art, the heroism of Spain, to the mysticism, too—but for that I really had to go to Avila.

I went there with Miss X., who was as great an admirer of St. John of the Cross as I. I was enchanted to see that the city was still almost exactly the same as it must have been in the time of St. Teresa. There were still the small donkeys laden with wares; neither trucks nor busses betrayed the fact that we were living in the twentieth century; the only concession to the present seemed the nylon stockings in the tiny shop windows.

St. Teresa's old convent of the Incarnation is a little outside the town. An electricity meter I saw must have been about the only innovation since the time she had been Prioress there; for I noticed that even the well outside seemed to be still in use. We were shown into a small dark room, now outside the enclosure, which was the confessional where St. John of the Cross used to hear the confession of St. Teresa. It was a strange sensation to stand in this place. Was it only my imagination that I felt it was still loaded, as it were, with spiritual energy that had emanated from these two great mystics who had shared here their deepest experiences.

My friend pulled out her rosary and touched the walls with it, asking me to do the same. This, surely, was bathos. If the faithful touched the black Madonna at Einsiedeln with their rosaries I could understand it, though I had refrained from doing so myself, as it is a popular practice that means nothing to me. But the walls of the confessional of St. John of the Cross, who had waged so persistent a war against anything smacking of superstition! I walked out of the place, an untouched rosary in my bag.

Otherwise I found Miss X., whom I had met in such an extraordinary way, a most congenial companion. Our artistic tastes were almost identical; when I went to the Prado with her we always stopped before the same pictures; we had the same predilections for certain saints, we both wrote on religious subjects. There was just one topic on which our views were diametrically opposed. The first time I had come to her house I had shocked her profoundly. I was wearing what I considered to be a very demure ordinary English cotton frock, with a V-shaped neck and sleeves ending just above the elbow. Of course I knew about Spanish church etiquette and usually walked about with a black silk jacket over my arm to attire myself suitably if I wanted to drop into a church. But I had not thought it necessary to take this garment with me when calling on a friend.

Miss X. was profoundly disturbed. That a woman who went to Mass every morning should dress so "immodestly!" I was trying to explain that we did not think such dress immodest in England. This was due, of course, to the heresy prevailing there. What a priest must think if a woman dressed like this should call on him! I replied that I had been walking about in just such a dress with various priests even in Rome, and the only remark this had ever evoked was an appreciative: "You look nice and cool." Miss X. was genuinely dismayed. According to her there was practically no other cause of immorality in the world than women's short skirts and sleeves. She herself lived up to her principles: even on the hottest days I have never seen her wearing anything but a long-sleeved black dress reaching to her ankles, with a collar almost up to her chin. I think she would have liked the pope to make infallible pronouncements about the inches of female arms, legs and throats that might be left uncovered without falling into mortal sin. In fact she had a kind of obsession about dress, modesty, and immorality.

It was not the first, though the most flagrant instance of Manicheism I had come across among Catholics. Sooner or later every human being comes up against the question of the body and, consequently, of sex. I had sometimes read in the lives of certain saints that they had waged war on their body, which they regarded as their most dangerous enemy. I had never liked these expressions. Surely God has given us our bodies as part of our very selves, our instruments necessary to work out our salvation. He has made them in two sexes, male and female, which He has given a natural attraction for each other in order to ensure the propagation of the race. All these things were God-given and therefore good. I could not see why, in order to be pleasing to God, a woman should cover herself up from top to toe in a shapeless black garment pretending she was sexless.

For chastity does not mean sexlessness. Since we were created male and female we cannot, and ought not even to try to, make ourselves neuters. I have known widows of the "devout" type who look back on their marriage in its sexual aspect as on something "unclean," something almost to be ashamed of. Yet, in the teaching of the Church, marriage is a sacrament, consecrating just this marriage act which some of the "pious" seem to think a kind of reluctantly condoned fornication. I have also known "spinsters" who imagine themselves superior to married women for being without sexual experience. And I have known even more people whose generally neurotic behavior and discontent with life is due to the fact that something had gone wrong in the sphere of sex.

Sex, surely, is something so fundamental in the human make-up that it cannot be abused, whether by over-indulgence or by repression, without injuring the whole personality. But what happens when a man or woman makes a vow of chastity? Does this not mean that sex is being repressed? The question was forced on me as I was discussing this matter of dress with Miss X., which cropped up again and again, as I needed but inadvertently to mention nylon slips as practical for travelling to set off the spark. Personally I think that if a chaste life produces such aberrations, it means that something has been repressed. Now we repress things if we leave them unused. But in a chaste life in the Christian sense sexual energy is not left unused, it is transformed into something else, as, in the natural sphere, water can be transformed into electricity. I like this comparison, because just as electricity has a greater force and a wider range of activity than water, so chastity is more powerful than the sex instinct from which it has sprung. Yet water retains all its beneficial qualities; and no one would dream of despising it because, as our basic drink, it does not produce electricity. Yet, for all its beauty and usefulness, even water can become stale and unwholesome.

This is the danger if sex is mistaken for something to be ashamed of, a subject altogether unmentionable even to oneself. Then we shall end up by seeing it everywhere, and the water, instead of being a source of energy, will stagnate and turn into an evil smelling pool, poisoning the whole atmosphere.

*   *   *   *   *

Since, despite my wasteful excursions, I still had a few pesetas left, I flew to Seville for two days, to get at least a glimpse of the south. I could hardly believe that I was still in Europe. I could not resist looking through the wrought-iron gates into every patio, and wandered for hours through the narrow streets, inaccessible to cars, over which awnings were spread from side to side to keep out the sun which was blazing from a cloudless October sky. The Alcazar with its exquisite fayence walls, its enchanting patios cooled by fountains, its formal gardens with orange trees and palms and myrtles seemed like a dream from the *Thousand and One Nights*. Only in the magnificent Cathedral I was once more back in Christendom, in the city of St. Isidore, a lexicographer, *salva reverentia*, like myself.

Back in Oxford I began work on Edith Stein in earnest. During the next months I literally lived in her—spiritual—company. It was an odd experience, for she attracted and repelled me in turns. There was her brilliant intellect, her absolute integrity, her selfless devotion to attract me. Yet, when I had first read about her, I had disliked her feminism and her earnestness. I could not help wondering how we should have reacted to each other had we ever met, and I had a sneaking suspicion at times that our so different temperaments might have clashed. As I was now trying to penetrate her character more deeply I realized that it would not be easy to give a convincing picture of her: she was first and foremost a scholar; the ordinary weaknesses of her sex seemed quite foreign to her; her interests were first philosophy and then God, there was little color in her life; yet, it was a life representative of our time, and she herself was one of the great women of the age.

While I was writing on her, groaning and smiling alternately, and carrying on a large correspondence with those who had known her, the Coronation began to cast its shadows. Though I was personally as thrilled as most of her subjects to have a charming young queen, the event would not have loomed quite so large on my horizon had it not been for Betty. Betty was a young American writer with whom I had first come into contact through my Therese Neumann book. In the course of our correspondence she had expressed the desire to come to Oxford to see me, and I had suggested she might like to come to the Coronation. She seemed enthusiastic about the idea and wrote back she was going to book rooms for all of us, my mother included, at a very expensive hotel in London. This sounded somewhat odd to me, but then Americans did odd things sometimes. Several weeks before Christmas she suggested she would give me a dictaphone as a Christmas present. By this time my native scepticism asserted itself. I was neither a Prime Minister nor an industrialist, not even an author of filmable bestsellers with three secretaries. Besides, I could not dictate—my best source of inspiration is a typewriter with an empty sheet in front of me. Betty wrote three detailed letters about the dictaphone and its merits, until I replied: Yes, thank you very much. I doubted whether it would ever arrive. My doubts were fully justified, for it never did. As Betty no longer mentioned her Coronation trip I surmised that the bookings at the "swell" hotel also existed only in her lively imagination. Then, a week before the event, a wild air letter arrived, starting: "We are off." By air, and would I come to the airport to meet her—without any further details as to time of arrival. It sounded crazy, but when I went shopping next, I thought I had better get the Stars and Stripes in addition to our collection of Union Jacks for the occasion.

But in all Oxford there was not one American flag to be had except a very large specimen which was both too expensive and unsuitable. It was just as well. For three days later a cable arrived: "Emergency. Father ill." I contented myself with a series of small tea parties to celebrate the event.

Almost immediately after, I set out for the Continent on a kind of literary Edith Stein pilgrimage, visiting most of the places (except those behind the Iron Curtain of course) where she had lived, and interviewing people she had known. It was a busman's holiday if ever there was one. I sat in archives studying manuscripts, before grilles of Carmelite convents questioning nuns who had a most irritating habit of branching off on some other subject just when I thought they were going to produce something really interesting. I even knelt in the same prie-dieu at Speyer which Edith Stein had used, for further inspiration. I found to my great satisfaction that the mood in Germany had changed since my last visit. They no longer despised us for putting up with rationing. It was all the Queen and the Coronation. I heard more than once: "We envy you your royal family—if we only had a monarchy like that." My aunt had a picture of the Queen I had sent her actually on her writing desk, and everybody was keen on the "coronation handkerchiefs" of which I had brought a large supply. One of them even found its way under a statue of our Lady in a nun's oratory.

After my return I could at last finish the Edith Stein biography, which I translated into German some time later. It was the first of my books which I translated myself into my own native language—a strange experience. I had been living in this country for about eighteen years now, during which I had spoken very little German, had written even less, and read scarcely any German books. I was quite frankly doubtful whether I should still be able to write a decent literary style. I must confess the first pages were difficult. This complicated syntax, so ideal for metaphysical verbiage, but such a recalcitrant instrument if one wanted to say things lucidly. These split-up verbs, these assortments of participles and infinitives cluttering along inconsequently at the end of a mammoth sentence—unless I was going to indulge in a breathless surrealistic staccato prose affected by some modern writers. I tried to steer a middle course between the two extremes, and had the satisfaction that the publisher's reader found only a few Anglicisms to correct, and that one of the reviewers complimented me on my clear and simple style. I have no hesitation to attribute this to the discipline of "plain English," in which obscurity is not considered a sign of "depth" but of insufficient clarity of thought.

Soon after Christmas I usually become restive and start making holiday plans. This time I wanted to go to Switzerland, where the controversy about the Therese Neumann book was in full swing, as the German translation had just come out. It had been translated by a Swiss priest who used a pseudonym. I wrote to him that I should like to come to Switzerland in the summer and to make his acquaintance on this occasion. This, as I thought most harmless suggestion, produced a quite staggering reaction. I was on no account to come to Switzerland if I wanted a peaceful holiday. I should have no rest from the devotees of Therese as soon as any Catholics there would be aware of my presence. As to visiting him—did I want to ruin his life completely? A *matrimonium clandestinum* would be the least of which people would suspect him. . . .

It seemed fantastic. I could only reply somewhat sarcastically that I was sorry Therese was so much more fortunate in her knights than I. Mine might be *sans reproche,* but they certainly were not *sans peur.* I thought his fears exaggerated, but as I had neither the talent nor the intention to play *femme fatale* to a priest, I abandoned my plan and went to France instead, where Therese Neumann is fortunately not a national asset.

The Lexicon was now in its last stages. Everybody was getting frantic with everybody else. Life became a nightmare of inaccurate references, misinterpretations, wrong editions cited. . . . Mr. Lampe, who had become professor in Birmingham some time ago, was putting in only rare appearances. He had accomplished the incredible: while collecting material for the Lexicon entry on *sphragis,* seal, he had become so interested in the subject that he wrote a book on it, *The Seal of the Spirit.* The book had long been published, but the Lexicon entry was still undone when I left.

By the end of 1954 I had been on the staff for over thirteen years. During the last years work had become increasingly burdensome to me, as my literary activities had developed. Besides, I was now no longer really needed; the cross-referencing and the revisions could be done by others more interested in these technical details than I. So, apart from a few hours in the early part of 1955 to help tie up some loose ends, my work on it came to an end after Christmas, 1954. It may sound exaggerated, but I felt as if I had been released from a long slavery. The monotony and the total absence of any creative activity had become almost unbearable. So, on the last day of the year, I went to church to sing the *Te Deum* with heartfelt gratitude and joy. Then I went home and brewed a punch to welcome the New Year.

Index

A NOTE ON THE TYPE

IN WHICH THIS BOOK IS SET

This book is set in Garamond, a type face considered by many as one of the most successful ever introduced. Claude Garamond, the designer of these beautiful types, was a pupil of Goeffroy Tory, a leader of the Renaissance in France, a university professor, artist, designer and printer who set out to place French on an equal footing with Latin and Greek as a language of culture. Garamond's evenness of color throughout the font is highly appreciated by book designers. The moderately strong fine lines tend to soften the effect, which is decidedly agreeable to many. This book composed by Wickersham Printing Company, Lancaster, Pa., and bound by Moore & Company of Baltimore. The typography and design of this book are by Howard N. King.

THE MONASTERY